Religion and
the American Future

Religion and the American Future

Editors
Christopher DeMuth
Yuval Levin

The AEI Press

Publisher for the American Enterprise Institute
WASHINGTON, D.C.

Distributed to the Trade by National Book Network, 15200 NBN Way, Blue Ridge Summit, PA 17214. To order call toll free 1-800-462-6420 or 1-717-794-3800. For all other inquiries please contact the AEI Press, 1150 Seventeenth Street, N.W., Washington, D.C. 20036 or call 1-800-862-5801.

Library of Congress Cataloging-in-Publication Data

Religion and the American Future / edited by Christopher DeMuth and Yuval Levin.
    p. cm.
  Includes bibliographical references and index.
  ISBN-13: 978-0-8447-4259-5
  ISBN-10: 0-8447-4259-7
  1. United States—Religion. 2. Religion—Forecasting. I. DeMuth, Christopher C. II. Levin, Yuval.

  BL2525.R46145 2008
  200.973'0905—dc22

                                                      2008002991

12 11 10 09 08   1 2 3 4 5 6 7

Printed in the United States of America

This book is dedicated to the memory of
Elizabeth Brady Lurie

Scholar, philanthropist, friend

Contents

Introduction:
Religion and the American Future

Yuval Levin

Modern liberal democracy has always seen the containment of religious passions as among its most crucial and most difficult tasks. Arising in the wake of bloody religious wars in Europe, the liberal project sought to quell the fighting by establishing a scheme of procedural justice which made actions, not beliefs, the measure of men and which did not depend on common answers to fundamental questions of divinity and humanity. The state would protect a few essential rights that might be grounded in broad premises about God but did not require very particular theological commitments, and religion would for the most part be a private matter, not a subject for public contention. "Everyone is orthodox to himself,"[1] John Locke wrote, and the liberal order he imagined would have its citizens respect that fact but also largely ignore it, for the sake of peace.

From the beginning, some have worried that this treatment of religious questions as not meriting the attention of the polity would smother religious belief, and flatten the souls and lives of citizens by rendering them ignorant of and uninterested in the deepest truths about themselves. And indeed the liberal democratic attitude toward religion, combined with the enormous material success achieved by the world's liberal societies, has certainly led in many places to declining interest in religious tradition and practice.

But America has been something of an exception. "On my arrival in the United States," wrote Alexis de Tocqueville in 1835, "it was the religious aspect of the country that first struck my eye."[2] A great many subsequent visitors have agreed. Yet here, too, the liberal order has done a fine job of averting religious conflict. Sectarian violence has been vanishingly rare, even as religious fervor and commitment have barely abated at all—and indeed in some respects have intensified through American history.

No one secret can explain this resilience of American religion. We are a different people than our European cousins, with a different history that has produced quite different instincts and habits. In America, rather than smother religious belief, liberal democracy has in some respects energized it through a constant—and, for the most part, a constructive—tension. Religious conflict has been avoided not by depleting the energy of our various sects but by uniting them in temperate but steady opposition to the cultural predilections of the liberal society itself.

Religion has become the chief foil of every prominent secular institution in America. Science—the flagship of the modern project—can hardly be discussed without mention of its religious critics. The law—the arena in which every important American notion eventually fights for its life—is ever confounded with complex dilemmas of religious freedom and coercion. The excesses of American art are held to account by almost no one except the religiously motivated. And in our politics these days, the religious voter is sought after with fervor, and displays of public religiosity unimagined a generation ago are common practice for politicians of both parties. Religion is an active, living force in every corner of American life and is everywhere in tense and often quite uneasy contact with the liberal society.

All of this has tended to unite the sects in America, and so to minimize interreligious conflict, yet at the same time it has energized the broad community of believers. In each of the areas of friction and tension, the secular faction and the religious faction both feel besieged and under threat by an overwhelming force threatening to crush them. Each somehow has managed to persuade itself it is fighting for its life against the other. The question of religion and secularism is therefore a live and open question in America in a way it has simply ceased to be in Europe (at least for now, while Europe remains largely blind to the challenge of Islam). And it is a question perhaps best understood as a series of individual encounters between religious believers and the institutions of the liberal society of which they are part: religion and science, religion and the law, religion and art, and so more broadly: religion and secularism.

In October of 2006, the American Enterprise Institute brought together a distinguished group of scholars to take up the question of religion in America on precisely these terms: to consider each of these encounters individually, to think through their combined significance, and to take into account also the very different but surely quite instructive experience of Europe. The workshop involved a series of prepared papers—one on each of the encounters just mentioned—with a brief prepared response to each, and then discussion of the subject. The participants sought, above all, to consider the future of American religion, and the place of religion in the future of the nation. This volume brings together those papers and responses, as well as brief selections from the ensuing discussion.

The papers and discussions defy a succinct summation, and reward a thorough reading. But if any single theme emerges from the whole, it is a sense that the constructive tension that has sustained American religion is here to stay, and with it also our uniquely religious and therefore uniquely serious liberal society. American religion faces profound threats from the secular society that surrounds it, and in some respects also poses deep challenges to that society. But these threats and these challenges continue to have the effect of sending Americans back to their first principles, and so of keeping us—more than any other modern society—constantly in contact with our founding ideals, secular and religious alike. That unending interaction with our past offers hope for religion, and so for the American future. And it offers hope as well that the liberal democratic experiment might not require the ultimate smothering of religious passions for the sake of secular peace. As this volume makes clear, there is much that should worry us as we cast our glance forward, but there is also much for us to draw upon in preparing for and contending with the challenges to come.

The workshop from which this volume emerges was sponsored by the W. H. Brady Program in Culture and Freedom at the American Enterprise Institute, and the papers and discussions that follow are a powerful example of precisely the kind of inquiry the program has always pursued: an engagement with the problems of freedom and culture in American society. They offer a glimpse into the future of American religion, and so of America itself.

Notes

1. John Locke, *Letter Concerning Toleration*, ed. James H. Tully (Indianapolis: Hackett Publishing Company, 1983), 23.

2 Alexis de Tocqueville, *Democracy in America*, trans. Harvey Mansfield and Delba Winthrop (Chicago: University of Chicago Press, 2000), 282.

PART I

Religion and Secularism

1

The End of the Secular Age

Michael Novak

We have, in recent years, observed two major events that represent turning points in the history of the 20th century. The first is the death of socialism, both as an ideal and as a political program, a death that has been duly recorded in our consciousness. The second is the collapse of secular humanism—the religious basis of socialism—as an ideal, but not yet as an ideological program, a way of life. The emphasis is on "not yet," for as the ideal is withering away, the real will sooner or later follow suit. . . . If one looks back at . . . [the past] century, one sees the rationalist religion of secular humanism gradually losing its credibility even as it marches triumphantly through the institutions of our society—through the schools, the courts, the churches, the media. This loss of credibility flows from two fundamental flaws in secular humanism.

—Irving Kristol[1]

After the death of Jacques Derrida (1930–2004), Professor Richard Wolin has called Jürgen Habermas the world's greatest living philosopher.[2] For some decades now, Habermas has wished to be thought of as an atheist. Yet in the last seven years, in unmistakable ways, he has begun to question the limits of secularism. He has also begun to express appreciation for at least a few aspects of those religions that offer a dimension of transcendence, and yet also profoundly defend the dignity, liberty, and responsibility of each human individual. He seems to have in mind, implicitly but not often expressly, religions of the Jewish and Christian type.

Habermas begins his critique, formulated over a number of essays and lectures, by noticing what many willfully overlook. *Secularism has been pushed into a new position in world history; it now appears to be the persuasion of a fairly small minority in a sea of rising religious commitment.* Two new facts led him to this conclusion. First, the thesis that the human world is becoming increasingly secular—"the secularization thesis"—appears to have been decisively falsified, in part because of secularism's own internal weaknesses. Second, a powerful religious awakening in the Third World, but also in other regions such as the United States and Eastern Europe, suggests that secularist Europe is the anomaly, not the norm.[3]

In the lifelong project of Habermas's work, the key concept of morality is "communicative discourse," discourse which arises from the ability of each partner to stand in the other's moccasins and to learn to sympathize with a viewpoint quite different from his own. Only in this way do we escape from the narrow egotism of never having engaged in real discourse with others.

Given that the resurgence of religion bids to swamp the atheist sections of the world, can secularists offer a coherent theory of why this is happening, and can they summon up the moral strength not only to tolerate, but also to respect, and then to enter into the viewpoint of, believers? Can they do so after so many generations during which they have been teaching cultural contempt for believers in God, the unenlightened, the people of the dark? These are the sorts of questions raised by Habermas's work.

A quick glance back is in order here. Feuerbach taught us that the relation of God and man is a zero-sum game, such that what is given to one is taken from the other. He taught, in addition, that it is man who creates God out of his own emotional needs, not God who creates man. Feuerbach's most famous student, Karl Marx, set out to eradicate religion as a form of opium that enervates the proletariat and renders them passive. Thus many of the "enlightened" held that the advance of science would isolate religion ever more narrowly, until it finally disappeared. After some decades of such teaching, when Nietzsche succinctly announced that "God is dead," he was only saying in a shocking way what many sophisticated Europeans already believed. Sigmund Freud added that the future of religion is *The Future of an Illusion.* This illusion, moreover, at least among serious people, will fade away. Religion is a neurotic dependency.

Plainly, these great analysts overlooked some important sources of vitality in the world around them. By the end of the twentieth century, the burgeoning force of religion around the world was undeniable. The question now may be less whether religion will survive than in what form secularism will survive. Will it come to seem dumbstruck, unable to communicate in the new "tongues," and increasingly isolated?

Habermas's Critique of Secularism

Habermas raises four questions about the limits of secularism that I will take up in turn. But let us look first at some recent statements that suggest a new openness to religion and religious points of view. Shortly after September 11, 2001, when nineteen Muslims—mostly graduate students and young professionals—flew airliners laden with aviation fuel into the Twin Towers of the World Trade Center in New York and into the low-lying Pentagon, Habermas gave a lecture on the occasion of receiving a major prize from the German Publishers and Booksellers Association. He shocked most listeners by taking up the subject of "Faith and Knowledge." His main theme was the need for toleration among secular humanists for religious people, and vice versa—and not just toleration, but mutual respect and open conversation.[4] He believed the future of civilization demanded no less.

A year later, in a brilliant, impassioned book entitled *The Future of Human Nature*, Habermas spoke out forcefully against biological engineering and human cloning.[5] He wrote of a human right to a unique human identity and expressed revulsion at a "human" artifact manufactured by others, a mere object among objects.

In 2004, he accepted an invitation—a challenge, in a way—to engage in public debate with Joseph Cardinal Ratzinger, then head of the Congregation for the Doctrine of the Faith and no liberal in theology, although a very learned, modest, and engaging man. (Ratzinger a year later was elected pope). Again, Habermas shocked many professors in the academy and journalists, too, by affirming openly the importance of religion for civilization and the obligation of secularism to engage with religion seriously and honestly. "Sacred scriptures and religious traditions," Habermas argued, "have preserved over millennia, in subtle formulation and hermeneutics, intuitions about error and redemptions, about the salvational outcome of a life experienced as hopeless."[6]

A reliable commentator explicates what Habermas was adding here to his earlier work: "Religious life keeps intact . . . a number of sensitivities, nuances, and modes of expression for situations that neither his own 'postmetaphysical' approach nor an exclusively rationalist society of professional expertise can deal with in a fully satisfactory manner."[7]

Cardinal Ratzinger, for his part, stressed the indispensable need for reason to diminish the "toxicity" sometimes present in religion. He also stressed the essential bond between Christianity and the Greek *logos*: reason and faith together, "summoned to mutual cleansing and healing."[8] This debate with Habermas foreshadowed the sturdy defense of reason that the new pope made at the University of Regensburg, where he had once been vice rector—the famous lecture to which many Muslims reacted not with reason but with violent demonstrations.[9]

The first question raised by Habermas's new explorations of uncharted ground between the secular and the religious worlds was this: *Did most secularists have the tools and, as well, the moral stamina to carry out an honest, respectful conversation, after so many generations of contempt for religion?*

Habermas raises a second question in the context of an earlier and little-noticed vein of thought developed in his masterwork, the two-volume *Theory of Communicative Action* (1981). In a section that bears a title in almost untranslatable German, signifying something like "The Putting into Words of the Sacred,"[10] Habermas argues that honesty commands secular people to recognize their linguistic and conceptual debts to Judaism and Christianity.[11] The question is, *Have secularists the honesty to admit these debts openly?*

Certainly Habermas is clear about the nature of these debts. For instance, he asserts that modern notions of equality and fairness are, as Richard Wolin puts it, "secular distillations of time-honored Judeo-Christian precepts."[12] Further, the contract theories of modern secular philosophy can scarcely be understood apart from the great prestige attached to the covenants so central to both Jewish and Christian history. Habermas clarifies that he is not speaking merely of matters of etymology or intellectual history. He means also the reverence for such themes as moral obligation and justice maintained in Jewish and Christian preaching and living. Without these, he judges, it is doubtful whether modern societies would be able to sustain their own scientific and political views.

In a more recent interview, Habermas names a substantial list of moral realities that secular life and thought do not sustain alone:

> For the normative self-understanding of modernity, Christianity has functioned as more than just a precursor or a catalyst. Universalistic egalitarianism, from which spring *the ideals of freedom and a collective life in solidarity, the autonomous conduct of life and emancipation, the individual morality of conscience, human rights, and democracy*, is the direct legacy of the Judaic ethic of justice and the Christian ethic of love.[13]

A third question about the limits of secularism arises out of Habermas's view that today we live in a postsecular society; certainly, he thinks, people in the United States do. Habermas sees this fact as having many benefits for secularism, but also as posing the danger that Judaism and Christianity might teach humans to undervalue worldly accomplishment, initiative, and action in favor of passivity before the will of God (Habermas is mindful of Nietzsche's impassioned claim that Judaism and Christianity are "slave religions," moved by passive-aggressive *ressentiment*). He also worries about those Christians who hold that the fall of Adam so seriously damages human nature that no intrinsic good can come from it.

Are there many such Christians left in optimistic America? Does Habermas correctly grasp the Christian theologies of the fall? A professor at a Calvinist college in the American Middle West once told me the best way to describe original sin: "Anyone who says that man is totally depraved can't be all bad." Has Habermas forgotten for a moment Max Weber's interpretation of the immense outburst of economic energy precisely among those Christians who most feared their own moral failures, failures that might indicate they were not among the elect? (I myself think that Weber was inexact in this diagnosis; but the workings of doctrine in daily life are quite subtle and complex.)[14]

Habermas's third question is, *Will most secular women and men see the wisdom in Habermas's diagnosis that, from time to time, the best and highest secular ideals—human rights, solidarity, equality—benefit*, as Wolin writes, *"from renewed contact with the nimbus of their sacral origins"*?[15]

In 2005, in a lecture at Lodz University in Poland on "Religion in the Public Sphere," Habermas posed a fourth question for secular men and women: *Are they ready to admit that toleration is always a two-way street?* Religious persons, he suggests, must be ready to learn toleration not only for each other's convictions and commitments, but also for those of atheists, agnostics, and other secularists. In a similar way, nonbelieving secularists must learn to appreciate the creeds, reasoning, and convictions of their fellow human beings who are believers. "For all their ongoing dissent on questions of world views and religious doctrines," says Habermas, "citizens are meant to respect one another as free and equal members of their political community."[16] Those on all sides must be ready to stand in the shoes of the other in order to see the other's point of view "from within."

As Pierre Manent has pointed out, the history of the last six or seven generations seems to show that Christianity has had an easier time identifying with democracy, and has done so more successfully, than secular people have done in standing in the shoes of Christians and other citizens energized by ancient and constantly self-renewed religions in their midst.[17] Habermas's question, then, is whether secularists have sufficient moral energy to redress this imbalance.

For religious people, Habermas poses a test. Among themselves, they may explain their convictions and their reasons for holding them in the language of faith, and even of the Bible. But in public life, those believers who enter into politics or activism have a special obligation to employ a "neutral" secular language. Perhaps Habermas is thinking of the situation of France or other secular European nations with high proportions of Muslim citizens. Perhaps he wants to put pressure on Muslims to step out of their own traditional stances and enter into the viewpoints of others. Perhaps he believes that the preponderance of people in those nations are secular, so that among them secular speech is the most readily accessible. Whatever his motives, his warning is that unless language in the public sphere (and here he means specifically governmental offices) is solely secular, some religious groups will feel themselves slighted, and social divisiveness will result. Still, Habermas is far more open than John Rawls on these matters. In his lecture "Religion in the Public Sphere," Habermas writes:

The citizens of a democratic community owe one another good reasons for their public political interventions. Contrary to the restrictive view of Rawls and Audi, this civic duty can be specified in such a tolerant way that contributions are permitted in a *religious as well as in a secular language*. They are not subject to constraints on the mode of expression in the political public sphere, but they rely on joint ventures of translation to have a chance to be taken up in the agendas and negotiations of political bodies. Otherwise they will not "count" in any further political process.[18]

In "Faith and Knowledge," Habermas adds, "The liberal state has so far imposed only upon the believers among its citizens the requirements that they split their identity into public and private versions. That is, they must translate their religious convictions into a secular language before their arguments have the prospect of being accepted by a majority."[19] For his part, Habermas does not want to put believers at a disadvantage, although he holds that all parties, including believers, must do their best to give reasons understandable to the other parties. So he lays burdens on both believers and unbelievers: "The search for reasons that aspire to general acceptance need not lead to an unfair exclusion of religion from public life, and secular society, for its part, need not cut itself off from the important resources of spiritual explanations, if only so that the secular side might retain a feeling for the articulative power of religious discourse."[20]

By contrast, the assumption that Rawls and others make is that the secular mode of speech is actually "neutral." In the experience of many believers of various faiths, it is anything but neutral. Speech limited to secular categories has its own totalistic tendencies. It penalizes or even quarantines those with religious points of view, whose insights and public arguments by this rule are not given due weight by narrowly secular officials. Curiously, in a set of lectures at the University of Virginia in 1928, Walter Lippmann made a parallel observation about the famous Scopes trial three years earlier. In a lecture framed as a conversation, the "Fundamentalist" says to his counterpart the "Modernist":

In our public controversies you are fond of arguing that you are open-minded, tolerant and neutral in the face of conflicting

> opinions. That is not so. . . . Because for me an eternal plan of salvation is at stake. For you there is nothing at stake but a few tentative opinions, none of which means anything to your happiness. Your request that I should be tolerant and amiable is, therefore, a suggestion that I submit the foundation of my life to the destructive effects of your skepticism, your indifference, and your good nature. You ask me to smile and to commit suicide.[21]

The Modernist does not grasp the total surrender he is asking the person of faith to make by submitting one source of knowledge (faith) to another (reason), when the latter seems to him inferior.[22]

The parallel challenge that Habermas throws down for secular people, then, is an even newer one: since they now live in a postsecular age, they must not be content with understanding social realities only in a secular way. They must enter into dialogue with believers and be willing to see the world from their perspective, just as is expected of believers vis-à-vis secularists.

If the tender roots of something like universal democracy are ever to survive and spread around the world, these conceptions—these breakthroughs for a universal ethos of public communication, and mutual reaching out to understand others from within—make an indispensable contribution. But these new rules for public discourse also renegotiate the historical preeminence that "the enlightened" assign themselves, and the language of contempt by which they have taken believers less than seriously. These rules call upon secularists, too, to be learners, and to master the new morality of communicative discourse, a morality that calls for mutual respect.[23]

Some Newly Discovered Incapacities of Secularism

For many generations secularists have assumed that the triumph of secularism is assured and, indeed, fast approaching. Predictions of the disappearance of religion have been many. So it has been difficult for secularists to absorb their new situation, and more difficult still to learn of significant deficiencies in their own philosophy and moral capacities. Their philosophy is noble, and we are all in its debt. Their moral resources are many and admirable. It is quite clear that without religion some can live good and noble lives. But there are also in the secularist worldview certain significant incapacities.[24] Irving Kristol, who is cited at the start, mentions in particular two. The first is that

> the philosophical rationalism of secular humanism can, at best, provide us with a statement of the necessary assumptions of a moral code, but it cannot deliver any such code itself. Moral codes evolve from the moral experience of communities, and can claim authority over behavior only to the degree that individuals are reared to look respectfully, even reverently, on the moral traditions of their forefathers. It is the function of religion to instill such respect and reverence. Morality does not belong to a scientific mode of thought. . . . One accepts a moral code on faith— not on blind faith but on the faith that one's ancestors, over the generations, were not fools and that we have much to learn from their experience.[25]

The prevailing moral code of the West was, for centuries, informed by the wisdom of our forefathers, but in the vision of human nature and destiny developed by secular humanism, that old code is no longer relevant. It has, accordingly, become more and more attenuated. That biting challenge of Nietzsche still nags at our conscience: if God is really dead, by what authority do we say any particular practice is prohibited or permitted? In the resulting moral disarray in our society, the most urgent moral questions have also become unsettled: "How shall we raise our children? What kind of moral example should we set? What moral instruction should we convey?" A society uncertain in its answer to these questions is likely to "breed restless, turbulent generations,"[26] some of whom are likely to seek more authoritative answers somewhere, anywhere. We know this can happen. It happened to a smart and amicable young German friend of Albert Camus, who took quite seriously the chatter in the cafes of Paris about the meaninglessness of individual life, and *therefore* joined the Nazi Party, and gave his all for the triumph of his nation, his greatest good.[27]

The second flaw in secular humanism that Kristol identifies is even more fundamental:

> If there is one indisputable fact about the human condition it
> is that no community can survive if it is persuaded—or even
> suspects—that its members are leading meaningless lives in a
> meaningless universe.[28]

Secular humanism, Kristol goes on, instructs people to respond to the ultimate meaninglessness of human life by making something worthwhile of
"autonomy" and "creativity." Yet why, in a meaningless world, is creativity
better than passivity, or autonomy better than submission? Thus even these
bright goals are undermined by skeptical nihilists, neopagans, and tor-
mented existentialists such as Nietzsche, Heidegger, and Sartre. Later still,
secular humanism has come to be mocked by postmodernists, deconstruc-
tionists, and structuralists. That is why something has gone out of the self-
confidence of secularism. "Secular humanism is brain dead even as its heart
continues to pump energy into all of our institutions."[29]

But these animadversions of Kristol address only some of secularism's
incapacities, as I will now suggest.

Secularism Cannot Combat Moral Decadence. Ever since the fall of
Rome, historians and philosophers have noted how often civilizations fall
by way of moral decadence. What tools does secularism possess to arrest
such decadence? How does a secularist society even diagnose moral decadence? By whose standards?

The relativism in secularist thought, the tendency of secularism to make
morality a matter of description rather than prescription, makes these questions hard to answer. The secularist emphasis on the autonomous and unencumbered individual often leads to a wholly relativistic theory of the good.
For instance, Judith Jarvis Thompson argues that the good is whatever an
autonomous person chooses as a good.[30] Such definitions deprive secularists of any ground on which to measure moral decadence, whether in a single person or in an entire culture. Moreover, precisely insofar as they define
the good as whatever a person chooses, such definitions are inconsistent
with everyday speech, and strip human critical faculties of any useful role.

By contrast, historians teach us that the United States, chiefly because
of its Protestant heritage, has experienced at least three "Great Awakenings."
Nobel Prize–winner Robert Fogel has written that the country is in the

throes of a rolling wave, not yet crested, of a fourth Great Awakening.[31] This return to tradition and family values, to serious work and self-discipline, is not limited to religious people, let alone the Religious Right. But the source of this and earlier renewals seems to be several important Jewish and Christian religious teachings: for instance, a high standard for what counts as fidelity to God and to moral duty (the opposite of sin); a call to repentance; a demand for conversion of life; and a possibility of "being born again" (not necessarily by accepting Jesus Christ, but at least by a new openness to the transcendent and to moral seriousness).

Thus, even among people fallen deep into the slough of moral decadence, an inner call to awaken and resume the path of duty, self-governance, and personal dignity can sometimes be faintly heard. This inner call (in the biblical view) bears the promise of divine assistance, which imparts inner powers entirely beyond the strength of the autonomous and unencumbered will. From this promise, many have drawn courage. Even those who do not believe in divine assistance may well observe changes in behavior among those who do.

Abraham Lincoln explained early in his political career why such new awakenings are necessary. Moral life, Lincoln observed, proceeds in cycles of three or more generations, cycles that end in a slow but steady decline. Thus, the generation that won the independence of the United States was revered for its courage and its amazing steadfastness in the face of defeat, desolation, and lack of popular support. (Almost two-thirds of the people either sided with the British or sat back to watch, uninvolved.) The children of this great generation tried to live up to the high example of their fathers but often failed. In the next generation, the grandchildren were weary even of hearing about their heroic grandparents, and preferred more pleasant paths. Lincoln called this process a bombardment of courage and devotion by "the silent artillery of time."[32]

For secularists, a kind of Newtonian law of inertial moral decline presents two problems, both noted at the beginning of this section: By what public moral standard ought decline and progress to be measured? And what tools are available to the secularist for converting citizens from their downward drift to new levels of discipline, self-government, duty, and honor? The progressive remedies are "consciousness raising," "education," and "raising public awareness." But such remedies imply publicly available universal standards, and moral exemplars to constitute, as it were, a moral avant-garde. The moral relativism of far too many secularists prevents these remedies from getting under way.

Secularism's Promise of a Universal Ethic of Reason Has Failed. The secularism stemming from the Enlightenment has been unable to keep its promise of forging a universal consensus about an ethic based on reason alone. Today ethical schools of thought may be more divided than ever. According to the distinguished philosopher Alasdair MacIntyre, there is now so little common ground shared by the various schools of thought that rational ethical debate has been reduced to exclamatory cheering sections that, faced with an ethical proposition, erupt into "Hurrah!" or "Boo!"[33]

Professors in countless classrooms in many different disciplines report that students have already been taught that when they are faced with any moral proposition, the proper response is: "That's just your opinion." They are resistant, then, to resolving disagreements by reasoned arguments. They aver: "You choose your goods, and I'll choose mine." Reasoned debate is replaced by naked will. I *choose*. Don't ask me to give reasons, I just choose.

This circumstance seems to be what Nietzsche meant when he observed that no man of reason should rejoice in the death of God. Experience would soon show, he was certain, that with the death of God arrives the death of reason. If reason is a compass, it requires a North Star. If it is a tool for getting to the truth, it presupposes about truth a regulative principle of this sort: *even if no one yet possesses the truth, we must agree that the presentation of evidence through reasoned argument is the most reliable path for coming closer to the truth—and that there is a truth to come closer to.*[34]

Further, mutual conversation about evidence that is available to all parties is the best guide for figuring out how to come closer to the truth of things. An old way of putting this is that civilization is constituted by reasoned conversation. Civilized humans converse with one another, argue with one another, offer evidence to one another. Barbarians club one another.[35]

Of course, the utility of evidence depends on there being truths to be discovered, or at least to be more closely approximated. Thus, a regulative idea of truth is an essential constituent of any civilization worthy of reasoning animals. Without it, no conversation can amount to more than

conjoined soliloquies. There is no evidence to point to, no mutual acceptance of rules of discourse.

But if God is dead, so also is the regulative idea of truth. If all is chance,
random, and inherently meaningless, reason has no North Star; its needle
spins aimlessly.

At the death of God, therefore, Zarathustra wept.

Secularism Cannot Address Human Suffering, Tragedy, and Evil. As Irving Kristol pointed out more than ten years ago, secularism has little to say
about human suffering, brokenness, tragedy, remorse, and evil. Secularism is
not altogether speechless in the face of death, sin, suffering, and human
tragedy. Yet its voice does sound faint. It is simply not very satisfying to those
who feel pain at life's extremities. And pain is unavoidable: hardly a conversation with a neighbor passes by without one learning of a person struggling
with a horrible cancer or dealing with a terrible accident. It is not that secular humanism offers so little comfort, but that it cannot see *meaning* in suffering and self-sacrifice, which are everyday and common events.

Secularism also offers little in the way of remedy to those who have
deliberately, consciously done something evil, and now repent of it. Such
persons cannot be fooled by "therapy"; they know exactly what they did
and that they chose deliberately to do it. They are not seeking "understanding," but rather the removal of real guilt for real evils that they have
committed. Knowing that these deeds cannot be undone, they feel remorse
bite the more deeply.

Nor is secularism comforting to the weak and the vulnerable, who in
the mad struggle for survival of the fittest do not feel well positioned. What
has secularism to say to the vulnerable that it does not borrow directly from
Judaism and Christianity? Both Bertrand Russell and Richard Rorty have
confessed that they simply stole one of their central social values, compassion (or, in the new word, solidarity), from Jesus Christ, and certainly not
from Aristotle, Plato, Kant, or Nietzsche.[36] Borrow where you can, they say.

Secularism May Not Survive Islamofascism and Demographic Trends.
What are the long-term prospects of existing secular societies such as those
in Europe and the United States? Two difficulties stand out. The first is this:
faced with an extreme ideology such as Islamofascism, which has been

conceived in white-hot passions (such passions as *ressentiment* and hatred, bloodlust, the death-wish), with what can relativism arm itself in its own defense? Some of the most sensitive members of a secularist community are liable to make excuses for murderous opponents, and to plead for better understanding, tolerance, and pacification. Since they have no standard of moral truth that they might appeal to, they may rejoice in bringing down their own leaders if these are of a different political party, even if this means giving heart to the enemy.

The second difficulty is a demographic one. Secularism seems to give no motive to young men and women to have children in sufficient numbers to reproduce themselves, plus a little more, to allow for future growth. In fact, secularism seems to serve up motives for *not* having children, whether out of perceived moral duties to "the environment," or fears of "overpopulation," or simply a preference for enjoying a relatively carefree life, unencumbered by the long-enduring and difficult responsibilities of child raising.[37] There appears to be very little writing in the contrary direction.

Possibly, too, the conditions of the social welfare state—high taxes, small apartments, heavily regulated living arrangements, the weakening of personal responsibilities both to the older and to the younger generation—have the unintended consequence of discouraging child raising. The unspoken but demoralizing perception that the welfare state has made far more promises than it can possibly satisfy only compounds this problem. In any case, a certain foreshortening of the future, a certain cultural pessimism, seems to be a natural concomitant of the social welfare society. Tocqueville predicted a "new soft despotism" that would result from an unchecked drift toward social equality, untempered by a fierce love for individual liberty and personal responsibility. In that event, under "democracy" he feared a dread sameness, an enervation, and a coarsening of life.[38]

Secularism's Atheism and Agnosticism Are Not Tenable. Since secularism means, and intends to mean, the death of God, can it propose an alternative to religion? Atheism is not a rational alternative; it is a leap in the dark. No person can possibly prove a negative and thus be certain that there is no God.

That is why agnosticism has come to seem a more modest, skeptically open, and humanistically attractive position. Yet it does have one central flaw. Cardinal Ratzinger and Marcello Pera point it out in their acute diagnosis of the sickness of the West, *Without Roots: The West, Relativism, Christianity, Islam.*[39]

Pera and Ratzinger argue that the flaw in agnosticism lies in its holding back, which is appropriate only for those who do not act. As a spectator sport, agnosticism is at least understandable. Yet every day women and men have to go down into the arena of action. They must make decisions, and when they do, their actions fall under the principles of one theory—or else of that other one. They cannot go on making decisions *etsi Deus non daretur*, as if God does not exist, without having effectively made a pivotal decision about God. In every big decision they make they will, one way or the other, take sides. They will act in a way cognizant of God's will and respectful of it, as a friend would act in the presence of a friend. Or else they will act in a way that violates God's will, as if there were no God, or at least as if there were no way of knowing what his will *is* here and now. One can, in short, pretend to think as an agnostic, but the pressures of actually choosing how to act, this way or that way, oblige one to declare one's relationship to God, willy-nilly. In action, there are no agnostics.[40]

Now it may be possible for extraordinary and unusual people to go on acting as if God does exist, even if they are atheists or agnostics. But it seems unlikely that whole societies can do that—and highly doubtful that ordinary, commonsense people can do that for long, across more than three generations. To be sure, religious societies are also riven by sin. (Every Catholic mass opens with the simple public confession of meeting as a community of sinners, much as a meeting of Alcoholics Anonymous opens with a ritual by which one person after another rises to say, "I am an alcoholic." Not one word more, nor one word less. No excuses, no explanations.) And churches, too, have perennial problems with laxity, backsliding, and sheer moral disorder. But the churches also have means and methods for addressing the problem of moral failure.

Atheism and agnosticism do not, and where they flourish, one may expect to find a certain moral carelessness seeping into common life, a certain slacking off, a certain habit of getting away with things. Secularism may be livable among the highly educated or gifted, but its effects on the less educated seem to be less comforting.

One effect, for instance, may be a coarsening of daily intercourse, as we now seem to be experiencing in America, looking back nostalgically to the time when one could leave home with the door unlocked. A number of British writers down the years have recalled with pleasure the old sweetness and courtesy imbued into the culture by Methodism in its early generations. Another effect, among the rough-and-tumble sort in any population, may be a greater sense that there is no price to pay (even within one's own conscience) for thuggishness and the exhibition of brute will.

Atheism and agnosticism, moreover, seem to offer few reasons why those who are religious—Muslims, for example—should change their religious commitments, even when these lead to violence. Why should they exchange experience, clarity, and certainty for relativism? And if they do not, what fault in that can relativists discern? To be alarmed by violence deployed in the name of religion—as in the bloody murder of Theo Van Gogh in the Netherlands— is to cease being relativist, to discover the reality of evil, and to stand on the verge of resolving to combat it. Judaism and Christianity, one may think, explain this sequence better than current-day secular humanism.

Secularism Weakens the Culture of Science. A pernicious result of the flourishing of atheism and agnosticism is an undermining of the power of reason. One hardly ever meets these days the cocky rationalist of one hundred years ago, secure in his powers of logic and scientific reasoning. The pretense of nihilism, exhibited by genteel people who lack seriousness in the poses they take, flies under the flag of "postmodernism." Aiming to undermine all standards set by reason, postmodernism subordinates the strength and legitimacy of reason to the supervening interests of class, gender, sexuality, and race.

Postmodernism has already made crippling inroads into various fields of science (environmental sciences, for instance), and has begun to corrupt schools of medicine and law. It has aspired to rule the humanities and social sciences, even in major universities. One reason postmodernism has gone so far is that the sort of reason that lifted up the Enlightenment is not altogether well-suited to justifying itself. Reason, as we are learning again, can be used to undermine reason. Reason has also been used to undermine the morale and moral self-confidence of those whose whole lives have been committed to the Enlightenment, by calling them warmongers, or insensitive robots, and the like in order to impugn both their standing in the community and their own sense of self-worth.

Science depends upon a supportive culture, and a measure of social admiration, that make worthwhile all the sacrifices of acquiring a scientific education and professional practice—and that enable the scientist to stiffen the spine against temptation. Science is not just a methodology; it is a set of habits and practices, supported by a culture of a particular kind. This culture is characterized by commitment, discipline, and hard work; it requires honesty and trustworthiness in the reporting of findings, as well as cooperation with colleagues, since science these days is seldom for lone rangers.

If the life of reason is as much a culture as a method, then a great many persons and institutions must be committed to its disciplines, its aims, and its long-term support. Yet it is not clear that science alone, or reason alone, particularly on the basis of atheism or agnosticism, can long inspire such a cultural commitment. If everything is at the end of the day a result of chance, what exactly is the point of a commitment to reason? Reason seems to be out of harmony with the fundamental nature of reality. The humanist who in all things seeks reason while insisting that, at bottom, there are no reasons is tangled in a spider's nest of self-contradictions.

Sometimes reason is portrayed as a set of individual flashlights in a great darkness, held and directed by solitary individuals, committed like Sisyphus to climbing a steep and difficult mountain. Every time he approaches the top, however, Sisyphus is knocked meaninglessly back to the valley floor.

How long, in the face of ultimate pointlessness, can a culture sustain the experience of the frustration of reason and still continue to attract young people to the necessary disciplines? Say this much for it: classical metaphysics was at this point self-consistent.

Religio-Secular Pluralism

Whatever the incapacities of secularism—and surely there are others not enumerated here—it is not clear at this point whether secularism can endure much longer. There is a fifth question raised by Habermas, one that troubles him more than any of the others: *How can a small island of people committed to reason and to science long survive in a great ocean of peoples who see in science and reason engines of demoralization and cultural decadence?* [41]

André Malraux once wrote that "the twenty-first century will be religious, or not at all." But I do not believe that the postsecularist age will necessarily be, or even should be, a religious age. It may be something altogether different.

What, then, might a postsecular age look like? Habermas seems to talk good sense when he writes that in the world after September 11, 2001, secular and religious women and men of the West need each other, not only if they are to survive, but also if they are to put together all the elements of a sustainable humanistic culture. While it is true that the long contest between secularism and religion is still in doubt—with the latter, at the moment, assuming more powerful dimensions than the former had long predicted—we may at least mark out a ground on which both the people of the "secular" order and the people of the "sacred/transcendent" order (as distinct from particular churches and particular cultures) can begin to learn how to cooperate, to the advantage of both.

That such cooperation is necessary was stressed by Cardinal Ratzinger in his debate with Habermas. (It is not as pope or cardinal that Ratzinger is worth learning from, by the way, but as a man of great erudition, superior penetration, openness, and sympathy.) Ratzinger made three surprising points. First, the secular intellect will always be necessary to curb and to correct some of the toxic temptations of religion. Second, neither contemporary secular reason nor any individual religion has as yet adequately come to understand other powerful cultural currents on earth, or adequately begun to converse with them intelligently and profoundly. Relations at this point remain woefully superficial. Christianity and scientific rationalism must "admit de facto that they are accepted only in parts of mankind and are intelligible only in parts of mankind."[42] If we are ever to attain a planetary consensus on the reasonableness of certain moral principles—such as the Western tradition of natural law—we will need to interact far more deeply than anyone as yet has done with the Indian tradition of karma, the Chinese traditions of the Rule of Heaven, and the Islamic tradition of the will of Allah.

Ratzinger's third point, on which he seems to concur with Habermas, is that there are certain creative energies and intuitions that Christianity can bring to secular society. Christianity, after all, is by now found in virtually all nations on earth, and it numbers among its baptized members one-third of all people on earth. It is a fount of practical knowledge about other cultures. The secular is a legitimate regime, with its own special autonomy, rules, and privileges; but also with its own responsibilities and self-inflicted limitations. There can be, is, and ought to be conversation between the religious and the secular: each must be properly distinguished from the other, but when they are incarnated in particular persons, particular practices, and particular institutions, each typically owes much to the other.

The Catholic Church, for example, has over the centuries learned much from successive secular orders. From the East it learned a sense of the great mystery and lordliness of God—a more mystical and contemplative cast of mind. From the ancient Greeks, it learned to love reason, proportion, and beauty. From the Romans it learned stoic virtue, universal administration, and a practical sense of law. From the French it learned the upward flare of the gothic and the brilliance of *idées claires* and rapid wordplay; from the Germans, metaphysics, formidable historical learning, and metahistorical thinking; and from the Anglo-Americans, a dose of common sense (with its echoes of Aristotle) and a passion for the religious liberty of the individual conscience.

There is no point in repeating here the lessons that secularist culture, according to Habermas, has in its turn learned from Judaism and Christianity: intuitions; habits of mind, heart, and aspiration; new standards of compassion and even personal conscience; and the like. Even without sharing in Christian faith, secular persons ought in all fairness to give due recognition to their intellectual indebtedness.

Pluralism cannot mean mere mutual toleration. Even to say that pluralism means mutual respect, while far closer to the heart of the matter, is not enough. For the parties committed to it, pluralism must also mean learning from each other.

If a postsecular age is coming, it is not likely to be an age in which intelligent people set aside their skepticism about Judaism and Christianity, or their deep commitment to science and reason. But it will be, or ought to be, an age in which secular persons recognize at last that their own claim to universal superiority—the view of themselves as "enlightened" while others still walk in darkness—was premature. Not by pure secularism alone will the future be more fruitful than the immediate past. The times call for a planetary conversation among a multitude of human beings, for most of whom a sense for the sacral and the transcendent is as important as science and reason.

The choice between science and religion, or between the ways of reason and the ways of faith, is not an adequate human choice. Better is to take part in a prolonged, intelligent, and respectful conversation across those outmoded ways of drawing lines.

Notes

1. Irving Kristol, "The Future of American Jewry," *Commentary* 92.2 (August 1991): 24.

2. "It would seem that Habermas has justly inherited the title of the world's leading philosopher. Last year he won the prestigious Kyoto Prize for Arts and Philosophy (previous recipients include Karl Popper and Paul Ricoeur), capping an eventful career replete with honors as well as a number of high-profile public debates." Richard Wolin, "Jürgen Habermas and Post-Secular Societies," *Chronicle of Higher Education*, September 23, 2005, B16.

3. "At the beginning of the 20th century, a bare majority of the world's people, precisely 50 percent, were Catholic, Protestant, Muslim, or Hindu. At the beginning of the 21st century, nearly 64 percent belonged to these four religious groupings, and the proportion may be close to 70 percent by 2025." Timothy Samuel Shah and Monica Duffy Toft, "Why God Is Winning," *Foreign Policy*, July/August 2006, 40.

4. "The boundaries between secular and religious . . . are tenuous. Therefore, fixing of this controversial boundary should be understood as a cooperative venture, carried on by both sides, and with each side trying to see the issue from the other's perspective. Democratically enlightened common sense is not a singularity, but is instead the mental constitution of a public with many different voices." Jürgen Habermas, "Faith and Knowledge" (lecture given upon his acceptance of the Peace Prize of the German Publishers and Booksellers Association, Frankfurt, Germany, October 14, 2001), available at http://www.nettime.org/Lists-Archives/nettime-l-0111/msg00100.html.

5. Habermas, *The Future of Human Nature* (Oxford: Polity Press, 2003).

6. Habermas, quoted in Virgil Nemoianu, "The Church and the Secular Establishment: A Philosophical Dialog between Joseph Ratzinger and Jürgen Habermas," *Logos* 9.2 (Spring 2006): 26.

7. Ibid.

8. Joseph Ratzinger, quoted in ibid., 30.

9. On the Regensburg address, see the insightful essay by Lee Harris, "Socrates or Muhammad? Joseph Ratzinger on the Destiny of Reason," *The Weekly Standard* 12.3 (October 2, 2006): 30–35.

10. Habermas, *Theorie des kommunikativen Handelns*, 2 vols. (Frankfurt, Germany: Suhrkamp, 1981). The phrase Habermas uses to express his idea is "*Versprachlichung des Sakrals.*"

11. Habermas affirmed this view in a 2005 lecture: "Ever since the Council of Nicaea and throughout the course of a 'Hellenization of Christianity,' philosophy itself took on board and assimilated many religious motifs and concepts of redemption, specifically those from the history of salvation. Concepts of Greek origin such as 'autonomy' and 'individuality' or Roman concepts such as 'emancipation' and

'solidarity' have long since been shot through with meanings of a Judaeo-Christian origin." Habermas, "Religion in the Public Sphere" (lecture presented at the Holberg Prize Seminar, November 29, 2005), 19.

12. Wolin, "Jürgen Habermas and Post-Secular Societies," B16.

13. Habermas, quoted in Wolin, "Jurgen Habermas and Post-Secular Societies," B16, emphasis added.

14. See Michael Novak, "Max Weber Goes Global," *First Things*, April 2005, 26–27.

15. Wolin, "Jürgen Habermas and Post-Secular Societies," B16.

16. Habermas, "Religion in the Public Sphere" (lecture, Lodz University, 2005), 7.

17. Pierre Manent, "Christianity and Democracy (Part I)," in *A Free Society Reader*, ed. Michael Novak, William Brailsford, and Cornelius Heesters (Lanham, MD: Lexington Books, 2000), 109–115.

18. Habermas, "Religion in the Public Sphere," 12–13.

19. Habermas, "Faith and Knowledge."

20. Ibid.

21. Walter Lippmann, *The American Inquisitors: A Commentary on Dayton and Chicago* (New York: The Macmillan Company, 1928), 62–63, 65–66.

22. The Fundamentalist responds: "You admit that all history shows how few men have been able to live a moral life without the conviction that they were obeying a divine will. You then point out a few unusual men, a few stoics perhaps, a few Epicureans, a few followers of Spinoza, a few pure and disinterested spirits among the scientists, and you ask me to believe that what this trifling minority has achieved through innate moral genius, the great humdrum mass of mankind is to achieve by what you optimistically describe as education. I do not believe it." Ibid., 56–57.

23. "In short, post-metaphysical thought is prepared to learn from religion while remaining strictly agnostic. It insists on the difference between certainties of faith and validity claims that can be publicly criticized; but it refrains from the rationalist temptation that it can itself decide which part of the religious doctrines is rational and which part is not." Habermas, "Religion in the Public Sphere," 20.

24. "Secular humanism gave us answers for 500 years that no longer seem adequate even to many who tried hard to be faithful to them. That is why so many far-seeing souls announce that we have come to the edge of the Enlightenment and are stepping forth into something new, untried, not yet transparent." Novak, "The Most Religious Century," *New York Times*, May 24, 1998.

25. Kristol, "Future of American Jewry," 25.

26. Ibid.

27. Albert Camus recounts a letter from a German friend: "The greatness of my country is beyond price. Anything is good that contributes to its greatness. And

in a world where everything has lost its meaning, those who, like us young Germans, are lucky enough to find a meaning in the destiny of our nation must sacrifice everything else." Albert Camus, "First Letter," *Resistance, Rebellion, and Death*, trans. Justin O'Brien (New York: Alfred A. Knopf, 1961), 5.

28. Kristol, "Future of American Jewry," 25.

29. Ibid.

30. Judith Jarvis Thompson, *The Realm of Rights* (Cambridge, MA: Harvard University Press, 1990).

31. Robert William Fogel, *The Fourth Great Awakening and the Future of Egalitarianism* (Chicago: University of Chicago Press, 1999).

32. "A living history was to be found in every family—a history bearing the indubitable testimonies of its own authenticity, in the limbs mangled, in the scars of wounds received, in the midst of the very scenes related—a history, too, that could be read and understood alike by all, the wise and the ignorant, the learned and the unlearned. But *those* histories are gone. They can be read no more forever. They *were* a fortress of strength; but, what invading foeman could *never* do, the silent artillery of time has done; the leveling of its walls." Abraham Lincoln, "Address to the Young Men's Lyceum of Springfield, Illinois, January 27, 1838," in *Abraham Lincoln: Speeches and Writings 1832–1858*, ed. Roy P. Basler (New York: Literary Classics of the United States, 1989), 36.

33. Alasdair MacIntyre, *After Virtue* (Notre Dame, IN: University of Notre Dame Press, 1981).

34. For a fuller treatment of truth as a regulative ideal, see Novak, "Caritapolis: A Universal Culture of Mutual Respect," in *The Universal Hunger for Liberty: Why the Clash of Civilizations Is Not Inevitable* (New York: Basic Books, 2004), 37–38.

35. "Barbarism is the lack of reasonable conversation according to reasonable laws. The depreciation of language accompanies the depreciation of the currency in the decline of civilization. . . . Civilization is formed by men locked together in argument. From this dialogue the community becomes a political community." Thomas Gilby, *Between Community and Society: A Philosophy and Theology of the State* (London: Longmans, 1953), 93.

36. In a review of *Plato and Europe* by Jan Patocka, the Czech philosopher and martyr (1907–77), Rorty writes: "Jerusalem should share the credit with Athens for making Europe what it has become. The Christian suggestion that we think of strangers primarily as fellow sufferers, rather than as fellow inquirers into Being, or as fellow carers for the soul, should have a larger role than Patocka gives it. The waves of joy of 1989 cannot plausibly be traced to the sense that judgment had been rendered on Socrates' judges, as opposed to the belief that a lot of people who had been humiliated and shamed would now be able to stand up and to speak. Separating out the roles of Socrates and Christ in the history of Europe is a notoriously tricky business, but surely Patocka oversimplifies things

when, like Heidegger, he approvingly quotes Nietzsche's comment that 'Christianity is Platonism for the people.' Might not a sense that charity and kindness are the central virtues have caught on, and helped make Europe what it became, even if some eager Platonists had not grabbed control of Christian theology?" Richard Rorty, "Review of *Plato and Europe*," *New Republic* 205, no. 1 (July 1991): 37. Bertrand Russell makes an analogous argument in *Why I Am Not a Christian* (Girard, KS: Haldeman-Julius Publications, 1929). For more on this subject, see Novak, "How Christianity Changed Political Economy," in *Three in One: Essays on Democratic Capitalism*, 1976–2000, ed. Edward W. Younkins (Lanham, MD: Rowman & Littlefield, 2001), 194–201.

37. For more on demography, see Mark Steyn, "It's the Demography, Stupid!" *New Criterion* 24 (January 2006): 10.

38. "I am trying to imagine under what novel features despotism may appear in the world. In the first place, I see an innumerable multitude of men, alike and equal, constantly circling around in pursuit of the petty and banal pleasure with which they glut their souls. Each one of them, withdrawn into himself, is almost unaware of the fate of the rest. . . . [Government] does not break men's will, but softens, bends, and guides it; it seldom enjoins, but often inhibits, action; it does not destroy anything, but prevents much being born; it is not at all tyrannical, but it hinders, restrains, enervates, stifles, and stultifies so much that in the end each nation is no more than a flock of timid and hardworking animals with the government as its shepherd." Alexis de Tocqueville, *Democracy in America*, trans. George Lawrence, ed. J. P. Mayer (New York: Anchor Books, 1969), 691–92.

39. Joseph Ratzinger and Marcello Pera, *Without Roots: The West, Relativism, Christianity, Islam*, trans. Michael F. Moore (New York: Basic Books, 2006). At the time he wrote the book, Pera was president of the Italian Senate.

40. Arguing against Derrida's deconstructionism, Ratzinger and Pera write: "People no longer believe in 'ultimate' foundations. . . . Only philosophers in their classrooms can afford the luxury of not taking practical decisions; not so the man of the street, the politician, the head of state." Ibid., 19.

41. Habermas, "Faith and Knowledge," German Publishers and Booksellers Association, Frankfurt, Germany, October 14, 2001.

42. Ratzinger, quoted in Nemoianu, "Church and the Secular Establishment," 30.

2

A Response to Michael Novak

Roger Scruton

I am in broad agreement with Michael Novak that the conflict between the religious and the secular worldviews has entered a new phase, that secularism has, for a variety of reasons, lost some of its militant character, and that a new dialogue is needed between believers and skeptics if the West is to face the future with confidence. I agree with him, too, in seeing the spread of postmodernism as in part the result of the loss of religious faith. In Novak's imagery, God was the pole to which the truth-seeking compass of reason once turned. Now the compass spins at random, coming to rest along no line of force.

However, there are one or two things with which I take issue in Professor Novak's argument, and one or two ways in which I would like to supplement its principal points. My first objection is to Professor Novak's opening sentence, which exhorts us to praise Habermas as the world's greatest living philosopher, and Derrida as his predecessor in that position. Derrida, it seems to me, was a charlatan, whose peculiar brand of intoxicating nonsense did much to create the postmodernist orthodoxy which Novak rightly deplores. Habermas is a better thinker than that—it would be hard to be a worse one. As last living representative of the Frankfurt School, he tinkered for many years with Marxist categories and tried to find new ways of shaping the anticapitalist message. His lifelong theme has been the crisis of legitimacy faced by capitalist societies, a crisis that could be overcome only by the usual alliance of left-wing intellectuals with carefully selected, and duly deferential, members of the working class.

Only in *The Theory of Communicative Action* did Habermas begin to grow up. And that book is to be commended in advocating dialogue, negotiation, and sympathy in the place of the old Marxist "struggle." But I cannot find anything new in it that helps me to understand what we should communicate about, or how we might give heart to our world. If the *only* message is, let's talk, I wonder why we need two volumes of inspissated jargon to convey it. And the dialogues that Habermas now advocates, in the wake of September 11, are noticeable for the voices that they exclude: no nationalists, no social conservatives, no premodernists, and no fervent free-marketeers will be invited to the table when the postmodern future of mankind is plotted in the Habermasian bunker. By excluding so much of ordinary humanity from his chatter-house, Habermas *avoids* the real questions that confront us, recommending that we discuss them only to avoid discussing them.

The first of these questions has to do with human nature. Without a theory of human nature that shows the reality of our religious need, there is no way of pushing secularism into the corner that Professor Novak believes it to be already in. The most powerful current of secularism today is not, I think, the postmodernism to which Professor Novak takes exception, but the view advanced by Richard Dawkins and his followers, according to which human beings are "survival machines" in the service of their genes. This view is expressed by Dawkins, and his many followers, with a kind of militant zeal that recalls the dogmatic atheism of T. H. Huxley and the first Darwinians. According to Dawkins there is nothing more to human nature than the complex workings of a particularly sophisticated survival machine, and our own self-image as free agents animated by a rational soul is simply an illusion—a shadow cast by language, with no substance of its own. Dawkins goes on to argue that religion is both irrational and dangerous, the result of the colonization of the human brain by a peculiar virus or "meme," which spreads from brain to brain like meningitis, and kills off the competing powers of rational argument. Like genes and species, memes are Darwinian individuals, whose success or failure depends upon their ability to find the ecological niche that enables reproduction.

Now, faced with a page of Derrida, and knowing that this drivel is being read and reproduced in a thousand American campuses, I have often found myself tempted by the theory of the meme. The page in my hand is clearly the product of a diseased brain, and the disease is massively infectious: Derrida admitted as much when he referred to the "deconstructive virus." All the same, I am not entirely persuaded by this extension by analogy of genetics.

The theory that ideas have a disposition to propagate themselves by appro-
priating energy from the brains that harbor them recalls Molière's medical
expert (*Le malade imaginaire*), who explained the fact that opium induces
sleep by referring to its *virtus dormitiva*.

Nevertheless, even if we don't accept the theory of the meme, we still
have to confront both the reductionist view of human nature that Dawkins
advances, and the associated belief that there is no such thing as religious
truth. The mysteries of religion, Dawkins will say, exist in order to forbid all
questioning, thus giving religion the edge over science in the struggle for
survival, but no edge at all in the search for truth. In any case, why are there
so many competitors among religions, if they really are searching for the
truth? Shouldn't the false ones have fallen by the wayside, like refuted theories in science? And how does religion improve the human spirit, when it
seems to authorize the crimes now committed each day by Islamists, which
are in turn no more than a shadow of the crimes that were spread across
Europe by the Thirty Years War?

In the face of this kind of challenge, it is not enough to point, as Michael
Novak does, to the fact that many of the most cherished values of the secular Enlightenment owe their origins and their propagation to our two great
religions. That may show the innate superiority of Judaism and Christianity over Islam—but it is a superiority judged in secular terms. In a way, it is
a point to the secularist when we argue that Christianity, for example, is the
true source of values like democracy and human rights. For that is to justify Christianity in terms of the things of this world, rather than in terms of
its vision of our final end. It is to justify Christianity as the precursor of
Enlightenment, not Enlightenment as the residue of Christianity. To answer
Dawkins and his followers, we need to show that our nature is not adequately represented by the theory of the selfish gene, that religious beliefs
are not irrational viruses but doctrines which aim at the truth—even if it is
a truth beyond the empirical world, concerning matters that lie outside the
scope of natural science.

The great error of the selfish gene theory, it seems to me, is in misidenti-
fying the kind to which we human beings belong. It is true that we are animals, and true therefore that the laws of genetics apply as much to us as they
do to ants, bees, and tapeworms. But we are also persons; and it is as persons
that we relate to each other, not as animals. What is needed is a philosophy

of the person that will show the ways in which interpersonal attitudes carve out a space for religion, and the ways in which they implant in us the states of mind—guilt, hope, longing, atonement—which point of their own accord towards a personal God. In the absence of this philosophy it will not really help us to describe the inadequacies of the secular vision, or the way in which, having lost confidence in God, it loses confidence in truth also. For there is a way of losing confidence which is also a way of gaining it: post-modernist skepticism can at any moment become postmodernism with teeth, tearing away at ordinary cultural certainties with all the ferocity of an inner disappointment. If we have no way of supporting those ordinary certainties, then we provoke the postmodernist attack on them. Remember that it is never strength that is attacked but only weakness.

I would hope, therefore, that Michael Novak would amplify his argument with a positive theory of human nature, one that will show just why the available secular visions are inadequate: just why they misrepresent what we truly are. As I see it, human conduct admits not merely biological explanation, but explanation of another kind, in which free choice, reason, accountability, and self-consciousness play a determining role. And this kind of explanation is, it seems to me, irreducible to the categories of biology. If it is possible to sustain that view, then we are on the way towards victory over secularism and all that it means. However, it is certainly not Habermas who is going to help us here; I place more trust in Max Scheler, though of course his phenomenological method belongs to the past, and needs to be sent to the Wittgensteinian laundry before it can be worn again.

There is one other thought that I should like to add to Professor Novak's exposition, which is this: the failure of secularism is not in the first instance an intellectual failure; it is a moral failure. It does not provide to people what they need in order to survive and flourish. It does not provide a crucial component in human earthly happiness, which is the sense of membership. Religions, by contrast, are a call to membership—they provide customs, beliefs, and rituals that unite the generations in a shared way of life, and implant the seeds of mutual respect. In a way, this is what provokes people to attack them. Like every form of social life, religions are inflamed at the edges, where they compete for territory with other faiths. Hence there are religious wars, and in these wars the gift of mercy is often in short supply.

Unlike Dawkins, I don't regard this fact as a damning criticism of religion. On the contrary. To blame religion for the wars conducted in its name is like blaming love for the Trojan War. All human motives, even the most noble, will feed the flames of conflict when subsumed by the territorial imperative. Take religion away, as the Nazis and the Communists did, and you do nothing to suppress the pursuit of *Lebensraum*. You simply remove the principal source of mercy in the ordinary human heart and so make war pitiless: atheism found its proof at Stalingrad.

Nevertheless, there is a tendency, fed by the sensationalism of television, to judge all human institutions by their behavior in times of conflict. Religion, like patriotism, gets a bad press among those for whom war is the one human reality, the one occasion when the Other in all of us is noticeable. But the real test of a human institution is in peacetime. Peace is boring, quotidian, and also rotten television. But you can learn about it from books. Those nurtured in the Christian faith know that Christianity's ability to maintain peace in the world around us reflects its gift of peace to the world within. It is that peace which secularism destroys: it leaves us without the principal resources of the lonely heart, which are prayer, confession, atonement, and the love of God—all of them paths back to membership in this world, and a preparation for blessedness in the next.

Muslims say similar things, and so do Jews. So who possesses the truth, and how would you know? We don't know, nor do we need to know. All faith depends on revelation, and the proof of the revelation is in the peace that it brings. Rational argument can get us just so far, in raising the monotheistic faiths above the muddled world of superstition. It can help us to understand the real difference between a faith that commands us to forgive our enemies, and one that commands us to slaughter them. But the leap of faith itself—this placing of your life at God's service—is a leap over reason's edge. This does not make it irrational, any more than falling in love is irrational. On the contrary, it is the heart's submission to an ideal, and a bid for the love, peace, and forgiveness that even that old bore Habermas is seeking, since he, like the rest of us, was made in just that way.

3

Commentary

Irving Kristol

I am not so certain that the kind of discourse and conversation Michael Novak envisages is the way to go. A German philosopher may have the perception that when the Second Coming eventuates, all the PhDs and all the Doctors of Divinity will be gathered in one place to engage in an endless conversation. If Dante is present, he will know exactly where to put that spectacle.

Arguing about religion makes no sense, in my opinion, if it means arguing about theology. Theology is a given; it's not going to change as the result of argument among the sects. It may change for other reasons, but no Christians are going to change their theology because Jews criticize them or vice versa. The more they know of their own theology, the more invincible they are to the force of that kind of argument.

More than thirty years ago, I was discussing with a good friend of mine, who is a professor at the Jewish Theological Seminary, what they did at the seminary. I said, "You know, you really need a good course on the history of Christian thought. After all, we live in a Christian civilization. Rabbis should know a lot more about Christian thought than they do." He flatly disagreed: "Jews are very suspicious of rabbis who claim to know a lot of Christianity. They're not going to give them positions in their community, taking care of their children." He had a point.

Theology is not a fruitful point of contact between the religions. Morality is. There is an important difference between Judaism and Christianity. In Judaism, morality trumps theology, practically always. In Christianity, theology trumps morality, frequently enough. After all, our revelation is the Ten Commandments, for ordinary people, in their daily life. It is not intended just for saints or to effect the transvaluation of humanity—just what they eat, and how to eat it. I think, therefore, that Jews have no problem with other religions if their moral code is, more or less, parallel to the Jewish moral code. We let all righteous people into heaven. Not every religion does so, however.

I'm not certain, then, about the benefits of these "dialogues." They're best conducted not by people who have any connection with the religion, but by intellectuals who find fun fooling around with ideas, talking about this religion, about that religion.

Let me make one final point about religious awakenings. I would love to have a religious revival without a religious awakening. I am frightened by religious awakenings. I think we are witnessing a major religious awakening in the world right now in Islam. What's happening in Islam is a major awakening, based on a hatred of the West, and the discovery that there is a very effective technology with which you can fight the West, namely suicide bombers.

This awakening is transforming Islam. People who say that Islam needs a reformation generally imagine that such a reformation would make Islam more liberal. But it could just as easily make it more vivid and more ferocious. We have to remember, especially in our particular time and place, the danger of a religious awakening out of control.

Peter Berkowitz

I think there is an underlying shared logic to Michael Novak's argument and Roger Scruton's response. First, what most people now know as liberalism is one form of liberalism. Let's call it the reflection of secular triumphalism. Modern liberalism arose to grapple with a variety of problems, but especially to find a political solution to the wars of religion in Europe, a political solution to the problem posed by a multiplicity of religions. In a sense, then, early modern liberalism is more suited to our postsecular age than the liberalisms of Rawls and Habermas.

But early modern liberalism has a defect discussed by various authors in this volume, Leon Kass especially. That defect is reductionism. Liberalism celebrates rights but neglects duties. It reduces the moral life to the following of rules, or the computing of pleasure and pain, and it truncates the scope of reason, so that reason equals natural science—no more, no less.

Early modern liberalism had an antireligious tendency, even as it responded to a problem that is our problem: how do you deal with a world in which there are a multiplicity of clashing religions? Thus as we're entering this postsecular age, or having entered it, we need this early modern liberalism more than ever. Yet it has this defect.

Where do we go from there? Perhaps this is the key question: would it be helpful to work with some of the central goods of this early modern liberalism, but against its antireligious tendency? Among its goods are its respect for reason, its skepticism, understood as an insistence on the limits of reason, its generosity towards difference, its toleration of that with which it disagrees. Could we not focus on these goods within early modern liberalism to develop a way of thinking that was more open to traditions outside the liberal sphere, traditions that would leaven and enliven liberalism? Could doing so offer a way of thinking about politics that not only provides a framework within which various religions can live with each other, but is open to competing claims?

PART II

Religion and Politics

4

The Faith-Based Vote
in the United States:
A Look toward the Future

John C. Green

Although long given to hyperbole, American political discourse reached
new levels of excess after the 2004 presidential election, especially with
regard to the impact of religion on voting. Hardly were the ballots counted
than disappointed liberal commentators attacked religious conservatives for
reelecting George W. Bush, comparing them to Islamic extremists.[1] Such
denunciations were followed by a spate of books decrying the political
power of religious conservatives and their plans to impose a "theocracy" on
the country.[2] The objects of this commentary were vocal as well: leaders of
the Christian Right paused from their usual denunciations of "secularists"
to take credit for the Republican victory and policy changes they felt were
sure to follow.[3] But they soon returned to the attack, accusing liberal elites
of waging a "war on Christians."[4]

From a factual point of view, this rhetoric is an overstatement: there is
little evidence for either an impending "theocracy" or a "war on Christians"
in the United States. However, such rhetoric indicates just how controversial faith-based politics has become. In part, this dispute reflects real disagreements over cultural issues, such as abortion and marriage, on which
many religious communities have taken sides. But it also reflects the close
political division of the electorate, where even small groups of voters—
including religious communities—can influence election outcomes. In
sum, the caustic commentary reveals America's diverse religious communities to be an important part of a highly polarized politics.

41

This reality raises several questions. What does the future hold for faith-based politics? Will the present controversies and circumstances continue, or are changes on the way? Will religion be more or less of a factor in future elections?

This essay is an investigation of these questions. It begins with a description of the major religious communities in the United States and of how they voted in the 2004 election. Next, it glances back to the 1988 election to see how faith-based politics was different at that time. Finally, it reviews the religious and issue bases for the major-party voter coalitions. This information, along with the 2006 election results, is used to evaluate two scenarios for the future of faith-based politics: a continuation of cultural conflict or its decline.

Religious Communities and the 2004 Presidential Vote

A good place to begin is with a description of the major religious communities in the United States and how they voted in 2004. Using a special survey of the American public (see the appendix for details), table 1 lists twenty-two religious groups defined by religious affiliation, belief, and practice. Although the number of religious categories may appear excessive, it barely taps the diversity of American religion, and it illustrates the complexity of faith-based politics.

Religious Traditions. The basic building blocks of these categories (and the major sections in the table) are the major religious traditions, measured by self-reported denominational affiliation. These religious traditions include Evangelical, Mainline and Black Protestants, Catholics, Jews, and two composite categories of smaller traditions, Other Christians (such as the Latter-day Saints and the Eastern Orthodox) and Other Faiths (such as Muslims, Buddhists, and Hindus). Latino Protestants and Catholics are also separate categories because of their political importance (although they might be better thought of as ethnic sub-traditions). The final category is the Unaffiliated, representing the special case of the *absence* of affiliation with a religious tradition. Cruder references to these religious traditions are a staple of political discourse, such as the perennial interest

TABLE 1
RELIGIOUS COMMUNITIES AND THE PRESIDENTIAL VOTE, 2004

	Size	Two-Party Vote	
	Percentage of Population	Percentage for Bush	Percentage for Kerry
Evangelical Protestants			
Traditionalist Evangelical	10.7	87.9	12.1
Centrist Evangelical	9.7	70.4	29.6
Modernist Evangelical	3.3	57.1	42.9
Nominal Evangelical	1.5	56.5	43.5
Mainline Protestants			
Traditionalist Mainline	4.5	65.6	34.4
Centrist Mainline	5.5	49.1	50.9
Modernist Mainline	4.4	43.1	56.9
Nominal Mainline	2.0	31.0	69.0
Minority Protestants			
Latino Protestant	2.6	62.9	37.1
Traditionalist Black Protestant	4.2	18.2	81.8
Less Traditional Black Protestant	5.1	17.5	82.5
Catholics			
Traditionalist Catholic	4.2	73.9	26.1
Centrist Catholic	7.4	52.3	47.7
Modernist Catholic	3.8	38.1	61.9
Nominal Catholic	2.1	28.9	71.1
Latino Catholic	4.5	31.4	68.6
Other Traditions			
Other Christians	2.8	80.0	20.0
Jews	1.9	26.7	73.3
Other Faiths	2.6	22.0	78.0
Unaffiliated			
Unaffiliated Believers	4.8	37.0	63.0
Seculars	9.0	29.5	70.5
Atheists, Agnostics	3.4	20.0	80.0
ALL	100.0	51.2	48.8

SOURCE: Fourth National Survey of Religion and Politics, Bliss Institute University of Akron, 2004, available at http://pewforum.org/publications/surveys/green-full.pdf.
NOTE: N=4,000 overall, 2,750 post-election.

in the "Catholic vote" and the turnout of black Protestants. But without doubt the most common focus is on the "religious Right" and "fundamentalists" of one kind or another. Indeed, even the harsh rhetoric about faith-based voting takes for granted the importance of religious affiliation, albeit in a pejorative fashion.

Religious Traditionalism. The religious traditions in table 1 are further divided where practicable into four categories based on traditional religious beliefs and practices. As the name implies, "traditionalists" are the most likely to hold traditional religious beliefs (such as belief in a personal God and in heaven and hell) and to engage in traditional practices (such as regular worship attendance and frequent prayer). In contrast, "modernists" are the most likely to hold modern beliefs and to engage in fewer traditional practices. "Centrists" fall in between the traditionalists and modernists in these regards, while "nominals" report few religious beliefs or practices of any kind. The unaffiliated population is divided into three roughly analogous categories based on other criteria, producing Unaffiliated Believers, Seculars, and self-identified Atheists and Agnostics.

Due to the small number of respondents, Black Protestants are divided into two categories, "traditionalist" and "less traditional" (combining centrists, modernists, and nominals). For the same reason, the four remaining religious categories were not subdivided at all, but there is reason to believe that the traditionalist-nominal distinctions may occur within some of these groups, such as Jews. (For more detail on the definition of these categories, see the appendix.)

The impact of religious traditionalism on the vote has been widely recognized by political observers, most famously in the form of the "God gap" in voting.[5] There is a good bit of truth behind the "God gap," but religious traditionalism includes religious practices as well as beliefs. In any event, the "God gap" has helped fuel the fierce rhetoric about faith-based politics.

The first column in table 1 lists the relative size of these religious categories. These data quantify the religious diversity of the American public. For instance, the largest group, Traditionalist Evangelical Protestants, accounts for only about one-tenth of the adult population. Most of the categories are one-half this size or smaller. In fact, many of these categories must be viewed with caution because of the small number of cases. Clearly, there is no simple "religious majority" in the United States, and as a consequence, faith-based electoral politics is inherently a process of coalition building.

Religion and the 2004 Presidential Vote. The remaining two columns in table 1 report the two-party presidential vote in 2004. These patterns illustrate the usefulness of these religious categories in understanding the presidential vote. To begin with, there are consistent differences within the three large Christian traditions based on traditionalism: the traditionalists always voted most for Bush and the nominals always voted most for Kerry—with the centrist and modernists always falling in between. For example, nearly nine of ten Traditionalist Evangelicals backed Bush, compared to a bit more than one-half of the Nominal Evangelicals. Similar divisions occurred among Mainline Protestants and Catholics, and even among the unaffiliated, where Unaffiliated Believers were seventeen percentage points less likely to vote for Kerry than Atheists and Agnostics.

However, religious affiliation also mattered to the presidential vote: Traditionalist Evangelicals (87.9 percent) were more Republican than Traditionalist Catholics (73.9 percent) or Traditionalist Mainline Protestants (65.6 percent). Likewise, Modernist Evangelicals (42.9 percent) were less Democratic than Modernist Mainliners (56.9 percent) or Modernist Catholics (61.9 percent). Affiliation was particularly important for religious minorities. For instance, Traditionalist Black Protestants hardly differed from their less traditional counterparts in terms of the Democratic vote. Note also the differences between Latino Protestants (62.9 percent for Bush) and Latino Catholics (68.6 percent for Kerry). Distinctive presidential preferences were also displayed by the Other Christians (80 percent for Bush) as well as by Jews and Other Faiths (73 and 78 percent for Kerry, respectively).

Of course, this simple table does not take into account other demographic factors that also affect the vote, such as income, education, and gender. However, taking these factors into account does not eliminate the connection between these religious distinctions and the vote. In fact, most of these demographic factors had an independent impact in 2004, with religion a powerful factor in head-to-head comparisons with other measures of demography.[6] That said, it is important to remember that religion is not the only thing that matters in elections.[7]

A Glance Back at the Recent Past

Table 1 documents the importance of the faith-based vote in 2004. Hyperbole aside, there was a reality behind the bitter commentary on faith-based politics. Simply put, some religious communities strongly backed President Bush's reelection, others strongly opposed it, and still others were more evenly divided.

Some of the patterns in table 1 are longstanding, such as the relationship between religious tradition and the vote, but other features are relatively new, such as the importance of religious traditionalism. Table 2 illustrates this change by looking at the same religious categories for the "Bush" vote in 2004 and 1988. The 1988 election was chosen as a point of comparison because there were comparable religious measures for both elections (see appendix for details). But there is a satisfying symmetry in comparing the election of the first President Bush to the reelection of the second President Bush.

The most important pattern in table 2 is found within the major religious traditions. Note that the differences in the Bush vote in 1988 between traditionalists and nominals are smaller and less consistent than in table 1. For example, there was no real difference in the 1988 Bush vote between Traditionalist Catholics (50.8 percent) and Modernist or Nominal Catholics (about 53 percent each). Although Traditional Mainline Protestants (62.7 percent) did vote more Republican than Nominal Mainliners (55.2 percent) in 1988, the Modernist Mainliners voted even more strongly for the GOP (68 percent) in that year. Meanwhile, the difference between Traditionalist Evangelicals (74.1 percent) and Modernist Evangelicals (59.8 percent) was just fourteen percentage points, roughly one-half of the analogous difference of thirty percentage points in 2004.

Thus between 1988 and 2004, a striking change occurred across the traditionalist-nominal divide within the three largest Christian traditions: traditionalists increased their Republican vote, while the modernists and nominals voted more Democratic. For example, Traditionalist Evangelicals became some fourteen percentage points more Republican by 2004, building on an already impressive Bush vote in 1988. Meanwhile, Modernist and Nominal Evangelicals voted more Democratic, the latter by a large margin. A similar pattern occurred among Catholics, with Traditionalist Catholics

TABLE 2
RELIGIOUS COMMUNITIES AND THE "BUSH" VOTE, 2004 AND 1988

	Percentage for Bush 2004	Percentage for Bush 1988	Change 2004–1988
Evangelical Protestants			
Traditionalist Evangelical	87.9	74.1	**13.8**
Centrist Evangelical	70.4	65.3	**5.1**
Modernist Evangelical	57.1	59.8	**-2.7**
Nominal Evangelical	56.5	92.3	**-35.8**
Mainline Protestants			
Traditionalist Mainline	65.6	62.7	**2.9**
Centrist Mainline	49.1	60.7	**-11.6**
Modernist Mainline	43.1	68.0	**-24.9**
Nominal Mainline	31.0	55.2	**-24.2**
Minority Protestants			
Latino Protestant	62.9	31.0	**31.9**
Traditionalist Black Protestant	18.2	7.7	**10.5**
Less Traditional Black Protestant	17.5	18.8	**-1.3**
Catholics			
Traditionalist Catholic	73.9	50.8	**23.1**
Centrist Catholic	52.3	47.9	**4.4**
Modernist Catholic	38.1	53.6	**-15.5**
Nominal Catholic	28.9	53.8	**-24.9**
Latino Catholic	31.4	23.4	**8.0**
Other Traditions			
Other Christians	80.0	65.6	**14.4**
Jews	26.7	23.6	**3.1**
Other Faiths	22.0	22.9	**-0.9**
Unaffiliated			
Unaffiliated Believers	37.0	70.4	**-33.4**
Seculars	29.5	50.3	**-20.8**
Atheists, Agnostics	20.0	46.2	**-26.2**
ALL	**51.2**	**53.0**	**-2.0**

SOURCES: First National Survey of Religion and Politics, Bliss Institute University of Akron, 1988; Fourth National Survey of Religion and Politics, Bliss Institute University of Akron, 2004, available at http://pewforum.org/publications/surveys/green-full.pdf.
NOTES: For 2004, N=4,000 overall, 2,750 post-election; for 1988, N=4,001 overall, 2,265 post-election (see appendix for details). Under column headed "Change 2004–1988," positive numbers mean a net gain in Republican ballots; negative numbers mean a net loss in Republican ballots.

becoming some twenty-three percentage points more Republican by 2004, while Modernist and Nominal Catholics went the other way (15.5 and 24.9 percentage points less Republican, respectively). An analogous shift occurred among Mainline Protestants, but with only small Republican gains among the already strongly Republican traditionalists.

Other changes over time shown in table 2 support these patterns. Note that Traditionalist Black Protestants increased their "Bush" vote, while the less traditional moved a bit the other way. Latino Protestants, Other Christians, Latino Catholics, and Jews also moved in a Republican direction (perhaps due to a greater number of traditionalist voters in their midst). Meanwhile, the unaffiliated groups deserted the GOP, posting double-digit shifts toward the Democrats between 1988 and 2004.

Hence the "Bush" era, broadly defined, saw the Republicans attracting more voters who were traditionally religious from across the religious landscape, while losing to the Democrat voters who were less traditional, less religious, and nonreligious. These dramatic changes occurred within the short span of five presidential elections. However, there is evidence that this process began as long ago as the 1972 election (with its culture clash between George McGovern's "new politics" and Richard Nixon's "silent majority"), when the worship attendance gap first appeared. This gap declined a bit through 1992 and then began a steady climb to 2004[8] and continued to grow in 2006.

Religious Communities and Presidential Voter Coalitions

These dramatic changes in faith-based voting did not go unnoticed by political observers. The intense commentary on faith-based politics is just one proof of this development. Some analysts focused on the religious basis for the change, dubbing it the "restructuring of American religion."[9] Others stressed the cultural nature of these divisions, noting a tension between "two cultures" with opposite aspirations[10] or announcing the advent of "culture wars."[11] Still others were impressed by the partisan nature of these changes, describing them as a "great divide"[12] or a "diminishing divide"[13]—depending upon one's perspective. To be sure, the details, origins, and implications of these changes have been hotly debated, with many scholars skeptical of their comprehensiveness, impact, and durability.[14] But even the skeptics recognize the presence of new religious elements in the major-party coalitions at the elite and mass levels.[15]

Table 3 reorganizes the data in table 1 to look at each party's voter coalitions in 2004. In the first column, the twenty-two religious communities are rearranged in order of the net Bush vote (the Bush vote minus the Kerry vote). The categories range from the most Republican group in 2004, Traditionalist Evangelicals (a net of 75.8 percentage points for Bush) to the least Republican group, Less Traditional Black Protestants (a net of –65.0 percentage points for Bush—and a net 65.0 points for Kerry).

For ease of discussion, this listing of the religious communities is subdivided into rough partisan groupings: "core" and "peripheral" GOP constituencies, evenly divided "swing" constituencies, and "peripheral" and "core" Democratic constituencies. The final two columns report the percentage of the total Bush and Kerry vote that came from each of the twenty-two religious categories. These columns provide a sense of the relative importance of the religious communities at the ballot box, in effect taking into account their relative size and level of turnout, along with their presidential preferences.[16]

Core Republican Constituencies. The four core Republican constituencies are Traditionalist Evangelicals; the composite category of Other Christians (with Latter-day Saints the largest group); Traditionalist Catholics; and Centrist Evangelicals (all with a net Bush vote of more than forty percentage points). The Traditionalist Evangelicals provided almost one-quarter of all of Bush's 2004 ballots, his single largest constituency. This group comes closest to being the "fundamentalists" of popular discourse and the core of the "religious Right." Centrist Evangelicals contributed another one-tenth of the Bush vote, so that when combined, these two evangelical groups made up more than one-third of all Bush's ballots. (If Modernist Evangelicals and Nominal Evangelicals in the peripheral constituencies are included, all Evangelical Protestants accounted for nearly two-fifths of the Bush total).

The four core Republican constituencies summed to almost one-half the Republican presidential vote. A glance back at table 2 reveals that all these religious communities moved in a Republican direction between 1988 and 2004.

TABLE 3
RELIGIOUS COMMUNITIES AND VOTE COALITIONS, 2004

	Net Two-Party Vote	Vote Coalitons	
	2004	Bush	Kerry
Core Republican			
Traditionalist Evangelical	75.8	23.4	3.4
Other Christians	60.0	4.3	1.1
Traditionalist Catholic	47.8	7.7	2.9
Centrist Evangelical	40.8	11.9	5.2
Peripheral Republican			
Traditionalist Mainline	31.2	7.0	3.9
Latino Protestant	25.8	2.6	1.6
Modernist Evangelical	14.2	2.8	2.2
Nominal Evangelical	13.5	1.5	1.2
Swing Constituencies			
Centrist Catholic	4.6	7.9	7.6
Centrist Mainline	−1.8	6.5	7.1
Peripheral Democratic			
Modernist Mainline	−13.8	3.3	4.6
Unaffiliated Believers	−26.0	2.0	3.6
Modernist Catholic	−23.8	2.8	4.9
Latino Catholic	−37.2	1.9	4.4
Nominal Mainline	−38.0	1.5	3.6
Core Democratic			
Seculars	−41.0	4.6	11.6
Nominal Catholic	−42.2	1.3	3.4
Jews	−46.6	1.4	4.1
Other Faiths	−56.0	1.4	4.0
Atheist, Agnostic	−60.0	1.5	6.4
Traditionalist Black Protestant	−63.6	1.4	6.7
Less Traditional Black Protestant	−65.0	1.3	6.5
ALL	2.4	100.0	100.0

SOURCE: Fourth National Survey of Religion and Politics, Bliss Institute University of Akron, 2004, available at http://pewforum.org/publications/surveys/green-full.pdf.
NOTES: N=4,000 overall, 2,750 post-election. Under column headed "Net Two-Party Vote," positive numbers mean a net Bush advantage; negative numbers mean a net Kerry advantage.

Peripheral Republican Constituencies. The four peripheral Republican constituencies were Traditionalist Mainline Protestants, Latino Protestants, Modernist Evangelicals, and Nominal Evangelicals (all with a net Bush vote of less than forty and greater than twelve percentage points). All told, these groups accounted for one-seventh of all Bush's ballots. Traditionalist Main-liners are in some respects the remnant of the once strong allegiance of the Protestant Mainline to the GOP. If Traditionalist Mainliners' contribution to the Bush coalition is added to that of Traditionalist Evangelicals and Catholics, the sum is almost two-fifths of all Bush's ballots. The combined Republican core and peripheral constituencies accounted for some three-fifths of all the Bush ballots.

Core Democratic Constituencies. For purposes of comparison, it is worth jumping to the bottom of table 3, which lists the core Democratic con-stituencies: the two categories of Black Protestants, Atheists and Agnostics, the composite Other Faiths category, Jews, Nominal Catholics, and Seculars (groups that had a net Bush vote of –40 percentage points or less). This var-ied collection of religious communities certainly fits with the legendary diversity of the Democratic Party.

However, these core constituencies were dominated numerically by two combinations: Black Protestants, which summed to roughly one-eighth of all Kerry's ballots, and nonreligious people, with the Seculars and the Atheists and Agnostics adding up to almost one-fifth of the Democratic vote. The lat-ter are the "secularists" of polemical discourse—and if all the nominals were added in, more than one-quarter of Kerry's votes came from people who were largely nonreligious, a figure slightly more than the support Bush received from Traditionalist Evangelicals. Taken together, all the core Democratic con-stituencies provided Kerry with more than two-fifths of all his ballots in 2004, a bit less than Bush received from the core Republican constituencies.

Peripheral Democratic Constituencies. Three of the five peripheral Democratic constituencies (all groups with a net Bush vote between –40 and –12 percentage points) were characterized by less traditional beliefs and practices: Modernist Mainline, Unaffiliated Believers, and Modernist Catholics. These groups might well be considered the core of the "religious Left." Together they contributed more than one-eighth of Kerry's ballots.

The Modernist Catholics are in some sense the remainder of the once formidable "Catholic vote" in the Democratic Party. Modernist Mainliners represent a gain for the Kerry campaign with a religious community that was Republican in 1988. Hispanic Catholics are an exception to these patterns, being at once more conventionally religious and quite Democratic.

Taken together, the peripheral Democratic constituencies provided Senator Kerry with more than one-fifth of his total vote. And if combined, the core and peripheral Democratic groups accounted for nearly two-thirds of all Kerry's ballots, a little more than the comparable figure for Bush from the Republican religious constituencies.

The Swing Constituencies. It is conventional wisdom that there were relatively few swing voters in 2004 due to the polarization of the electorate. This view certainly holds for religious "swing" constituencies, which numbered just two: Centrist Catholics and Centrist Mainline Protestants (groups nearly evenly divided on the net Bush vote). President Bush had a slight edge among Centrist Catholics and Senator Kerry a slight edge among Centrist Mainliners. These constituencies provided both candidates with about one-seventh of their total ballots.

It is worth noting that each candidate received crucial votes from the other party's religious constituencies. Roughly one-eighth of all Bush's ballots came from peripheral Democratic constituencies and another one-eighth from the Democratic core constituencies. If the swing constituencies are included, some two-fifths of President Bush's total ballots were found among religious constituencies that did not vote strongly Republican—and in most cases voted strongly Democratic. This figure is not trivial, being about the size of Bush's ballots from Evangelical Protestants as a whole or all the traditionalists combined.

Much the same can be said for the Democratic vote coalition. One-eighth of Kerry's votes came from core Republican constituencies, and roughly another one-twelfth from peripheral Republican groups. Indeed, Kerry received more than one-third of all his ballots from constituencies that did not strongly support him—most of which were in fact strongly opposed to his election. This figure is not trivial either: these more traditional religious voters were about as important to Kerry as all his ballots from the unaffiliated, nominal, and modernist groups combined.

Presidential Voter Coalitions and Issues

Thus both Bush and Kerry assembled complex religious coalitions in 2004. Bush relied on Evangelicals and traditionalist Christians, while Kerry depended on the nonreligious, less religious, and less traditionally religious as well as religious minorities. These patterns are the factual basis for the hyperbolic rhetoric surrounding faith-based politics. However, both campaigns had to find a substantial number of votes from beyond their party's core religious constituencies. On balance, Bush was a bit more successful than Kerry in this regard, but the reverse could easily have occurred (which is what happened in 2006, as will be shown below).

Issue priorities and positions were central to building these complex coalitions. Table 4 lists the twenty-two religious communities by the net Bush vote (as in table 3) and then reports each group's position on indices of cultural, foreign policy, and economic issues (see the appendix for further details of these measures).

The first column under each type of issue reports the *net conservatism* of the religious category (the percentage of conservatives minus the percentage of liberals on that issue; a positive number means the group is on balance conservative, and a negative number means it is on balance liberal).

The second column in each case represents the *salience* of the issue type to the religious category (the percentage of the group that said the issue was "very important" to their vote in the 2004 election). Taken together, these simple measures provide a convenient summary of the issue orientations of the religious communities in 2004.

Cultural Issues. In 2004, most of the Republican constituencies had, on balance, conservative positions on cultural issues, such as abortion and marriage. Not surprisingly, the most conservative group was Traditionalist Evangelicals, with a net cultural conservatism of 68 percentage points. This group was an outlier compared to the other core GOP constituencies, which were markedly less conservative in this regard, and included Traditionalist Catholics (49.1 percentage points); Other Christians (35.4); Latino Protestants (29.5); Centrist Evangelicals (24.3); and Traditionalist Mainliners (20.6). Modernist Evangelicals were even less culturally conservative (9.8), while the Nominal Evangelicals were quite liberal on these issues (−44.0).

TABLE 4

RELIGIOUS COMMUNITIES, PARTISANSHIP, AND ISSUE POSITIONS, 2004

	Net Vote	Cultural Issues	
	Bush	Net Position	Important
Core Republican			
Traditionalist Evangelical	75.8	68.0	83.7
Other Christians	60.0	35.4	63.8
Traditionalist Catholic	47.8	49.1	71.7
Centrist Evangelical	40.8	24.3	55.2
Peripheral Republican			
Traditionalist Mainline	31.2	20.6	60.4
Latino Protestant	25.8	29.5	55.1
Modernist Evangelical	14.2	9.8	51.7
Nominal Evangelical	13.5	−44.0	29.6
Swing Constituencies			
Centrist Catholic	4.6	−9.9	30.3
Centrist Mainline	−1.8	−19.5	35.4
Peripheral Democratic			
Modernist Mainline	−13.8	−32.8	32.2
Unaffiliated Believers	−26.0	2.1	36.8
Modernist Catholic	−23.8	−37.0	21.4
Latino Catholic	−37.2	−3.3	40.5
Nominal Mainline	−38.0	−55.0	42.6
Core Democratic			
Seculars	−41.0	−51.2	37.9
Nominal Catholic	−42.2	−65.4	30.0
Jews	−46.6	−67.1	49.0
Other Faiths	−56.0	−45.1	40.8
Atheists, Agnostics	−60.0	−78.5	40.0
Traditionalist Black Protestant	−63.6	53.8	64.0
Less Traditional Black Protestant	−65.0	11.8	37.2
ALL	2.4	0.0	49.3

SOURCE: Fourth National Survey of Religion and Politics, Bliss Institute University of Akron, 2004, available at http://pewforum.org/publications/surveys/green-full.pdf.

Foreign Policy Issues		Economic Issues	
Net Position	*Important*	*Net Position*	*Important*
38.8	75.8	45.4	40.6
−1.8	84.2	16.2	61.4
12.5	79.2	16.0	48.1
10.6	79.0	6.5	55.6
8.9	78.5	19.6	54.7
4.8	69.4	7.5	51.0
−6.9	79.3	0.8	55.2
−1.7	92.6	−10.0	55.6
0.7	81.8	−1.7	60.4
−1.3	81.5	−6.3	60.0
−2.3	77.9	6.9	50.6
−30.8	89.7	11.4	66.2
7.1	87.0	−11.0	58.0
−9.5	74.1	−8.4	71.4
−3.7	81.3	−7.4	61.7
−13.4	80.3	−7.2	61.8
11.7	68.6	−3.5	58.0
24.0	87.5	−38.7	68.8
−24.0	85.7	−35.6	56.3
−18.5	78.8	−20.8	62.6
−13.1	80.4	−31.7	76.0
−25.3	74.7	−25.4	87.5
0.0	79.6	0.0	58.4

NOTES: N=4,000 overall, 2,750 post-election. Under columns headed "Net Position," positive numbers mean a net conservative advantage (cultural, foreign policy, or economic issues); negative numbers mean a net liberal advantage on issues. Columns headed "Important" indicate percentage reporting an issue as "very important" to the respondent's vote.

A different picture, however, emerges for the salience of cultural issues. Traditionalist Evangelicals reported the highest salience for cultural issues, but the cultural issues were salient to most of the Republican religious constituencies: 50 percent or more of all but one of these groups (Nominal Evangelicals) said cultural issues were "very important" to their 2004 vote. So there is some factual basis for the claim by liberal elites that the "religious Right" played a major role in the Republican coalitions in 2004.

Cultural issues were less prominent among the swing constituencies. Centrist Catholics (–9.9 percentage points) and Mainline Protestants (–19.5) held modestly liberal views on these questions, with about one-third reporting cultural issues as salient.

In contrast, most of the Democratic constituencies held strongly liberal views on cultural issues. For example, Atheists and Agnostics had a net conservatism score of –78.5 percentage points. Other groups also had low net scores: Jews (–67); Nominal Catholics (–65); Nominal Mainliners (–55); and Seculars (–51). And the Other Faiths (–45), Modernist Catholics (–37), and Modernist Mainline Protestants (–32.8) were more modest in their liberal leanings. Thus the claim by religious conservatives that secular voters played a major role in the Democratic coalitions also has some basis in fact.

However, note that nearly all of these religious groups assigned lower levels of importance to cultural issues compared to the Republican constituencies. Indeed, just one group approached the 50 percent mark (Jews). And there were some exceptions to the pattern of cultural liberalism. For example, Traditionalist Black Protestants had a fairly high net conservatism score (53.8 percentage points) and nearly two-thirds regarded cultural issues as salient—figures exceeded only by the Traditionalist Evangelicals. Less Traditional Black Protestants, the Unaffiliated Believers, and Latino Catholics were also much less culturally liberal than other Democratic groups, but assigned relatively low salience to cultural issues.

Foreign Policy Issues. Overall, the Republican religious constituencies tended to be conservative on foreign policy issues, such as the war on terrorism and the war in Iraq. Traditionalist Evangelicals were once again the most conservative, with a net conservatism score of 38.8 percentage points. The other GOP religious constituencies were much less conservative, and three of them (the Other Christians along with Modernist and Nominal

Evangelicals) held modestly net liberal positions on foreign policy issues. The swing constituencies were nearly evenly divided on foreign policy. As one might expect, many of the Democratic constituencies had net liberal views on foreign policy, including Unaffiliated Believers (–30.8 percentage points), Less Traditional Black Protestants (–25.3), the Other Faiths (–24.0), and Atheists and Agnostics (–18.5). Many of the remaining groups were more modest in their liberal leanings, although some had net conservative positions, including Jews (24.0) and Nominal Catholics (11.7).

Thus, foreign policy issues were less divisive among the religious communities than cultural issues in 2004. One reason for this pattern is that many Americans held moderate views on these matters. In addition, attitudes towards the war on terrorism and the war in Iraq tended to offset each other, the former favoring the Republicans and the latter helping the Democrats. More importantly, foreign policy issues were uniformly salient across these religious communities. For example, the lowest score was for Latino Protestants, where 69 percent reported foreign policy to be "very important" to their vote. Most groups scored substantially higher, including 92.6 percent among Nominal Evangelicals, 89.7 among Unaffiliated Believers, and 87.5 among Jews.

Economic Issues. The Republican religious constituencies also tended to hold conservative positions on economic issues, such as social welfare programs and taxes. Once again Traditionalist Evangelicals were the farthest to the right, with a net conservatism score of 45.4 percentage points. The other GOP constituencies, such as Traditionalist Mainline Protestants (19.6), Other Christians (16.2), and Traditionalist Catholics (16.0) were less strongly conservative. The remaining Republican constituencies were even less conservative on balance, with the Nominal Evangelicals holding on balance liberal views (–10.0).

Here, too, the swing constituencies were fairly evenly divided. And a variety of economic issue positions were found among the Democratic religious constituencies. The most liberal group on the economy was the Jews, with a net conservatism score of –38.7 percentage points, followed closely by the Other Faiths (–35.6), Traditionalist Black Protestants (–31.7), Less Traditional Black Protestants (–25.4), and Atheists and Agnostics (–20.8). Most of the remaining groups had more modestly liberal views on economic issues, and two groups, Modernist Mainline Protestants and Unaffiliated Believers, had modestly conservative positions.

Thus, like foreign policy issues, economic issues were less divisive among these religious communities than cultural issues. Economic issues were salient across the religious landscape. On the Republican side, 50 percent or more of all but two groups said that such issues were "very important" to their vote. The two exceptions are interesting: Traditionalist Evangelicals (40 percent) and Traditionalist Catholics (48 percent), two of the groups among the most culturally conservative. Economic issues were generally more salient to the Democratic constituencies, with every group scoring 50 percent or better. Economic issues were most important to Less Traditional Black Protestants (87.5 percent); Traditionalist Black Protestants (76 percent); and Latino Catholics (71 percent). Interestingly, the swing constituencies also regarded economic issues as important (60 percent each).

A Look toward the Future

This account of religion and the 2004 presidential vote provides a baseline for speculating about the future. Of course, many departures from these patterns are possible, depending on the special circumstances of particular campaigns. But two likely scenarios suggest themselves: cultural conflict continues, or cultural conflict declines. After discussing each scenario, we will take a brief look at the results of the 2006 congressional election, which contains some evidence supporting each scenario.

Scenario 1: Cultural Conflict Continues. This scenario is the easiest to imagine because it is the continuation of the trend among religious communities up to 2004. The origins of this trend are well-enough known that only a brief sketch of them is necessary. The present cultural conflict over sexual behavior and family life appeared on the political agenda in the early 1970s, and for more than thirty years this conflict slowly altered the major-party coalitions, giving the Republicans a strong traditionalist element in their voter coalition, while the Democrats acquired modernist and secular components in theirs. Indeed, a portion of this shift from 1988 to 2004 was illustrated in table 2. No doubt such cultural conflict was also related to changes in America's place in the world and alterations in its economy, but as table 4 shows, cultural issues became one of the critical factors in creating the core and peripheral religious constituencies for both parties. This scenario assumes that such conflict will persist into the future.

Cultural Issues and the Republican Coalition. At the moment, Republicans cannot ignore cultural issues in elections. For one thing, the strong proponents of cultural conservatism, Traditionalist Evangelicals, have become an extremely valuable electoral constituency for the GOP. As table 3 shows, it would be difficult for any Republican presidential candidate to replace this constituency at the polls. So the problem facing the GOP is how to keep this crucial community minimally happy without alienating other groups of voters also necessary for a winning coalition. While only a minority of Traditionalist Evangelicals is likely to vote Democratic, many could stay home on election day—a threat regularly articulated by conservative Christian leaders.

Thus, the GOP faces the challenge of managing a traditionalist coalition within the party's base. Other such constituencies besides Traditionalist Evangelicals include Traditionalist Catholics and Other Christians, groups for whom cultural issues are salient, but who are less conservative. Here some lingering theological differences among these groups may reduce political cooperation. A 2008 presidential bid by Mitt Romney, the Mormon governor of Massachusetts, will provide a test of the strength of party management, since many Traditionalist Evangelicals are quite critical of the Latter-day Saints on religious grounds.[17]

A second tier of culturally conservative groups includes Latino Protestants, Centrist Evangelicals, and Traditionalist Mainline Protestants. These groups are a step less conservative on cultural issues and consider such issues a bit less salient than do Traditionalist Evangelicals. These differences show up on issues such as stem cell research. Just as important, these groups often dislike the hard-edged political style of the Christian Right.

Finally, a third tier of voters, which includes Traditionalist Black Protestants, are cultural conservatives from outside the Republican fold. These voters typically hold liberal or moderate views on other issues, imposing limits on the effectiveness of cultural appeals. To a lesser extent, this pattern applies to Latinos. In 2004, the harvest of such votes was small but important.

Through 2004, the Republicans have had considerable success in managing this traditionalist alliance. For one thing, Traditionalist Evangelicals have become so firmly wedded to the GOP that party leaders have had some flexibility on cultural issues. As table 4 shows, Traditionalist Evangelicals are also the most conservative of the religious constituencies on foreign policy and economic issues. To a large extent, foreign policy and economic issues have reinforced the effects of cultural issues among the Republican constituencies. But these issues also allowed Bush to attract needed votes from groups that are not culturally conservative, such as Nominal Evangelicals, Centrist Catholics, and Mainline Protestants.

This coalition building has been aided by the high level of importance assigned to cultural issues by most of the Republican religious constituencies. Bush and the congressional Republicans pursued policies that enjoyed wide support among their religious constituencies, including the federal ban on late-term abortions and the appointment of conservative judges to the federal courts. Meanwhile, the cultural liberalism of the Democratic coalition—and especially some of its most prominent leaders—has helped maintain the Republican allegiance of the traditionalist groups.

Cultural Issues and the Democratic Coalition. Democrats cannot ignore cultural issues at the ballot box either. Although the Democratic coalition is more complex, many of its members hold strongly liberal perspectives on cultural issues, including Atheists and Agnostics, Seculars, Nominal Catholics and Mainliners, and Jews,. Some of these groups are as strongly liberal on cultural issues as the Traditionalist Evangelicals are conservative, and overall, these constituencies have a higher level of cultural liberalism than their counterpart groups in the GOP have of cultural conservatism. But with the exception of Jews, these groups are typically organized not in explicitly religious terms, but by liberal social movements and interest groups active in Democratic Party politics (although it is worth noting that atheist, humanist, and secularist organizations are becoming increasingly vocal in electoral politics).

As shown in table 3, it would be quite difficult for a Democratic presidential candidate to replace these voters at the polls. The Democrats face the challenge of keeping culturally liberal groups minimally happy while not alienating other voters necessary for victory. The threat that these groups might stay home on election day is real enough, but some of them, especially the Unaffiliated, have had lower levels of turnout than their counterparts in the GOP coalition.[18] Thus, stimulating turnout among some cultural liberal voters represents a special problem for the Democrats.

There are also cultural tensions between these strongly liberal groups and other elements of the Democratic coalition, in particular Black Protestants, especially the Traditionalists, and to a lesser extent, Latino Catholics and the Unaffiliated Believers. Black Protestants and Latino Catholics are quite conservative on cultural issues, while the others are moderate. A further problem lies with Centrist Catholics and Mainline Protestants, and also with Modernist Catholics and Mainliners. All four communities are markedly less liberal on cultural issues than the Unaffiliated. Operationally, this might mean that the Democratic constituencies can unite on protecting basic abortion rights, but not on promoting same-sex marriage.

Another challenge is the issue of religion itself. Modernists and members of minority religions take faith quite seriously and approach cultural issues on the basis of religious values. But many in the secular and nominal groups do not, and some are openly disdainful of religion. Dislike of religion among these groups is a problem for Democrats reaching out to voters in swing or Republican religious constituencies.

Through 2004, the Democrats have been reasonably successful at managing their alliance of cultural liberals. However, what gave them most leverage was not cultural issues but economic ones. For instance, the strong priority given to economic matters by Black Protestants and Latino Catholics, combined with their economic liberalism, helped cement their ties to the Democratic Party. A similar situation may have obtained for Modernist Catholics. Similarly, foreign policy issues, especially the Iraq War, appear to have contributed to the Democratic votes of Modernist Mainline and the Unaffiliated Believers in 2004.

While the Republicans were aided by the high salience of cultural issues in their religious constituencies, the Democrats may have benefited from the lower salience of these issues in most of the Democratic religious constituencies. However, one cost of lower salience may be that the Democrats have not gotten the same level of performance at the polls from their most liberal constituencies on cultural matters. Indeed, in 2004 Bush was able to take a small but significant number of votes from cultural liberals on the basis of other issues.

The Limits of Cultural Conflict. One implication of this analysis is that the current type and level of cultural conflict could persist in the future, especially if the political parties manage their coalitions effectively. Indeed, some Republican and Democratic presidential hopefuls in 2008 may well base their strategies on continued cultural conflict. At this writing, Senator Sam Brownback of Kansas appears to be a good example in the GOP, since his campaign is predicated on mobilizing religious conservatives. Ohio Congressman Dennis Kucinich may be an example on the Democratic side, and another candidate representing religious and secular liberals may eventually emerge. But could cultural conflict become an even bigger factor in faith-based politics? The baseline data for 2004 suggest that there are limits to the electoral value of cultural conflict, and this argues against its further expansion.

These limits can be seen by a simple experiment that alters one factor in the 2004 election results, leaving everything else the same. The alteration assumes that all the religious communities cast their presidential ballots on the basis of their positions on cultural issues, if they reported cultural issues to be salient. Thus, a cultural conservative with cultural priorities who actually voted for Kerry in 2004 would now vote for Bush, and vice versa. In essence, this assumption requires everyone to have voted their cultural views and priorities with perfect consistency.

This experiment with the 2004 election alters each party's voter coalitions. The core Republican constituencies become a bit more Republican, and the GOP makes big gains among Latino Catholics and Black Protestants. Among Traditionalist Black Protestants, for example, the Bush vote doubles to 35 percent. At the same time, Kerry makes gains among the less religious and nonreligious, reducing the Bush vote among Atheists and Agnostics as well as Seculars and Jews, and attenuating Republican support among the swing constituencies of Centrist Mainliners and Catholics. (As we will see below, something like this happened in 2006.) Interestingly, Kerry makes only modest advances among Republican constituencies, largely because there are few cultural liberals among these groups. But the most telling feature of this experiment is the net result: Bush wins the popular vote by just about the same margin as in the actual election.

A slightly different result holds for an experiment where issue salience is removed from the mix, thus assuming that all voters simply vote their cultural views. Here the Bush votes among the less religious and nonreligious decline sharply, and the Republicans lose the swing constituencies. These losses more than offset the Bush gains among minority Christians, so that the results are the reverse of the Bush electoral win.

So if 2004 is a good guide, the net gains from expanding cultural conflict might not be worth the effort and the risk for either party. In fact, the only clear source of gain would be some kind of asymmetrical change. For example, the Republicans would need to collect the cultural conservatives from Democratic religious constituencies, while holding on to cultural liberals in the swing and Democratic constituencies; the reverse would be the case for the Democrats. The interaction of cultural views and salience would likely make such an outcome improbable.

Scenario 2: Cultural Conflict Declines. The possibility that cultural conflict could decline is implicit in the foregoing discussion. After all, if there were to be a decline in the salience of cultural issues or a shift in public opinion on these matters, other issue domains could become more salient to voters. Under these circumstances, faith-based politics might resemble what they were in 1988, when divisions within religious communities were less important than they became by 2004. However, cultural conflict could also decline in the absence of a dramatic change in the raw material of faith-based politics. Here two possibilities suggest themselves: a "politics of cultural moderation" or a "politics of issue displacement." In many respects, these approaches reflect the normal process of political adjustment by political parties and their candidates.

The Politics of Cultural Moderation. One way to reduce cultural conflict is for candidates to adopt moderate positions on cultural issues. Moderation may be difficult in a highly polarized political environment, especially in presidential campaigns, but the costs of cultural conflict can provide incentives for it. In fact, prominent Republicans and Democrats have proposed this approach.[19]

From the perspective of 2004, the prime targets for a moderate Democrat would be Centrist Catholics and Mainline Protestants. As table 4 shows, this group as a whole is modestly liberal on cultural issues, but it contains many cultural moderates and conservatives. A moderate position on cultural issues might well make it possible for a Democratic candidate to win some votes outright, but if not, to at least get a hearing on other kinds of issues.

Cultural moderation could also yield gains among Republican religious constituencies, and in this regard, the largest strategic implications are for Centrist Evangelicals. One of the largest religious communities listed in table 1, they have become part of the GOP base. However, they are less culturally conservative than Traditionalist Evangelicals, and even less conservative on foreign policy and economic issues. Many of these voters were never especially comfortable with the Christian Right, or for that matter with the stricter religiosity of their traditionalist coreligionists. Many identify personally with George W. Bush, but less so with his policies or with the Republican Party. Thus, Centrist Evangelicals may be open to a broader political agenda that goes beyond the core cultural issues. And in fact, some moderate Evangelical leaders have proposed just such an expansion on topics such as global warming, antipoverty programs, and international human rights.

But how much moderation would be necessary to attract new voters? A significant concession on abortion restrictions might be enough, but this approach would risk the ire of the cultural liberals in the Democratic coalition. Anything that would reduce the salience of cultural issues among the targeted religious constituencies would help. Here one possibility is for candidates to discuss their faith in highly personal terms and avoid discussing possible linkages of their faith to cultural issues. Such an approach would require a carefully calibrated mix of appeals—such as Bill Clinton deployed in the 1992 presidential campaign. Several candidates for the 2008 Democratic presidential nomination may test this approach, including Illinois senator Barack Obama and New York senator Hillary Clinton.

Republicans could adopt this approach as well. For instance, a culturally moderate Republican might compete even more effectively for Centrist and Modernist Mainliners, bringing some of them back into the Republican fold. They might also do well with Centrist and Modernist Catholics and Unaffiliated Believers. Here the concessions might be some restrictions on abortion while preserving its availability early in pregnancy, and support for stem cell research. As with Democrats, such concessions would risk the ire of the traditionalists in the GOP coalition.

The Politics of Issue Displacement. Another approach is to displace cultural issues with other types of issues. Of course, issue displacement occurs regularly in politics as new issues gain prominence and old ones fade away. Indeed, some argue that the rise of cultural issues in the 1970s was a displacement of economic issues.[20] Election-specific issues and controversies, such as a scandal or an international crisis, often displace other issues temporarily. However, politicians can deliberately seek to displace current issues by altering their salience.

This approach has been undertaken by elements of the "religious Left" since the 2004 election. In common parlance, the term "religious Left" has two meanings. On the one hand, it can mean people with "liberal" or modernist theology, such as Michael Lerner's "spiritual progressives." On the other hand, it can mean religious traditionalists and centrists who have a "liberal" politics, such as Jim Wallis and the "red-letter Christians."[21]

The case of "red-letter Christians" offers a good illustration of the politics of issue displacement. The salient issue for the red-letter Christians is poverty, and they argue for increased antipoverty programs on the basis of biblical teachings. Indeed, the label refers to a common approach to Bible publication in which the words of Jesus are printed in red. The implication is that if one read the Bible literally, one would give priority to Jesus's statements on caring for the poor over other concerns. This change in priorities is justified by the same religious values that justify opposition to abortion and same-sex marriage. Indeed, red-letter Christians are careful to point out that they are pro-life and pro–traditional marriage. Simply put, they are asking Christians to displace cultural issues in favor of poverty when they cast a ballot.

Although many red-letter Christians are formally nonpartisan, this approach would likely benefit the Democratic candidates in the immediate future. Such issue displacement could attract some votes from traditionalist groups, particularly Traditionalist Catholics and Mainline Protestants, religious communities with well-developed positions on a collective response to poverty. It could also have an impact among Centrist Evangelicals, Catholics, and Mainliners. The danger for Democrats, of course, is that appeals to such religious voters would create problems with cultural liberals within their ranks.

In fact, red-letter Christianity is likely to have the most appeal for Modernist Catholics, Modernist Mainliners, and Modernist Evangelicals, the other major part of the "Religious Left." These groups share some similar religious perspectives and have recently moved away from their traditionalist coreligionists at the ballot box. These groups also tend to be culturally liberal. Such a development could help the Democrats at the polls, but these groups already vote Democratic on balance.

It is one thing, of course, to seek ecumenical support for one of the basic values of Christianity, and quite another to translate it into an electoral program. Perhaps the closest contemporary example of a politician with this approach is the 2004 Democratic vice-presidential nominee, John Edwards, and his populist argument about "two Americas," one rich and one poor. A religious element could be added to such an approach in 2008.

The politics of issue displacement can be practiced by Republicans as well as Democrats. In fact, George W. Bush's "compassionate conservatism" had a similar political goal, one of displacing economic issues (social welfare programs) with cultural issues (faith-based social services and accountability in public education). Although largely directed at centrist groups, "compassionate conservatism" resonated most with existing Republican religious constituencies.

Perhaps a better example of issue displacement by President Bush involves foreign policy. Bush sought and received considerable support in the 2004 election from swing and Democratic constituencies that might otherwise have voted Democratic on economic issues. But here, too, it was religious traditionalists who most strongly supported the war on terrorism and the "Bush Doctrine" of preventative war. In fact, some Christian Right leaders tried to describe the war against terrorism as a "family value" in the 2006 campaign. Even in 2004, foreign policy created significant divisions between each party's religious constituencies—and the pattern of public opinion on foreign policy has become less favorable to the Republicans since then.

Some Evidence from the 2006 Election

In 2006, Democrats won control of both houses of Congress for the first time in twelve years. Overall, the election was close, with Democrats winning 52 percent of the two-party congressional vote nationwide, essentially reversing Republican winning margins in the 2002 congressional elections. Table 5 reports some additional findings on the congressional vote by major

TABLE 5
RELIGIOUS GROUPS AND THE CONGRESSIONAL VOTE, 2002–6

	2006		2004		2002		Change '04-'06	Change '02-'06
	Rep	Dem	Rep	Dem	Rep	Dem		
Weekly Attending Evangelical Protestant	76	23	78	20	80[a]	19[a]	3	4[a]
Less Observant Evangelical Protestant	61	38	67	31	61[a]	38[a]	7	0[a]
Weekly Attending Mainline Protestant	59	38	63	36	62[a]	37[a]	2	1[a]
Weekly Attending White Catholic	52	47	58	41	54	44	6	3
Less Observant Mainline Protestant	47	51	51	47	52[a]	47[a]	4	4[a]
Less Observant White Catholic	46	53	50	49	46	51	4	2
Other Faiths	29	66	36	57	41	52	9	14
Unaffiliated	25	72	35	61	36	58	11	14
Nonwhites	24	75	26	72	22	76	3	-1
Jews	11	87	21	77	32	67	10	20
ALL	46	52	50	47	51	46	5	6

SOURCES: National Election Pool, National Exit Polls, 2006; National Election Pool, National Exit Polls, 2004; and Voter News Service, National Exit Polls, 2002. Estimates derived from Pew Research Center, "House Voting Intentions Knotted, National Trend Not Apparent," November 3, 2002, http://people-press.org/reports/display.php3?ReportID=164.
NOTE: a = estimates derived from a 2002 Pew Research Center Election Weekend Survey.

religious groups in the 2006, 2004, and 2002 elections. These data do not have the extensive religion measures used in the previous tables, but affiliation and worship attendance allow for a crude proxy of more exact religious communities. For ease of comparison to the previous tables, the religious groups are arranged by Republican congressional vote; the far-right-hand columns report the change in the Democratic vote over the period (see the appendix for more details).

The order of religious groups in table 5 is remarkably similar in all three elections, and it closely resembles the patterns in table 3. Weekly Attending Evangelicals (a proxy for Traditionalist Evangelicals) were the strongest Republican group in all cases, and Weekly Attending Mainliners and Catholics (also proxies for the relevant traditionalists) always voted more Republican than their less observant coreligionists (less-than-weekly attenders who are a proxy for centrists, modernists, and nominals). Jews and Unaffiliated also voted Democratic, as did Nonwhites (a combination of Black Protestants and Hispanics, among others). Other Faiths is a truly diverse category, and it therefore makes sense that this group would be on balance Democratic.

Thus the basic pattern of faith-based voting in 2004 held in 2006. So how did the Democrats win? First, they obtained much stronger backing from Democratic constituencies than in the previous elections. For example, Jews increased their support for Democratic congressional candidates by ten percentage points over 2004 and twenty percentage points over 2002. The victors also improved their support among the Unaffiliated (by eleven and fourteen percentage points, respectively) and the Other Faiths (nine and fourteen percentage points). And they made more modest gains among less observant Christians, especially Less Observant Evangelicals (seven percentage points over 2004). Here, Nonwhites were a modest exception, with just a three percentage point gain over 2004 (and a 1 percent loss over 2002).

In addition, Democratic congressional candidates made inroads into Republican religious constituencies. They picked up six percentage points over 2004 among Weekly Attending Catholics (but just three percentage points over 2002), and made smaller gains among Weekly Attending Evangelicals (three and four percentage points, respectively) and Weekly Attending Mainliners (two and one percentage points).

These patterns can also be seen in table 6, which reports the congressional vote by frequency of worship attendance. In 2006, Democrats gained at every level of attendance, but they gained least among the most religiously observant voters, and most among the least observant. The net result was that the "attendance gap" widened in 2006, from eighteen percentage points in 2002 to twenty-nine percentage points in 2006. Put another way, the attendance gap worked in favor of the Democrats in 2006.

TABLE 6
WORSHIP ATTENDANCE AND THE CONGRESSIONAL VOTE, 2002–6

Worship Attendance	2006 Rep	Dem	2004 Rep	Dem	2002 Rep	Dem	Change '04-'06	Change '02-'06
More than weekly	60	38	61	37	61	37	1	1
Weekly	53	46	57	42	57	41	4	5
Monthly	41	57	49	50	46	52	7	5
A few times a year	38	60	43	55	47	50	5	10
Never	30	67	36	60	41	55	7	12
Attendance gap	-30	29	-25	23	-20	18	6	11

SOURCES: National Election Pool, National Exit Polls, 2006; National Election Pool, National Exit Polls, 2004; and Voter News Service, National Exit Polls, 2002.
NOTE: Attendance gap calculated by subtracting the vote of top row from bottom row in each column.

Implications for the Future. What do these data tell us about the future of faith-based politics? Such evidence must be viewed with caution, since congressional elections are quite different from presidential contests. With this caveat in mind, the 2006 results provide some support for both scenarios, the continuation of cultural conflict and its decline. On the first count, the expansion of the attendance gap strongly suggests the persistence of cultural divisions—a pattern that extends to the impact of attendance within the largest religious traditions. Indeed, the Democrats more fully exploited the less observant (and less traditional) part of the religious landscape. As one of the experiments with the 2004 vote showed, John Kerry might have been elected president if this kind of pattern had obtained.

Perhaps in 2006, the less traditional, less religious, and nonreligious voters increased their backing for Democrats in reaction to the influence of religious traditionalists among Republicans. Certainly the intense attacks on religious conservatives by liberal elites laid the groundwork for such a shift. However, this change may also have reflected increased opposition to the war in Iraq and anger with President Bush. In any event, these data show at least a temporary expansion of one side of the faith-based divide.

Meanwhile, the traditionalist alliance among Republicans largely held firm in the congressional vote. Weekly Attending Evangelicals strongly backed Republican congressional candidates, despite expectations that they might defect in large numbers. In addition, Weekly Attending Mainliners and Catholics also stayed in the Republican column, basically returning to their levels of GOP congressional support in 2002. The fierce assault on secular liberals (and the Democratic Party) by conservative Christian leaders may well have been a factor in these results. From this perspective, the loyalty of traditionalist voters prevented the Republican defeat from becoming a rout.

However, given the Democratic gains among less observant voters, the Republicans would have needed an increase among the more observant to win the popular vote. Instead they suffered some losses across the board, a result that provides some evidence for the decline of cultural conflict. In 2006, the Democrats improved their support among Republican religious constituencies over 2004 and especially over the vote for President Bush in that year. Less Observant Evangelicals and Weekly Attending Catholics were most important in this regard, with Democrats gaining at a rate greater than their overall improvement in the congressional vote. They also made some modest inroads among Weekly Attending Evangelical and Mainline Protestants.

Did these particular Democratic gains come from the politics of moderation or the politics of issue displacement? The best evidence is for the former: some of the most successful Democratic candidates ran as cultural moderates with an emphasis on their faith, including Bob Casey in the Pennsylvania senate race and Ted Strickland in the race for governor of Ohio. In fact, these candidates had an even better showing among key religious groups than the national Democratic congressional vote. For example, in Pennsylvania, Casey won 59 percent of the white Catholic vote, an impressive fourteen percentage point gain over the 2000 Democratic candidates. There is less evidence in these data for issue displacement of the sort advocated by religious progressives. But it is certainly possible that it occurred in particular races. Such gains may well have been masked by the major issue displacements of the 2006 campaign: the war in Iraq and corruption.

Thus the 2006 election suggests that both scenarios for the future of faith-based politics are possible. Perhaps a more important question is which approach is likely to be more successful for the major political parties. The answer will be known soon enough, perhaps as early as 2008.

Appendix: Surveys, Religious Categories, and Issue Indices

The Surveys. This essay is based on the Fourth National Survey of Religion and Politics, conducted by the Bliss Institute at the University of Akron in collaboration with the Pew Forum on Religion & Public Life, with additional support provided by the Paul B. Henry Institute for the Study of Christianity and Politics at Calvin College and the William R. Kenan, Jr. Endowment at Furman University.[22] The survey was a national random sample of adult Americans (eighteen years or older), conducted in the spring of 2004 (N=4,000). The initial sample was then re-interviewed after the 2004 election (N=2,730).

This survey was the fourth in a series of surveys conducted at the University of Akron. The 1992 survey (1992 pre-election N=4,000 and post-election N=2,265) is used to estimate the 1988 vote based on voter recall. A careful comparison with other surveys from 1988 reveals the estimate to have a high degree of accuracy.

The 2006 Data. These data come from the 2006, 2004, and 2002 exit polls and were developed at the Pew Research Center with the help of Scott Keeter and Greg Smith.[23]

Religious Tradition. All the National Surveys of Religion and Politics contained an extensive series of questions to determine the specific religious affiliation of respondents as accurately as possible. Despite the precision of this measure, there are some ambiguous responses, which are coded with the aid of other religious variables, including "born again" status, religious identities, and worship attendance. These affiliations were then recoded into the eleven religious traditions in table 1. This standard classification is based on the formal beliefs, behaviors, and histories of the denominations or churches involved, with the most detail dedicated to sorting out the many kinds of Protestants in the United States. Black Protestants and Latinos were separated on the basis of race and ethnicity.

Religious Traditionalism. The National Surveys of Religion and Politics contain extensive measures of religious belief and behavior. Five belief items were found in all four surveys (view of the Bible; belief in God; belief in the afterlife; view of the devil; and view of evolution) along with five behavior items (frequency of worship attendance; frequency of prayer; frequency of Bible reading; frequency of participation in small groups; and level of financial contribution to a congregation). In most cases, these items had the same question wording across surveys. However, in a few cases improvements in question wording over time produced some differences between surveys. In order to maintain the same conceptual basis for the traditionalism scale, these items were adjusted by means of other religious measures not used in the overall analysis so as to have the same range and frequency as the items in the 2004 survey.

The final belief and behavior items were then subjected to separate factor analyses in each of the surveys. The factor loadings were quite similar on all these analyses. Belief and behavior factor scores were then generated and the two scores were subjected to a second factor analysis to extract the underlying traditionalism. This final factor analysis also generated a factor score, which was adjusted to the mean score for all four surveys for each religious tradition. This adjustment was very modest but corrected for the peculiarities of each survey.

In the final step, the adjusted traditionalism scale was divided into four categories within the three largest religious traditions. The cut-points were the mean traditionalism scores of four levels of religious salience. These cut-points were chosen because they were specific to the religious traditions, unambiguous, and consistent across surveys. Also, traditional religiosity stresses the importance of religion over other aspects of life. The Unaffiliated Believers were defined by scoring in the top two-thirds of the belief factor score in each survey.

Although this categorization process is complex, it was remarkably robust, with a wide range of alternative measures, methods, and cut-points producing essentially the same results.

Issue Indices. The cultural, foreign policy, and economic issue indices were created by dividing factor scores into three equal parts, one containing the most conservative third of respondents, one the most liberal third of respondents, and the remaining third the most moderate respondents. Cultural issues included abortion, marriage, gay rights, stem cell research, and school vouchers. Foreign policy issues included the Iraq War, support for a preemptive war, the role of the U.S. in the world, whether the U.S. should mind its own business in the world, and whether the U.S. should work through international organizations. Economic issues included level of government spending and taxes, whether to increase taxes on the middle class to help the poor, whether to increase taxes on the wealthy to help the poor, the need for government assistance to help the disadvantaged, and support for the Bush tax cuts.

Notes

1. Paul Marshall, "Fundamentalists & Other Fun People," *Weekly Standard*, November 22, 2004, 16–18.

2. Ross Douthat, "Theocracy, Theocracy, Theocracy," *First Things* 165 (August/September 2006): 23–30.

3. Alan Cooperman and Thomas Edsall, "Evangelicals Say They Led Charge for the GOP," *Washington Post*, November 8, 2004, A1.

4. Cooperman, "'War on Christians Is Alleged," *Washington Post*, March 29, 2006, A12.

5. Steve Thomma, "Americans' Religious Practices Serve As Gauge of Political Choice," *Philadelphia Inquirer*, December 2, 2003.

6. Laura R. Olson and John C. Green, "Symposium—Voting Gaps in the 2004 Presidential Election," *PS: Political Science and Politics* 39 (July 2006): 443–72.

7. Andrew Kohut, John C. Green, Scott Keeter, and Robert Toth, *The Diminishing Divide: Religion's Changing Role in American Politics* (Washington, D.C.: Brookings Institution, 2000).

8. Olson and Green, "Voting Gaps," 455–60.

9. Robert Wuthnow, *The Restructuring of American Religion* (Princeton, NJ: Princeton University Press, 1988).

10. Gertrude Himmelfarb, *One Nation, Two Cultures* (New York: Vintage Books, 2005).

11. James Hunter, *Culture Wars: The Struggle to Define America* (New York: Basic Books, 1991).

12. Geoffrey C. Layman, *The Great Divide: Religious and Cultural Conflict in American Party Politics* (New York: Columbia University Press, 2001).

13. Kohut et al., *Diminishing Divide*.

14. See Alan Wolfe, *One Nation, After All* (New York: Viking, 1988), and Morris Fiorina, Samuel J. Abrams, and Jeremy C. Pope, *Culture War? The Myth of a Polarized America* (New York: Pearson Longman, 2005).

15. Geoffrey C. Layman and John C. Green, "Wars and Rumors of Wars: The Contexts of Cultural Conflict in American Political Behavior," *British Journal of Political Science* 36.1 (2005): 61–89.

16. John C. Green, Corwin E. Smidt, James L. Guth, and Lyman A. Kellstedt, "The American Religious Landscape and the 2004 Presidential Vote: Increased Polarization," Pew Forum on Religion & Public Life, 2005, http://pewforum.org/docs/index.php?DocID=64.

17. See Lisa Anderson, "Can a Mormon be President? Romney Must Erase Electorate's Worries on his Faith for '08 Bid," *Chicago Tribune*, December 17, 2006, 6.

18. See Green et al., "American Religious Landscape."

19. On Republicans, see John Danforth, *Faith and Politics* (New York: Viking, 2006). On Democrats, see James E. Carter, *Our Endangered Values* (New York: Simon and Schuster, 2005).

20. David C. Leege, Kenneth D. Wald, Brian S. Krueger, and Paul D. Mueller, *The Politics of Cultural Differences: Social Change and Voter Mobilization Strategies in the Post–New Deal Period* (Princeton, NJ: Princeton University Press, 2002).

21. For the former, see Caryle Murphy and Alan Cooperman, "Religious Liberals Gain New Visibility," *Washington Post*, May 20, 2006, A01. For the latter, see Julia Duin, "Religious Left to Reclaim its Faith," *Washington Times*, September 19, 2006.

22. John C. Green and Steve Waldman, "The Twelve Tribes of American Politics," September 30, 2004, http://www.beliefnet.com/story/153/story_15355_1.html. Also see John C. Green et al., "American Religious Landscape."

23. Pew Forum on Religion & Public Life, "Understanding Religion's Role in the 2006 Election," http://pewforum.org/events/index.php?EventID=135.

5

Commentary

Christopher DeMuth

I would raise two general points in response to John Green's powerful argument.

First, moral and religious issues seem to have a special prominence in American politics, and are always emerging and reemerging, often in ways that shape elections and profoundly influence the way we govern ourselves. I think the prominence of these issues in our politics has to do not only with our religious character but also with our economic prosperity.

We have become a very rich society. The economic issues which were the most important domestic issues from the late nineteenth to the late twentieth century have become less salient because the struggle for existence and material welfare is less important in almost everybody's life—not everybody's, but almost everybody's. And while there are continuing efforts to keep economic issues alive, especially the Left's preoccupation with economic inequality and universal health insurance, these issues have never in the past twenty years connected with the general public.

At the American Enterprise Institute, we, too, spend a lot of time on economic issues, wringing our hands over budget deficits and profligate spending and tax and entitlement reform. Those are indeed very important issues, but they do not have the centrality in electoral politics and political debate that they once had.

In a very wealthy society, the major issues tend to concern what our prosperity is for and what we ought to do with our lives. Even within the traditional economic issues, we see cultural aspects starting to take the fore. In social security reform, for example, we are concerned not only about the financial balance sheets, but also about how our society will care for a vastly increasing older population. What are the duties of children to take care of their parents, and what should the government do to encourage them with those duties?

Tax policy is another example. In the past fifteen years, the traditional debates between supply-siders wanting to cut tax rates and tax-grabbers wanting to increase rates have been complicated by a new and powerful force: cultural conservatives wanting (and often getting) new and increased deductions and credits for child rearing and other forms of good behavior. I expect that these sorts of issues are going to continue to predominate, not as a result of anybody's political strategies but simply because they are becoming relatively more important in voters' immediate lives.

My second point concerns democratic moderation. To the extent that moral issues move from the courts to legislatures, and from the national legislature to state and local ones, there will be much stronger pressures for moderation on all sides. Courts are bound by doctrines and procedures that make it difficult for them to forge compromises; they speak in terms of rights and act in terms of specific commands. Legislatures have more flexibility, but at the national level politics tends to be highly symbolic, with politicians and activists using dramatic wedge issues to galvanize intense constituencies, which makes compromise difficult. To the extent that issues such as abortion, gay marriage, and the place of religion in public life become matters for democratic deliberation at lower, more local levels of government—where politics is perforce more practical and more constrained by competition among states and localities—the impulses for moderation and compromise will be stronger.

James Q. Wilson, in an important lecture at Harvard last year, said that the prominence of cultural and religious issues in our politics is contributing to increasing polarization, because moral positions are less amenable to compromise than economic positions. On the minimum wage, I say $10, you say $8, and we settle on $9. It is much more difficult to split the difference on issues of religious conviction or ethical principle.

I am unpersuaded by this argument. To the extent that matters are decided by legislatures, people who have strong views on different sides of issues of conduct and morality are forced to recognize that they live in a society with many people of equally strong, contrary views. On essentially every issue that we argue about in the realms of culture, religion, and morality, practicing politicians can find room for compromises that, while unprincipled and therefore objectionable to those of strong principle, are nevertheless necessary in a pluralistic society and may be appreciated for that reason.

Our prosperity moves us to argue, often heatedly, about moral, ethical, and religious issues. But our democracy can allow us to avoid tearing ourselves apart over them.

Joseph Bottum

John Green's discussion of faith-based voting leads me to reflect on the differences between religious and ethnic divisions in America, and on how the former have come to the fore as the latter have been fading in recent decades.

For many years in America, Catholic voters expressed themselves more as ethnic voters—as Italian or Irish or Polish. When the ethnic vote disappears, or the ethnic unity disappears from the Catholic vote, then you start to see the kind of breakdown in the Catholic vote that John Green points to, between traditionalist and mainline, between those who regularly attend mass and those who do not. In other words, there is no longer, within the sect or within the ethnic group, a vertical unity; instead it stratifies horizontally with other groups.

This is a pattern that we have started to see over and over again. Various people have used various names for it; I call it "mere religion." It includes a sense among serious believers that they have more in common with serious believers in other sects or even other religions than they have with the nonserious believers in their own sect.

Right before September 11, *Christianity Today* carried an article by a woman who had been in Istanbul and said how wonderful it was to see all the mosques and to feel such faith. Shortly thereafter, however, we had proof that Muslims at least have maintained the vertical unity and have not developed the horizontal, with its attitude of "We are all on the same side on this issue, so it is okay that you are not a Muslim."

But that creates a problem in America: Do we actually want there to emerge in the United States something that resembles a Christian Democratic Party and a secularist party? Do we want these issues to push us further and further apart? I believe that the issue of abortion, especially the *Roe v. Wade* ruling, has been the single greatest cause of these divisive forces in recent decades. Of course, the United States has a much stronger abortion license than any European country, precisely because we did not get it democratically in this country. We got it by court fiat. If there emerges something like these new political parties—defined by religious belief or the absence of it—American exceptionalism is exactly what is on the line.

PART III

Religion and Science

6

Permanent Tensions,
Transcendent Prospects

Leon R. Kass

Naomi (age 4): Where did the first person come from?

Polly (age 7): Well, there are two answers, but what do you think?

N: I think there was a big tree that broke in half, and, POP, out came a person.

P: Oh, that's interesting. You might be right, but here are the two answers. The Jewish answer is that God created Adam and Eve, and all people came from them. The Public answer is that people came from monkeys.

Mother: And where did the monkeys come from?

P (quick as a wink): From God!

Father: But what was before the monkeys?

P: *Tehom.*

Parents: (confused looks on their faces)

P: You know, like the first part of *Bereshith* [Genesis], "*Veha'arets hayeta tohu vavohu vehoshekh 'al-peney tehom.*" ["And the earth was unformed and void, and darkness was on the face of the deep (*tehom*)."]

Western civilization would not be Western civilization were it not for biblical religion, which reveres and trusts in the one God, who has made known what He wants of human beings through what is called His revelation, that is, through scripture. Western civilization would not be Western civilization were it not also for science, which extols and trusts in human reason to

83

disclose the workings of nature and to use the knowledge gained to improve human life. These twin sources of Western civilization—religion and science (or, before science, philosophy), divine revelation and human reason—are, to say the least, not easily harmonized. One might even say that Western civilization would not be Western civilization without the continuing dialectical tension between the claims and demands of biblical religion and the cultivation of autonomous human reason.

The tension between religion and science is an old story, as the names of Galileo, Giordano Bruno, and Darwin remind us. So too are efforts to overcome these tensions and to harmonize their seemingly disparate teachings; Isaac Newton spent the better part of his intellectual life on matters theological. The tensions between philosophy and religion (pagan as well as biblical) are even older, as the names of Socrates and Lucretius remind us; the former was convicted of impiety, the latter wrote as an explicit enemy of piety. In the Middle Ages, philosophical and religious giants, Aquinas and Maimonides, undertook great labors to synthesize the teachings of Aristotle with the teachings of scripture, Christian and Jewish; in the former case, the harmony could go only so far, in the latter case, it was not readily accepted by the religious community as being Jewish.

Given its long history, one might have thought that this subject had been wrestled to the mat, with little new to be said or done that could render a decisive verdict. Yet, for understandable reasons, it persists as a lively and increasingly relevant topic of cultural tension and public controversy, most visibly in recent debates over the teaching of evolution or stem cell research. From the one side we have arguments for "intelligent design," advanced by Christian believers and their scientific friends, intending not merely to show the limitations of orthodox Darwinism but also to shore up the scriptural account of creation. From the other side, we have arguments for unfettered scientific research, advanced by scientists and their secular friends, alleging that moral opposition to destructive embryo research represents the renewal of the Church's attack on Galileo and the independence of human reason.

Yet it is clear that these notorious controversies are but skirmishes in what appears to be a larger contest of worldviews, a contest deemed by some, and feared by others, to be irreconcilable, especially in light of the emergence of the robust biological sciences of genetics, neurobiology, and evolutionary psychology. We have had an outpouring of writings on the subject, many of them by biologists,[1] some who come as harmonizers, some who appear in battle dress. Among the harmonizers, paleontologist and popular-science author Stephen Jay Gould argues that science and religion are "non-overlapping magisteria"; entomologist and sociobiologist E. O. Wilson (himself an atheist) invites Christians to join hands with naturalists in the great task of preserving "the creation"; and physician and molecular geneticist Francis Collins, the head of the Human Genome Project, describes his own turn from atheism to Christianity, stemming largely from what he encountered in medicine and science.[2] Among the warriors, biologist and bio-prophet Richard Dawkins and philosophy professor Daniel Dennett offer purely naturalistic and evolutionary accounts of the origin of human religions and document what they regard to be the evils that belief in God has wrought.[3] The atheist British philosopher Antony Flew, who once declared that the teachings of evolution made the biblical account of creation "plumb unbelievable," recently converted to theism for reasons similar to those advanced by proponents of intelligent design.[4] The Templeton Foundation, committed to the goodness and truth of both science and Christianity, sponsors research that it hopes will demonstrate their perfect compatibility. And the Church itself has not been idle on this subject: the late Pope John Paul II writes an encyclical, *Fides et Ratio*,[5] that aims to show that reason and faith are finally not at odds—though, to be precise, the pope was concerned with showing Christianity's harmony with philosophical reason rather than with the special kind of rationalism that is modern science.

Amid these claims and counterclaims, it seems that we cannot escape this subject, fully aware that the last word will probably never be said. Indeed, it is important that we pay it careful attention, for the stakes are high: at issue are the moral and spiritual health of our nation, the continued vitality of science, and our own self-understanding as human beings and as children of the West.

The relation of science and religion is a venerable subject of scholarship, but it is not one of mine, though I have spent time studying on both sides of the street. I have practiced science, thought about its human significance, and offered philosophical critiques of the scientific understanding of living nature and of man. I have more recently taken up the study of the Hebrew Bible, motivated in part by a search for wisdom but also by a desire to see for myself whether biblical teachings can still be affirmed (or need to give ground) in the face of the findings of modern science. But regarding the relation of science and religion, I have mainly watched the cultural conflicts from the sidelines, dismayed by the rancor and sloppy thinking that is often displayed by partisans on all sides. At the same time, I have also been less than satisfied by the noble efforts of wishful-thinking harmonizers to make all conflict go away.[6] Accordingly, I aim here not for original insights but rather for some simple clarity, hoping to set forth certain plausible truths about the state of the question, present and projected. Because I offer a synoptic overview, my comments necessarily will be general (probably much too general), largely abstracted from the particular concrete issues where science and religion might meet in controversy—issues that include cosmological origins, natural teleology, creation and evolution, the human soul, free will, the status of human reason, the morality of scientific research, the sources of morality, and the ultimate cause of all that is. Still, I hope that my general observations may also be useful for anyone considering those more particular, sensitive subjects.

Preliminary Distinctions

I begin with a few preliminary stipulations about terms and procedure. First, the terms "religion" and "science" are complicated and ambiguous, each worthy of long and deep inquiry. The world knows innumerable religions, and even the so-called great religions, East and West, differ profoundly in their conceptions of divinity, nature, man, reason, morals, spirituality, and the purpose of it all. Moreover, the identification of religion with "faith"—and hence the reformulation of our topic under the heading of "faith and reason"—is, I would argue, a regrettable oversimplification and, indeed, the cause of much of the difficulty we face in thinking about science's relation to religion. Religions are about much more than faith, and many (I would even say most) of the teachings of biblical religion are neither irrational nor unreasonable. The focus on "faith" in these discussions may well reflect Christianity's emphasis on the supreme importance of *belief* and the affirmation of *doctrine* and *creed* as compared with matters of *practice, ritual,* and *lawful observance*—a subject to which I will return briefly at the end. But Enlightenment rationalism, for its part, welcomed the dichotomy, which served the purpose of an attack on religion as "irrational."[7]

"Science," too, is supremely ambiguous, referring (in its modern meanings[8]) both to a *methodical art* for gaining knowledge and to the accumulated *knowledge* itself. Both need to be distinguished from a strictly scientific *outlook* on life and the world, which in its most developed form has been called "*scientism*," a quasi-religious faith in the sufficiency of modern science to give a full account of our world, human life emphatically included. One need not be scientistic to practice science, and most scientists are not. Indeed, many a scientist is also a self-identified member of one or another religious community, though part of our concern here is whether any easygoing compatibility of, for example, Darwinism during the week and Christianity on the Sabbath is rationally defensible and free of contradiction.

Since our theme is religion and the *American* future, I will for present purposes use "religion" to refer mainly to Christianity and Judaism,[9] overlooking for the most part all the important differences between them (and the disagreements within each), both in idea and in practice. By "science" I will mean modern Western science, the globally successful effort to understand how things work—of which mathematical physics is the jewel and foundation—based on a method of discovery uniquely invented for this purpose, and ultimately imbued with a philanthropic aspiration to use that knowledge for the relief of man's estate and the betterment of human life.[10]

The second preliminary point concerns how to conduct such an inquiry. The relation between religion and science is, of course, not a scientific question, though scientists may freely speak about it. Likewise, although religious leaders also pronounce on this subject, neither is it a religious question. So the question arises: if not on the terrains of science or religion, on whose terrain, and in what terms, shall we take up this question? For many people, this will be a matter of private conscience and personal testimony; and there are well-known cases of people who have experienced religious insight that clarifies for them, and perhaps also for their readers and hearers, just how scientific reason and a particular faith are to be harmonized—or not. For others this is a matter for psychology or scientific anthropology, for example, Freud's attempts at psychodynamic explanations for religious belief or evolutionary psychologists' attempts to give bio-historical accounts of how primitive human beings first turned to religious belief—and why we in our enlightenment no longer need to. There is also a sociological approach: we could do empirical research on the shifting beliefs of Americans about God and man, in relation to new scientific findings and claims, say, in cosmology, genetics, or neuroscience.

My approach here, in contrast, will be philosophical. For insofar as the relation between religion and science is regarded as a genuine *question*, it is a matter for philosophy: it is both the subject and object of a quest for wisdom. Such an approach, I admit straightaway, carries its own hazards of distortion, since it risks treating science and (especially) the various religions *from the outside*, and not in the terms in which they understand themselves. Accordingly, thoughtful Jews and Christians and knowledgeable scientists may well not recognize themselves in my account. Nevertheless, looking in the mirror that I am providing will, I hope, stimulate salutary reflection.

With these preliminaries disposed of, let me outline the discussion that follows. Although any religion, as a human (and more-than-human) institution, comprises much more than the knowledge or truths it propounds, the primary point of contact and contest between science and religion happens to be about truth. Hence the central question here is this: how do matters stand between the truths discovered by science and the truths revealed by biblical religion, between the truths that can send a man to the moon and the truth spoken in the Torah or the truth that will make you free? My answer is divided into three parts: first, some remarks about knowledge and truth in general and their implications for religious teachings; second, remarks about knowledge of man and his place in the whole; and third, remarks about knowledge of how human beings ought to live—in short, matters epistemological, anthropological, and ethical-spiritual. My main goal will be to show, in each case, the limits—the *permanent* limits—of scientific knowledge and truth, and hence the enduring power and relevance of the perspectives and concerns, and also the specific teachings, of biblical religion.[11]

At the same time, however, I must insist that the discovery of science's double partiality—its incompleteness and its bias—does not by itself vindicate either the necessity or the truth of any particular alternative religious account: to discover that there are lacunae in science's account of the origins of the universe or limitations in the doctrine of evolution by natural selection does not entitle us to conclude that the biblical account of special creation must be correct. Indeed, no comfort to the harmonizers, I would maintain (and will point out in passing) that certain crucial biblical teachings, of immense importance to both Judaism and Christianity, may be in trouble, should science's underlying *heuristic* assumptions about nature and nature's lawfulness be taken as gospel ontological truth. Yet, and on the other hand, I will in a final section suggest that friends of biblical religion have no reason to fear that the Bible will be replaced as a true source of profound and elevating human instruction.

The Limited Knowledge of Modern Science

What kind of knowledge is science, and how is it related to the truths promulgated by biblical religion? Are these, as the late Stephen Jay Gould argued, "non-overlapping magisteria," each with its own canons of evidence and legitimate claims, but—despite apparent contradictions between them—perfectly compatible domains, neither capable of refuting or replacing the other? Or should we rather insist that there cannot be contradictory "truths" about the one world? For either the world is eternal or it came into being; if it came into being, either it was created by God or it was not; if there is divinity, either there is one God or many gods; either man is the one god-like ("image of God") creature or he is not; either his soul is immortal or it is not; either he has free will or he does not; either God has made known to man what He requires of him or He has not. It is, I trust, not just the residual scientist in me that insists that there cannot be more than one truth about the one world, even if we human beings can never know it to the bottom.

This premise of a single, universal truth is indeed one of the starting points of modern science, and it is science's reliance on methodical reason to discover such truth that makes possible its transnational and trans-religious appeal.[12]

If Buddhists or Muslims or Christians want to describe the relation of pressure to volume in a gas at constant temperature or the motion of falling bodies, they will necessarily embrace the equations that are Boyle's law or the law of universal gravitation. Indeed, the quest for *indubitable* knowledge, universally accessible and rationally expressible, was the radical new goal of modern science, rebelling against a two-thousand–year history of intellectual controversy and disagreement on nearly all matters hitherto discussed by scholars. As Descartes put it, "There is nothing imaginable so strange or so little credible that it has not been maintained by one philosopher or other."[13]

By the stringent standard of indubitability, a critique similar to Descartes' could be applied now as well as then to some of the central teachings of the world's great religions. Anyone can doubt or deny creation or immortality or the resurrection of the dead without self-contradiction; but no one can deny that the square built on the hypotenuse of a right triangle is equal to the sum of the squares built on the other two sides. In order to gain knowledge as indubitable as mathematics, the founders of modern science had to reconceive nature in objectified (mathematical) terms and to change the questions being asked: no longer the big questions regarding the nature of things, pursued by rare wisdom-seekers, but quantifiable problems regarding an objectified nature, soluble by ordinary mathematical problem-solvers. If the history of modern science could be viewed not retrospectively from the present, but prospectively from its origins in the early seventeenth century, we would be absolutely astonished at what science has been able to learn about the workings of nature, objectively reconceived.

Nevertheless, despite its universality, its quest for certainty, its reliance on reason purified from all distortions of sensation and prejudice by the use of mathematical method, and the reproducibility of its findings, science does not—and cannot—provide us with absolute knowledge. The reasons are not only methodological but also substantive, and not merely substantive but also intrinsic and permanent.

The substantive limits of science follow from certain fundamental aspects of scientific knowledge and from science's assumptions about what sorts of things are scientifically knowable. They stem from science's own self-proclaimed conceptual limitations—limitations to which neither religious nor philosophical thought is subject. This is not because science, being rational, is incapable of dealing with the passionate or subrational or spiritual or supernatural aspects of being. It is, on the contrary, because the rationality of science is but a partial and highly specialized rationality, concocted for the purpose of gaining only that kind of knowledge for which it was devised, and applied to only those aspects of the world that can be captured by such rationalized notions. The peculiar reason of science is not the natural reason of everyday life captured in ordinary speech, and it is also not the reason of philosophy or religious thought, both of which are tied to—even as they seek to take us beyond—the world as we experience it.[14]

Consider the following features of science and their contrast with the realm of ordinary and rationally graspable experience. First, science at its peak seeks laws of nature, ideally expressed mathematically in the form of equations that describe precisely the relationships among changing measurable variables; science does not seek to know beings or their natures, but rather the regularities of the changes that they undergo. Second, science—especially biology—seeks to know how things work and the mechanisms of action of their workings; it does not seek to know what things are, and why. Third, science can give the histories of things but not their directions, aspirations, or purposes: science is, by self-definition, non-teleological, oblivious to the natural purposiveness of all living beings. Fourth, science is wonderful at quantifying selected *external* relations of one object to another, or an earlier phase to a later one; but it can say nothing at all about the *inner* states of being, not only of human beings but of any living creature. Fifth, and strangest of all, modern science does not care much about causation; because it knows the regularities of change, it can often predict what will happen if certain perturbations occur, but it eschews explanations in terms of causes, especially of ultimate causes.

In a word, we have a remarkable science of nature that has made enormous progress precisely by its metaphysical neutrality and its indifference to questions of being, cause, purpose, inwardness, hierarchy, and the goodness or badness of things, scientific knowledge included.

Let me illustrate these abstract generalizations with a few concrete examples. In cosmology, we have seen wonderful progress in characterizing the temporal beginnings as a "big bang" and elaborate calculations to characterize what happened next. But from science we get complete silence regarding the status quo ante and the ultimate cause. Unlike a normally curious child, a cosmologist does not ask, "What was *before* the big bang?" or "*Why* is there something rather than nothing?" because the answer must be an exasperated "God only knows!"

In genetics, we have the complete DNA sequence of several organisms, including man, and we are rapidly learning what many of these genes "do." But this analytic approach cannot tell us how the life of a cockroach differs from that of a chimpanzee, or even what accounts for the special unity and active wholeness of cockroaches or chimpanzees, or the purposive effort each living being makes to preserve its own specific integrity.

In neurophysiology, we know vast amounts about the processing of visual stimuli, their transformation into electrochemical signals, and the pathways and mechanisms for transmitting these signals to the visual cortex of the brain. But the nature of sight itself we know not scientifically but only from the inside, and then only because we are not blind. As Aristotle pointed out long ago, the eyeball (and, I would add, the brain) has extension, takes up space, can be held in the hand; but neither sight (the capacity) nor seeing (the activity) is extended, and you cannot hold them in your hand or point to them. Although absolutely dependent on material conditions, they are in their essence immaterial: they are capacities and activities of *soul*—hence, not an object of knowledge for an objectified and materialist science.

Implications for Religion

Let me pause to draw out some implications for scriptural religion. On the one hand, the self-limited character of scientific knowledge is very good news for Christians and Jews. Eschewing philosophical speculation and metaphysical matters, science leaves those activities and domains free for complementary activities. Human beings will always ask questions of what and why, as well as of when and how. Human beings will always ask questions about the first cause and the end of days. Speculative philosophy and religion address these concerns and offer their own answers—albeit on grounds that must of necessity be "unscientific." If, for example, Genesis 1 offers a picture of the hierarchy of being, with man perched at its apex, the truth of that claim will not be based on scientific evidence; nor, as I will suggest at the end, is that truth likely to be confirmed or denied by scientific findings.

But, on closer examination, Stephen Jay Gould's live-and-let-live suggestion of complementary truths has its own limitations for the seriously religious. This is especially true for those whose reading of scripture is not only literal but literalist: those who think that the truths of scripture belong to the same category of knowledge as that which can be demonstrated or falsified by science or historical research—a misguided hypothesis, in my opinion, but popular nonetheless. So, for example, those who, like Bishop Ussher in the seventeenth century, would learn the precise age of the earth from scripture may be compelled to reconsider the veracity of the Bible, given the abundant evidence regarding the vast age of the cosmos. The fossil record, despite its lacunae, is an embarrassment to those who believe that the Bible teaches correctly the near-instantaneous appearance of all God's creatures—unless, of course, they retreat to the position (proposed seriously in the nineteenth century) that God seeded the earth's layers with fossils of creatures that never existed, precisely in order to test the faithful.

And then, finally, there is that old chestnut, still hard to crack, of miracles. Few of us, creatures of the present age, believe in miracles—in occurrences that suspend the laws of nature—events that we must hold to be, according to the regularities that science describes for us, "impossible." In this respect, we are all children of science, at least regarding our contemporary life on earth. So little do we believe in the possibility of miracles that many of us even have trouble imagining any occurrence so unusual or momentous that would shake our faith in the *im*possibility of miracles.

I once discussed this issue with a class of brilliant high-schoolers studying Descartes' *Discourse on Method*, where the students were dogmatically insisting that their faith in nature's abiding lawfulness could never be shaken, come what may. "What if," I confidently asked, "Descartes himself were suddenly to appear in the flesh right before us, not some Madame Tussaud dummy but the real René? Would you change your mind?" To my astonishment, no one was the least bit moved. Instead, invoking the laws of probability and the always-finite chance of even the rarest of events, the smart scientists in the class averred that the molecules that once accompanied the genius that was Descartes might, on their own, accidentally reunite to give us his reincarnation. I found their faith as touching as it was preposterous. Yet the irrationality of their zeal does not solve the problem for believing Christians and Jews, for whom big miracles surely matter; and attempts to harmonize science and religion cannot make this issue disappear.

Either God gave the law to the Israelites at Mount Horeb or He didn't; if not, the six hundred thousand witnesses were deluded, and those who accept that His Torah was His gift may need to reconsider. Either the Red

Sea parted and the sun stood still, or they didn't, in which case God's prov-idence on behalf of His people is less than it is cracked up to be—not an uncommon opinion among some post-Holocaust Jews. And, abundant claims for the harmony of faith and reason notwithstanding, either Jesus rose from the dead or he did not—a miracle from the point of view not only of science but of all reasonable human experience. Yet on the truth of his resurrection rests the deepest ground for the Christian faith in the divinity of Jesus and the promise of man's ultimate salvation in him.

About such astounding "irregularities," science not only casts doubt: it cannot abide them. This is, for science, no idle prejudice. And the reason is plain. If a willful and powerful God were capable of intervening in worldly affairs and suspending the laws of nature, genuine science would be impos-sible.[15] Its regularities would be mere probabilities, and its predictions would be entirely contingent on God's being out to lunch.

To my mind, it is a limping rejoinder to this challenge to say that an omnipotent God could still perform miracles and may someday do so again, but that He binds His power by His will for His own good purposes—hence, among other things, making science possible. This is too neat and too ad-hoc to be satisfying. And there is, I should add, nothing in scripture to support these apologetic fancies.

On top of this rather old difficulty about miracles in general—a diffi-culty Christians and Jews have apparently learned to live with—biblical religious teachings today face newer and more particular difficulties in relation to specific scientific developments, of which the possible tension between evolution and the Bible is only the most well-known example. Here I have in mind present and projected discoveries in genetics and neuroscience, and, even more, the *interpretations* of these findings in the theoretical (and often explicitly anti-religious) pronouncements of evolu-tionary psychologists: interpretations and pronouncements that are sup-ported but, in my view, hardly necessitated by those scientific discoveries. Today and tomorrow, major challenges are coming that affect not only specific religious dogmas, unique to each faith, but also the biblical under-standing of human nature and human dignity, central ideas in all scrip-tural religion.

This is where the next big battles may be anticipated, and where we may next turn.

Science, Human Nature, and Human Dignity

The epistemological limitations of the scientific understanding of the world is, for most of us all of the time and for all of us most of the time, not a source of disquiet. Who cares, really, that according to our physics this most solid table at which I am writing is largely empty space, or that beautiful colors are conceived of as mere mathematized waves? Almost no one even notices that science ignores the being of things, even living things, and approaches them in objectified and mechanistic terms. We start to fret only when the account comes home to roost, to challenge our self-understanding as free and self-conscious beings with a rich inner life.

This venerable self-conception, rooted in everyday human experience, has been reinforced by centuries of philosophical and religious teachings. Yet the challenge to it has been coming for a long time; indeed, it emerged with the origins of modern science in the seventeenth century and has been there for all to see. For several centuries, giants of Western philosophy, including Leibniz, Spinoza, and Kant, labored mightily to find a home for human freedom and dignity, now that all of nature had to be ceded to mechanistic physics. Today, those philosophical defenses are no longer being attempted, whereas the challengers—all adherents of scientism— have become increasingly bold.

The strongest summonses today come from an increasingly unified approach to biology and human biology—evolutionist, materialist, determinist, mechanistic, and objectified—combining powerful ideas from genetics, developmental biology, neuroscience, and evolutionary biology and psychology. At issue are not only what we think we are, but also our standing vis-à-vis the rest of living nature. Already Darwinism, in its original version 150 years ago, appeared to challenge our special standing: how could any being descended from subhuman origins, rather than created directly by the hand of God, claim to be a higher animal, never mind a godlike one? Indeed, orthodox evolutionary theory even denies that animals should be called "higher" or "lower," rather than just more or less complex: since all animals are finally in the same business—individual survival, for the sake of perpetuating their genes—the apparent differences among them are, at bottom, merely more or less complicated ways of getting the job done.

Materialistic explanations of vital events, even psychic events, leave no room for soul, understood as life's animating principle. Remarkably, our science of life has no interest in the question of what life is or what is responsible for it. Likewise, our science of the psyche has no interest in its proper subject: does any psychologist ask, "What is soul, that we are mindful of it?" Deterministic and mechanistic accounts of brain functions seem to do away with the need to speak of human freedom and purposiveness. The fully objectified and exterior account of our behavior—once the province of B. F. Skinner, today the grail sought by neuroscience—diminishes the significance of our felt inwardness. Feeling, passion, awareness, imagination, desire, love, hate, and thought are, scientifically speaking, equally and merely "brain events."

Never mind "created in the image of God": what elevated *humanistic* view of human life or human goodness is defensible against the belief, trumpeted by biology's most public and prophetic voices, that man is just a collection of molecules, an accident on the stage of evolution, a freakish speck of mind in a mindless universe, fundamentally no different from other living—or even nonliving—things? What chance have our treasured ideas of freedom and dignity against the reductive notion of "the selfish gene" (or, for that matter, "genes for altruism"), the belief that DNA is the essence of life, or the teaching that all human behavior and our rich inner life are rendered intelligible only in terms of neurochemistry and their contributions to species survival and reproductive success?

Many of our leading scientists and intellectuals, truth to tell, are eager to dethrone traditional understandings of man's special place, and use every available opportunity to do battle. For example, in 1997, the luminaries of the International Academy of Humanism—including the biologists Francis Crick, Richard Dawkins, and E. O. Wilson and the humanists Isaiah Berlin, W. V. Quine, and Kurt Vonnegut—issued a statement in defense of cloning research in higher mammals and human beings. Their reasons were revealing:

> What moral issues would human cloning raise? Some world religions teach that human beings are fundamentally different from other mammals—that humans have been imbued by a deity with immortal souls, giving them a value that cannot be compared to that of other living things. Human nature is held to be unique and

sacred. Scientific advances which pose a perceived risk of altering this "nature" are angrily opposed. . . . [But] as far as the scientific enterprise can determine . . . human capabilities appear to differ in degree, not in kind, from those found among the higher animals. Humanity's rich repertoire of thoughts, feelings, aspirations, and hopes seems to arise from electrochemical brain processes, not from an immaterial soul that operates in ways no instrument can discover. . . . Views of human nature rooted in humanity's tribal past ought not to be our primary criterion for making moral decisions about cloning. . . . The potential benefits of cloning may be so immense that it would be a tragedy if ancient theological scruples should lead to a Luddite rejection of cloning.[16]

In order to justify ongoing research, these intellectuals and others like them today are willing to shed not only traditional religious views but *any* view of human distinctiveness and special dignity, their own included. They fail to see that the scientific view of man they celebrate does more than insult our vanity. It undermines our self-conception as free, thoughtful, and responsible beings, worthy of respect because we alone among the animals have minds and hearts that aim far higher than the mere perpetuation of our genes. It undermines, as well, the beliefs that sustain our mores, practices, and institutions—including the practice of science.

The problem lies not so much with the scientific findings themselves but with the shallow philosophy that recognizes no other truths but these and with the arrogant pronouncements of the bioprophets. For example, in a letter to the editor complaining about a review of his book, *How the Mind Works,* the well-known evolutionary psychologist and popularizer Steven Pinker rails against any appeal to the human soul:

Unfortunately for that theory, brain science has shown that the mind is what the brain does. The supposedly immaterial soul can be bisected with a knife, altered by chemicals, turned on or off by electricity, and extinguished by a sharp blow or a lack of oxygen. Centuries ago it was unwise to ground morality on the dogma that the earth sat at the center of the universe. It is just as unwise today to ground it on dogmas about souls endowed by God.[17]

One hardly knows which is the more impressive, the height of Pinker's arrogance or the depth of his shallowness. He appears ignorant of the fact that "soul" need not be conceived as a "ghost in the machine" or as a separate "thing" that survives the body, but can be understood (à la Aristotle) to be the integrated powers of the naturally organic body. He has evidently not pondered the relationship between "the brain" and the whole organism or puzzled over the difference between "the brain" of the living and "the brain" of the dead. He seems unaware of the fact of emergent properties—powers and activities that do not reside in the materials of the organism but emerge only when the materials are formed and organized in a particular way; he does not understand that the empowering organization of materials—the vital form—is not itself material. But Pinker speaks with the authority of science, and few are able and willing to dispute him on his own grounds.

There is, of course, nothing novel about his form of reductionism, materialism, and determinism; these are doctrines with which Socrates contended long ago. What is new is that, as philosophies, they seem (to many people) to be vindicated by scientific advance. Here, in consequence, would be the most pernicious result of our technological progress, a result more dehumanizing than any actual manipulation or technique, present or future: the erosion, perhaps the final erosion, of the idea of man as noble, dignified, precious, or godlike, and its replacement with a view of man, no less than of nature, as mere raw material for manipulation and homogenization.

As a *cultural* matter, the challenge of soulless scientism is surely daunting, even dispiriting. With philosophical anthropology in hibernation, only religious teachings appear to support the intuitions of uninstructed human experience of the human. As the passages quoted above indicate, our secular elite is only too happy to charge these teachings with parochialism, dogmatism, and narrow cultural prejudice, all in the service of a rational, universal science. And they are above all determined to banish all such teachings and (especially) their proponents from public discourse about "scientific" matters such as cloning or euthanasia.

But take heart: as a *philosophical* matter, these challenges should not bother us. Without for a moment calling into question the elegance or accuracy of any genuine scientific findings, each of these challenges can be met, and even without turning to religion. An adequate philosophy of nature would know what to say.

Although the subject is too long to be adequately dealt with here,[18] the following summary points show once again the limits of any *merely* scientific approach. First, regarding our origins: a history of coming-into-being is no substitute for knowing directly the being that has come. To know man, we must study him especially as he is (and through what he does), not how he got to be this way. For understanding either our nature—what we are—or our standing, it matters not whether our origin was from the primordial slime or from the hand of a creator God: even with monkeys for ancestors, what has emerged is more than monkey business.

Second, regarding our inwardness, freedom, and purposiveness, we must repair to our inside knowledge. For even if scientists were to "prove" to their satisfaction that inwardness, consciousness, and human will or purposive intention were all illusory—at best, epiphenomena of brain events—or that what we call loving and wishing and thinking are merely electrochemical transformations of brain substance, we should proceed to ignore them. And for good reason. Life's self-revelatory testimony with regard to its own vital activity is more immediate, compelling, and trustworthy than are the abstracted explanations that evaporate meaningful lived experience by identifying it with some correlated bodily event. The most unsophisticated child knows red and blue more reliably than a physicist with his spectrometers. And anyone who has ever loved knows that love cannot be reduced to neurotransmitters. Regarding our life—passionate, responsive, appetitive, thoughtful, and active—we have inside knowledge that cannot be denied.[19]

Third, on the scientists' own grounds, they will be unable to refute our intransigent insistence on our own freedom and psychic awareness. For how are they going to explain our resistance to their subversive ideas, save by conceding that we must just be hard-wired by nature to resist them? If all truth claims of science—and the philosophical convictions that some people derive from them—are merely the verbalized expressions of certain underlying brain states in the scientists who offer these claims, then there can be no way to refute the contrary opinions of those whose nervous systems, differently wired, see things the opposite way. And why, indeed, should anyone choose to accept as true the results of someone else's "electrochemical brain processes" over his own? Truth and error, no less than human freedom and dignity, become empty notions when the soul is reduced to chemicals.

The possibility of science itself depends on the immateriality of thought. It depends on the mind's independence from the bombardment of matter. Otherwise, there is no truth, there is only "it seems to me." Not only the possibility for recognizing truth and error, but also the *reasons* for doing science rest on a picture of human freedom and dignity (of the sort promulgated by biblical religion) that science itself cannot recognize. Wonder, curiosity, a wish not to be self-deceived, and a spirit of philanthropy are the *sine qua non* of the modern scientific enterprise. They are hallmarks of the living human soul, not of the anatomized brain. The very enterprise of science—like all else of value in human life—depends on a view of humanity that science cannot supply and that foolish scientistic prophets deny at their peril, unaware of the embarrassing self-contradiction.

Science and the Moral Life

Yet, truth to tell, the deepest limitation of a scientized account of the human condition concerns not so much man as knower but man as an ethical and spiritual being—a being whose existence is defined not only by Kant's first great question, "What can I know?" but by his second and third great questions: "What ought I do?" and "What may I hope?" For man alone among the animals goes in for ethicizing, for concerning himself with how to live, and with better and worse answers to this question. Science, notwithstanding its great gifts to human life in the form of greater comfort and safety, is notoriously unhelpful in satisfying these great longings of the human soul.

One should acknowledge straightaway that science is not an immoral or non-moral activity. On the contrary, although the motivations and characters of individual scientists run the usual human gamut, the enterprise of science taken as a whole is animated by noble human purpose: a philanthropic desire to alleviate human misery and to improve human life. In addition, one can argue (and some scientists do) that they stand under a moral injunction— even a divine injunction—not only to love their neighbor but to vindicate their powers of reason and their capacities to do good and to heal the world. Discovering the truths about nature's workings can even be said to be a form of reverence: as Francis Bacon put it, knowledge rightly understood is "a rich storehouse for the glory of the Creator and the relief of man's estate."[20]

Moreover, the successful practice of science requires the exercise of many virtues: enterprise (in imagining new possibilities), self-discipline and perseverance (in doggedly pursuing a line of experimentation), courage (in risking failure), measure and judiciousness (in weighing evidence), and intellectual probity and integrity (in reporting data, crediting others, and giving an honest account to one's sources of financial support).

Science is also a social activity: much scientific research involves direct collaboration, and nearly all of it rests on explicit and tacit networks of cooperation; it therefore requires openness, trust, and (within the limits of scientific competition) generous sharing of materials and data. In my own experience, I have found that personal integrity, group morale, and the ease of interpersonal relations in a research laboratory are several cuts above what I have encountered in any other domain of academic life (including philosophy departments and divinity schools).

But these private virtues of scientists, as well as the overall ethical character of the scientific project, are not themselves the product of science. Science is notoriously (and deliberately) morally neutral, silent on the distinction between better and worse, right and wrong, the noble and the base. And although it hopes that the uses made of its findings will be, as Francis Bacon prophesied, governed in charity, it can do nothing to insure that result. It can offer no standards to guide the use of the awesome powers it places in human hands. Though it seeks universal knowledge, it has no answer to moral relativism. It does not know what charity is, what charity requires, or even whether and why it is good. Science cannot provide either confirmation of or support for its own philanthropic assumptions.

Such moral poverty need not be embarrassing, either to science or to religion. After all, science never claimed to speak on moral matters, and religion remains available to speak where science is silent—to teach us our duties, to restrain our vices, to lead us to righteousness and holiness. But the ability of religion to guide us in these ways depends in part on its ability to withstand not the morally neutral discoveries of science but the morally freighted, anti-religious campaigns that rely on and make use of a strictly scientific view of human life. And here, the news is hardly good.

No one should underestimate the growing cultural power of scientific materialism and reductionism. As we have seen, our prophets of scientism are increasingly peddling the materialism of science, useful as a heuristic hypothesis, as the one true account of human life, citing as evidence the powers obtainable on the basis of just such reductive approaches. Many laymen, ignorant of any defensible scientific alternative to materialism, are swallowing and regurgitating the shallow doctrines of "the selfish gene" and "the mind is the brain," because they *seem* to be vindicated by scientific advance. The cultural result is likely to be serious damage to human self-understanding and the subversion of all high-minded views of the good life.

Nowhere will this challenge be more readily felt than in the proposed uses of biotechnical power for purposes beyond the cure of disease and the relief of suffering. Going beyond therapy, we stand on the threshold of major efforts to "perfect" human nature and to "enhance" human life by direct biotechnical alterations of our bodies and minds. We are promised better children, superior performance, ageless bodies, and happy souls—all with the help of the biotechnologies of "enhancement."[21] Bioprophets tell us that we are en route to a new stage of evolution, to the creation of a post-human society, a society based on science and built by technology, a society in which traditional teachings about human nature will be passé and religious teachings about how to live will be irrelevant.

But what, then, will guide this evolution? How do we know whether any of these so-called enhancements is in fact an improvement? Why ought any human being embrace a *post*-human future? Scientism has no answers to these critical moral questions. Deaf to nature, to God, and even to moral reason, it can offer no standards for judging technological change to be progress—or for judging anything else. Instead, it tacitly preaches its own version of faith, hope, and charity: faith in the unqualified goodness of scientific and technological progress, hope in the promise of transcendence of our biological limitations, charity in promising everyone ultimate relief from, and transcendence of, the human condition—all to be achieved by the very defective beings whose imperfections allegedly make the project necessary. No religious faith rests on flimsier ground. And yet the project for the mastery of human nature proceeds apace, and most people stand on the sidelines and cheer.

So this is our peculiar moral and religious crisis. We are in turbulent seas without a landmark precisely because we adhere more and more to a view of human life that both gives us enormous power and, at the same time, denies every possibility of non-arbitrary standards for guiding its use.

Though well equipped, we moderns know not who we are or where we are going. We triumph over nature's unpredictabilities only to subject ourselves, tragically, to the still greater unpredictability of our capricious wills and our fickle opinions. Engineering the engineer as well as the engine, we race our train we know not where. That we do not recognize our predicament is itself a tribute to the depth of our infatuation with scientific progress and our naive faith in the sufficiency of our humanitarian impulses.

Despite the fact, as I have argued, that there is no philosophical reason to despair and that a philosophical and religious anthropology could meet the challenge of scientism, there are in fact large cultural reasons to worry. Can our religious traditions rise to the challenge? Can they defend their own truths?

The Truth of the Bible

To this point, I have largely addressed the relation between religion and science by focusing on the limitations of science. But what about the limits of biblical religion? What new difficulties does it face in the age of science? Can it survive and surmount them?

As an empirical matter, there can be no doubt that the growth of secularism and atheism in the West over the past few centuries, especially in the last fifty prosperous years, is at least in part connected to the success of science and technology—and of modern rationalism more generally—and also to the uses that have been made of science in explicit attempts to embarrass religious beliefs. Just as Lucretius long ago used Epicurus' doctrine of atomistic materialism to combat religious beliefs and to cure men of the fear of the gods, so many modern epicureans enlist the teachings of evolution and neuroscience as battering rams against the teachings of the Bible and the religions built upon it.

Assessing the success of this assault is a very complicated enterprise, not only sociologically but also philosophically. But it may be helpful, as a test case, to look at what has been a chief target of scientism, the opening chapter of the Bible and its account of creation. How should the teachings of Genesis 1 be affected by the discoveries of science? Can one still affirm the truths that it purports to teach? Conversely, can the biblical account of creation—including man's place in it—answer the shortcomings of the scientific account? The answers to these questions depend entirely on what Genesis 1 actually says and what it aims to accomplish in the hearts and minds of its readers.

In writing elsewhere on this subject, I have argued that the teachings of Genesis 1 are indeed untouched by the scientific findings that allegedly make them "plumb unbelievable."[22] Here is a summary of the major points. First, Genesis 1 is not a freestanding historical or scientific account of what happened and how, but rather a (literally) *awe*-inspiring prelude to a lengthy and comprehensive teaching about how we are to live. Second, it is not an account that can be either corroborated or falsified by scientific or historical studies: neither "creation science" or arguments about "intelligent design," on the one hand, nor evidence regarding the age of the universe or man's evolutionary origins and the workings of his brain, on the other hand, can strengthen or weaken decisively what one is supposed to learn from the creation story.

This is partly because, third, the Bible addresses its readers not as detached, rational observers moved primarily by curiosity and the desire for mastery over nature, but as existentially engaged human beings who need first and foremost to make sense of their world and their task within it. Genesis speaks immediately and truly to the deepest concerns of human hearts and minds in their normal—and permanent—existential condition. The first human question is not "How did this come into being?" or "How does it work?" The first human question is "What does all this mean?" and (especially) "What am I to do here?"

The specific claims of the biblical account of creation begin to nourish the soul's longings for answers to these questions. The world that you see around you, you human being, is orderly and intelligible (albeit against a background of chaos and threat of dissolution), an articulated whole comprising distinct kinds. The order of the world is as rational as the speech that you use to describe it and that, right before your (reading) eyes, summoned it into being. Most importantly, this noetic (rather than sensual) order of created things means mainly to demonstrate that, contrary to the belief of uninstructed human experience, the sun, the moon, and the stars are not divine, despite their sempiternal beauty and power and their majestic perfect motion. Nature is neither eternal nor divine;[23] its beginnings are owed neither to the sexual couplings nor to the warring struggles of gods and goddesses. Moreover, being is *hierarchic*, and man is the highest being in creation although not perfect—unlike all other created things save the heavenly firmament, man is not said by God to be "good." Man is alone a being that is *in the image* of God.

What does this mean? And can it be true? In the course of recounting his creation, Genesis 1 introduces us to God's *activities* and *powers*: God speaks, commands, names, blesses, and hallows; God makes and makes freely; God looks at and beholds the world; God is concerned with the goodness or perfection of things; God addresses solicitously other living creatures and provides for their sustenance. In short, God exercises speech and reason, freedom in doing and making, and the powers of contemplation, judgment, and care.

Doubters may wonder whether this is a true account of God—after all, it is only on biblical authority that we regard God as possessing these powers and activities. But it is indubitably clear, even to atheists, that we human beings have them, and that they lift us above the plane of a merely animal existence. Human beings, alone among the creatures, speak, plan, create, contemplate, and judge. Human beings, alone among the creatures, can articulate a future goal and use that articulation to guide them in bringing it into being by their own purposive conduct. Human beings, alone among the creatures, can think about the whole, marvel at its many-splendored forms and articulated order, wonder about its beginning, and feel awe in beholding its grandeur and in pondering the mystery of its source.

Note well: these self-evident truths do *not* rest on biblical authority. Rather, the biblical text enables us to confirm them by an act of self-reflection. Our reading of this text, addressable and intelligible only to us human beings, and our responses to it, possible only for us human beings, provide all the proof we need to confirm the text's assertion of our special being. The very act of *reading* Genesis 1 performatively demonstrates the truth of its claims about the superior ontological standing of the human. This is not anthropocentric prejudice, but cosmological truth. And nothing we might ever learn from science about *how* we came to be this way could ever make it false.[24]

In addition to holding up a mirror in which we see reflected our special standing in the world, Genesis 1 teaches truly the bounty of the universe and its hospitality in supporting terrestrial life. Moreover, we have it on the highest authority that the whole—the being of all that is—is "very good":

> And God saw every thing that He had made, and, behold, it was very good.
>
> (Genesis 1:31)

The Bible here teaches a truth that cannot be known by science, even as it is the basis of the very possibility of science—and of everything else we esteem. For it truly is very good that there is something rather than nothing. It truly is very good that this something is intelligibly ordered rather than dark and chaotic. It truly is very good that the whole contains a being who not only can discern the intelligible order but can also recognize that it is "very good"—who can *appreciate* that there is something rather than nothing and that he exists with the reflexive capacity to celebrate these facts with the mysterious source of being itself. As Abraham Joshua Heschel put it in *Who Is Man?*

> The biblical words about the genesis of heaven and earth are not words of information but words of appreciation. The story of creation is not a description of how the world came into being but a song about the glory of the world's having come into being. "And God saw that it was good." This is the challenge: to reconcile God's view with our experience.[25]

There is more. The purpose of the song is not only to celebrate. It is also to summon us to awe and attention. For just as the world as created is a world summoned into existence under command, so to be a human being in that world is to live in search of our summons. It is to recognize, first of all, that we are here not by choice or on account of merit, but as an undeserved gift from powers not at our disposal. It is to feel the need to justify that gift, to make something out of our indebtedness for the opportunity of existence. It is to stand in the world not only in awe of its and our existence but under an obligation to answer a call to a worthy life, a life that does honor to the divine-likeness with which our otherwise animal existence has been—no thanks to us—endowed. It is explicitly to feel the need to find a way of life for which we should be pleased to answer at the bar of justice when our course is run, in order to vindicate the blessed opportunity and the moral-spiritual challenge that is the essence of being human.

The first chapter of Genesis—like no work of science, no matter how elegant or profound—invites us to hearken to a transcendent voice. It provides a perfect answer to the human need to know not only how the world works but also what we are to do here. It is the beginning of a Bible-length response to the human longing for meaning and wholehearted existence. The truths it bespeaks—and which are enacted when the text is read respondingly—are more than cognitive. They point away from the truths of belief to the truths of action—of song and praise and ritual, of love and procreation and civic life, of responsible deeds in answering the call to righteousness, holiness, and love of neighbor. Such truths speak more deeply and permanently to the souls of men than any mere doctrine, whether of science or even of faith. As long as we understand our great religions as the embodiments of such truths, the friends of religion will have nothing to fear from science, and the friends of science who are still in touch with their humanity will have nothing to fear from religion. That we should have been given such a life-affirming teaching is, to speak plainly, a miracle.

Appendix: "Objectification" and Its Deficiencies[26]

There is one special feature of modern biology, a feature that is itself a cardinal premise of modern science altogether, that seems to be both most powerful in yielding new knowledge of biological events and, at the same time, *most* untrue to life: the principle of *objectification*. Understanding this fact is the intellectual key to understanding the gulf between scientific knowledge and the world it purports to capture and explain.

The term "objective" has a common colloquial meaning and a precise philosophical meaning, the former descending from the latter but without our knowing what distortions we have swallowed in the process. In common speech, we are inclined to use "objective" as a synonym for "true" or "real." Not only a scientist but any fair-minded person is supposed "to be objective": unprejudiced, disinterested, rational, free from contamination of merely personal—that is, "subjective"—bias or perspective, and able therefore to capture so-called "objective reality." "Objective reality" is the domain especially of the sciences, because the methodical pursuit of reproducible and shareable findings guarantees their objective status.

But this common view is misleading: "the objective" is not synonymous with "the true" or "the real." Pursuit of the distinction discloses, surprisingly, an unbridgeable gap between science and reality, and, of greater moment for us, between the science of biology and the living nature it studies. *For the so-called objective view of nature is not nature's own, but one imposed on nature, imposed by none other than the interested human subject.*

Here's how this works. An "object," etymologically, means that which is "thrown-out-before-and-against" us—thrown by, thrown-before-and-against, and existing for and relative to the human subject who "did the throwing." Not the natural world, *but the self-thinking human subject*, is the source of objectivity. The interested subject's demand for clear and distinct and certain "knowledge" leads him to *re*-present the given world before his mind, in an act of deliberate projection, through concepts (invented for the purpose) that allow him to operate mentally on the world with utmost (usually quantitative) precision. What cannot be grasped through such conceptual re-presentation drops from view. Only those aspects of the world that can be "objectified" (or quantified) become objects for scientific study. As the given, visible, and tangible world of our experience is banished into the shadows, the shadowy world of "concepts" gains the limelight and reconfigures everything in sight, giving things an "objectified" character that is at best only partially true to what they *are*.

A concrete example can make more vivid this abstract account of the abstracting character of scientific objectification. The classic instance of objectifying the world in fact concerns the world as visible and, by implication, with ourselves as its experiencing viewers. In a revolution-making passage in the *Rules for the Direction of the Mind*, Descartes sets the program of all modern science by radically transforming how we should approach the study of color:

> Thus whatever you suppose color *to be*, you cannot deny that it is *extended* and in consequence possessed of figure. Is there then any *disadvantage*, if, while taking care not to admit any new entity uselessly, or rashly to imagine that it exists . . . but merely abstracting from every other feature except that it possesses the nature of figure, we conceive the diversity existing between white, blue, and red, etc., as being like the difference between the following similar figures? The same argument applies to *all cases*; for it is certain that the *infinitude of figures* suffices to *express* all the differences in sensible things.[27]

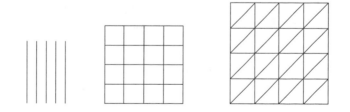

To see more clearly what is involved in "objectification" and how it distorts the very phenomena in the course of coming to "understand" them, let us go slowly through the passage, noting the following crucial points:

1. We are told to ignore the *being* or *nature* of color, and concentrate instead only on the "fact" that, because colored *things* are extended (that is, take up space), all *color* has figure or shape. ("Never mind," says Descartes, "what color really *is*. You cannot deny that *it* has figure.")[28]

2. We then must *abstract* from every feature of color *except* that it has the nature of *figure*. Why? Because doing so offers an advantage in knowing, yet a kind of knowing that is indifferent to existence, to what something really *is*. The knowledge acquired by objectification is indifferent or neutral to the *being* or *reality* of things.

3. The act of this reconception is a willful act of mind. Descartes *decides* or *chooses* to conceive the truth about color under the concept of figure. We do not, as knowers, try to catch the *natural* looks of *visible things*; instead, by decision, *we choose* to *conceive* (literally, "to grasp together") or represent before our grasping minds only *certain* aspects of the world.

4. Which aspects? Not the natures of colors, not the being of colors, but the *differences* among them ("the *diversity* existing between white, blue, and red"). We do not seek to know *things* through and through, but only their external—and measurable—*relations*.

5. The *natural* differences are "translated" into—or, rather, *symbolized by*—*mathematical* ones. The differences of color are represented by differences among similar figures. Why? Because if we configure things, we can then take their mathematical measure, using the radically new mathematics of quantity (featuring the number line and analytic geometry) that Descartes has invented for this purpose, a mathematics that introduced terms of arithmetic (traditionally the study of *discrete* multitudes) into the study of geometry (the study of *continuous* magnitudes). The analytic geometry of Cartesian space is the perfect vehicle for precise measurement of anything—space, time, mass, density, volume, velocity, energy, temperature, blood pressure, drunkenness, intelligence, or scholastic achievement—that can be treated as an extent or quantity or dimension.

6. Descartes' geometrical figures may be poor and passé as standing for the differences among the colors white, blue, and red, but the principle he proposes is not: today we still treat color in terms of "wave lengths," purely mathematical representations *from which all the color is sucked out*. This tells the whole story: *the objective is purely quantitative. All quality disappears.*

7. Objectification can be universalized, says Descartes: *all* the *differences* (that is, changes or relations) in sensible things—that is, in every being that exists in the natural world—can be expressed mathematically. The world—or more accurately, *changes* in the world—can be represented objectively, as differences among figures (or, eventually, in equations). The multifaceted

and profound world of things is replaced by a shadowy network of mathe-matized relations. Objectified knowledge is ghostly, to say the least.

In this classic example, we have the touchstone of all so-called objec-tive knowledge. The objectified world is, by deliberate design, abstract, purely quantitative, homogeneous, and indifferent to the question of being or existence. "Things" are "known" only externally and relationally. More-over, the symbolic representations used to handle the objectified world bear absolutely no relation to the things represented: a wave length or a mathe-matical equation neither resembles nor points to color.

No one gets very excited about the objectification of color, but we become suspicious when science tries to objectify the *viewing* of color or, worse, the *viewer*. And now we see why. By its very principle, "objective knowledge" of sight and seeing will not be—because it *cannot* be—true to lived experience; for lived experience is always qualitative, concrete, het-erogeneous, and suffused with the attention, interest, and engaged concern of the living soul. Real seeing can never be captured by wavelengths, absorption spectra of retinal cells, or electrical depolarizations and dis-charges in the objectified brain. Likewise also the inwardness of life, includ-ing awareness, appetite, emotion, and the genuine and interested relations between one living being and others, both friend and foe; or the engaged, forward-pointed, outward-moving tendencies of living beings; or the uniqueness of each individual life as lived in time, from birth to death; the concern of each animal (conscious or not) for its own health, wholeness, and well-being—none of these essential aspects of nature alive fall within the cramped and distorting boundaries of nature objectified.

Honesty compels me to interrupt this critique and to add one last and, indeed, astounding part of this tale, one that, I suspect, the reader already knows. Objectification works! For some reason, the many-splendored world of nature allows itself to be grasped by the anemic concepts of objective science. Never mind that it is partial, distorted, shadowy, abstract; the quan-titative approach has put men on the moon, lights on the ceiling, and pace-makers in our hearts. Somehow, it must be capturing well at least one aspect of being. But this aspect of being is not the whole or the heart of being; not by a long shot.

Notes

1. Until fairly recently, the religion and science question, insofar as scientists entered into it, was largely connected to matters cosmological, of interest mainly to physicists and astronomers; today, biologists are increasingly entering the discussions, because the vexing topics seem to emerge more from the scientific study of life, and especially of human life.

2. Stephen Jay Gould, *Rock of Ages: Science and Religion in the Fullness of Life* (New York: Ballantine Publishing Company, 1999); E. O. Wilson, *The Creation: An Appeal to Save Life on Earth* (New York: W. W. Norton, 2006); Francis S. Collins, *The Language of God: A Scientist Presents Evidence for Belief* (New York: Free Press, 2006).

3. Richard Dawkins, *The God Delusion* (New York: Houghton Mifflin, 2006); Daniel C. Dennett, *Breaking the Spell: Religion as a Natural Phenomenon* (New York: Viking, 2006).

4. "My Pilgrimage from Atheism to Theism: An Exclusive Interview with Former British Atheist Professor Antony Flew," http://www.illustramedia.com/IDArticles/flew-interview.pdf. Professor Flew had previously been quite clearly on the other side: "It is obviously impossible to square any evolutionary account of the origin of species with a substantially literal reading of the first chapters of Genesis." Antony Flew, "The Philosophical Implications of Darwinism," in *Darwin, Marx, Freud: Their Influence on Moral Theory*, ed. Arthur Caplan and Bruce Jennings (New York: Plenum Press, 1984), 10. See also my critical response, "Darwinism and Ethics: A Response to Antony Flew," in the same volume, 47–69, especially the section "Darwinism and the Bible."

5. Encyclical Letter, *Fides et Ratio*, of the Supreme Pontiff John Paul II to the Bishops of The Catholic Church on the Relationship between Faith and Reason, September 15, 1998; http://www.vatican.va/holy_father/john_paul_ii/encyclicals/documents/hf_jpii_enc_15101998_fides-et-ratio_en.html.

6. A personal confession: I am both intellectually and temperamentally a splitter rather than a lumper, preferring intellectual clarity gained by preserving illuminating distinctions (even if it comes at the price of living with psychic divisions) to psychic harmony gained by blurring important differences (especially if it comes at the price of living with muddled thinking).

7. Still, the Enlightenment learned the importance of the distinction from Christianity itself: its deepest truths, Christianity teaches, can be affirmed *only* by faith, seeing as they are utterly preposterous by the light of human reason. I refer especially to the Incarnation, the Crucifixion, and the Resurrection. See, for example, Paul's First Letter to the Corinthians.

8. My later discussion of the limitations of science may be helped by pointing out here, at some length, the radical differences between modern science and ancient science, against which modern science deliberately revolted. The most important

differences concern the purpose of science and, therefore, the character of knowledge sought. Although it is commonplace to distinguish *applied* from *pure* science (or technology from science), it is important to grasp the essentially practical, social, and technical character of modern science as such. Ancient science had sought knowledge of *what* things *are*, to be contemplated as an end in itself satisfying to the knower. In contrast, modern science seeks knowledge of *how* they *work*, to be used as a means for the relief and comfort of all humanity, knowers and non-knowers alike. Though the benefits were at first slow in coming, this practical intention has been at the heart of all of modern science right from the start.

But modern science is practical and artful not only in its end. In contrast with ancient science, its very notions and ways manifest a conception of the interrelation of knowledge and power. Nature herself is conceived energetically and mechanistically, and explanation of change is given in terms of (at most) efficient or moving causes; in modern science, to be *responsible* means to *produce* an *effect*. Knowledge itself is obtained productively: hidden truths are gained by acting on nature, through experiment, twisting her arm to make her cough up her secrets. The so-called empirical science of nature is, as actually experienced, the highly contrived encounter with apparatus, measuring devices, pointer readings, and numbers; nature in its ordinary course is virtually never directly encountered. Inquiry is made "methodical," through the imposition of order and schemes of measurement "made" by the intellect. Knowledge, embodied in laws rather than (as in ancient science) theorems, becomes "systematic" under rules of a new mathematics expressly invented for this purpose. This mathematics orders an "unnatural" world that has been intellectually "objectified," represented or projected before the knowing subject as pure homogenous extension, ripe for the mind's grasping—just as the world itself will be grasped by the techniques that science will later provide. Even the modern word "concept" means "a grasping together," implying that the mind itself, in its act of knowing, functions like the intervening hand (in contrast to its ancient counterpart, "idea," "that which can be beheld," which implies that the mind functions like the receiving eye).

And modern science rejects, as meaningless or useless, questions that cannot be answered by the application of method. Science becomes not the representation and demonstration of truth, but an *art*: the art of *finding* the truth—or, rather, that portion of truth that lends itself to being artfully found. Finally, the truths modern science finds—even about human beings—are value-neutral, in no way restraining, and indeed perfectly adapted for, technical application. In short, as Hans Jonas (*Philosophical Essays: From Ancient Creed to Technological Man* [Englewood Cliffs, New Jersey: Prentice Hall. 1974], 48) has put it, modern science contains manipulability at its theoretical core—and this remains true even for those great scientists who are themselves motivated by the desire for truth and who have no interest in that mastery over nature to which their discoveries nonetheless contribute, and for which science is largely esteemed by the rest of us and mightily supported by the modern state.

9. I am mindful of the fact that it is foolish today, even in the American context, to ignore the relevance and importance of Islam—and also of Buddhism, Hinduism, and the resurgent modern paganisms. But in America, our topic largely devolves into a discussion of science's relation to the Bible.

10. It is worth pointing out what modern science may owe, in purpose and in concept, to the Christian culture from which (and against which) it emerged. Its philanthropic spirit the modern scientific project clearly borrows from Christianity, with its emphasis on charity and love for downtrodden humanity universally considered, but redemption is to be supplied by *man acting here and now*, with the help of science and technology, rather than by God who has promised to redeem us hereafter. One might also argue that early modern science's insistence on indubitability as the standard for knowledge properly so-called is derived from the penchant for certainty that was the hallmark of traditional Catholic teaching about the divine. (In this connection, the dialectical—and nonspeculative, nontheological—ways of Jewish thinking embodied in the Talmud form an interesting point of comparison.) However much the worldview of modern science differs from that of Christianity, one suspects that modern science was logically as well as historically possible (and perhaps even likely?) only in the context of Christian civilization. To exaggerate in the direction of the truth: modern science is a natural, recognizable, but illegitimate (and finally rebellious?) child of Christian civilization.

11. Treating biblical religion as the venerable "champion" of instruction in these matters, and science as the relatively new and upstart "challenger," massively successful in its exploits and increasingly confident of its claim to full parity in truth telling with its elder rival, I am more interested in assessing the challenge science poses for religion than I am in seeing what science might learn from religion.

12. According to the famous biblical story of the city and tower of Babel, God multiplied the natural languages to permanently thwart the prideful project of self-sufficiency devised by humankind united by common speech and outlook. But that tale seems not to have anticipated the coming of a new, modern, universal, nonnatural "language," analytic geometry and calculus, which is intelligible across differences of natural language and culture and has today resurrected the ancient project of human mastery and self-re-creation.

13. René Descartes, *Discourse on the Method of Rightly Conducting the Reason and Seeking for Truth in the Sciences*, in *The Philosophical Works of Descartes*, ed. Elizabeth S. Haldane and G. R. T. Ross (Cambridge: Cambridge University Press, 1981), 90.

14. It is therefore worth calling into question arguments offered by those who seek to harmonize science and religion by assimilating the rationality of science with the rationality of the biblical God and His creation. They will point out, correctly, that God's creation according to Genesis 1, based on intelligible principles, proceeds through acts of intelligible speech. Or they will point out that the Christian God is a God of reason, because "In the beginning was the *logos* and the *logos*

was with God." But neither the intelligible principles of creation in Genesis 1 (separation, place, motion, and life) nor the *logos* spoken of in the Gospel of John are anything like the principles or mathematized *logoi* (ratios) of science. The former are tied to the distinctions of ordinary speech, which names qualitatively different natural kinds; the latter are tied to the concept of ontologically indifferent quantity, which homogenizes the differences of natural kinds (and even the difference between discrete and continuous quantity, between multitudes and magnitudes). For more on the conceptual peculiarities of modern science, and its radical difference both from ancient science and from ordinary human reasoning about life and the world, see the appendix at the end of this chapter.

15. Although Descartes has gained a great deal of fame for his proofs of the existence of God, the god to whose "existence" he is "devoted" is not the God of scripture. In listing the attributes of God he never speaks of His (its) omnipotence or goodness. In *Le Monde*, Descartes' major work whose publication he suppressed once he learned of Galileo's troubles with the Inquisition, we meet the true god of physics. He has only one attribute: *immutability!* (See René Descartes, *Le Monde, ou Traité de la Lumière* [*The World, or the Treatise on Light*], trans. Michael Sean Mahoney [New York: Abaris Books, 1979], 69). Descartes adds: "The knowledge of those laws [of motion] is so natural to our souls that we cannot but judge them infallible when we conceive them distinctly, nor doubt that, *if God had created many worlds, the laws would be as true in all of them as in this one.*" And further, "We will, if you wish, suppose in addition that *God will never make any miracle* in the new world [the one he is here reconceiving scientifically]" (75–77, emphasis added). Far from being omnipotent, the god of physics is "himself" bound by nature's immutable laws and nature's lawful motion. The divine, decisively defined as "eternal changelessness," is in fact indistinguishable from eternal, unchanging nature, acting according to immutable laws and therefore utterly immune to the sorts of miracles that are indispensable to scriptural teaching.

16. International Academy of Humanism, "Statement in Defense of Cloning and the Integrity of Scientific Research," May 16, 1997, http://www.secularhumanism. org/library/fi/cloning_declaration_17_3.html (accessed December 7, 2007).

17. Steven Pinker, "A Matter of Soul," *The Weekly Standard*, February 2, 1998, 6.

18. Interested readers should see, among others, Hans Jonas, *The Phenomenon of Life: Toward a Philosophical Biology* (Chicago: University of Chicago Press, 1982); Adolf Portmann, *Animal Forms and Patterns* (New York: Schocken Books, 1967) and *Animals as Social Beings* (New York: Viking Press, 1961); Erwin Straus, *Phenomenological Psychology* (New York: Basic Books, 1966) and *The Primary World of Senses* (New York: Free Press of Glencoe, 1968); Oliver Sacks, *Awakenings* (New York: Dutton, 1987); E. S. Russell, *The Directiveness of Organic Activities* (Cambridge, England: Cambridge University Press, 1945); and Marjorie Grene, *Approaches to a Philosophical Biology* (New York: Basic Books, 1968). For my own efforts, see *Toward a More Natural Science: Biology and Human Affairs* (New York:

The Free Press, 1985; paperback, 1988), especially chaps. 10–13, and *The Hungry Soul: Eating and the Perfecting of Our Nature* (New York: The Free Press, 1994; second edition, Chicago: University of Chicago Press, 1999).

19. The point has been exquisitely made in this poem by E. E. Cummings (called to my attention by Jackson Toby):

> "While you and i have lips and voices which
> are for kissing and to sing with
> who cares if some oneeyed son of a bitch
> invents an instrument to measure Spring with?"

20. Francis Bacon, *The Advancement of Learning*, bk. 1, 5.11.

21. For a thorough examination of these prospects and the attendant ethical and social issues, see *Beyond Therapy: Biotechnology and the Pursuit of Happiness*, a report from the President's Council on Bioethics (Washington, D.C.: Government Printing Office, 2003; New York: Reganbooks, 2003).

22. See Kass, *The Beginning of Wisdom: Reading Genesis* (New York: Simon and Schuster, 2003), especially chap. 1, "Awesome Beginnings." See also my "Evolution and the Bible: Genesis 1 Revisited," *Commentary* 96.5 (November 1988): 29–39.

23. One cannot exaggerate the importance the Bible attaches to this teaching, for the worship of nature is the "natural way" of human beings in the absence of biblical instruction (see also Deuteronomy 4:15–19). The point has been beautifully made by Harvey Flaumenhaft:

"Scholars nowadays give evidence that the ancient myths of many peoples are vestiges of records made before the time of written records; tales that recount the counting that makes up the stories in the sky, tales sometimes embodied more solidly in temples—in lines of sight those buildings furnish, or in the numbers of their bricks and models. All over the world, special numbers strangely recur; strange details related to those countings of what happens in the sky are found in accounts that do not seem to be related to the sky, or related to each other. Before the people of the book, it seems that cosmic bookkeepers did their work, impressing in the memories of men their celestial accountancy.

"That is why the Bible says in the beginning that what shines forth from up above is not divinities themselves but mere creations of divinity. What the heavens recount is the glory of that unique divinity which made them, we are told, and the worship of what shines forth in the heavens is the lot of all the peoples other than the recipients of this instruction given in the Bible. In the biblical instruction, idol worship is associated with the worship of the stars. Both are forms of what is rejected by the biblical instruction with its awesome either-or. Divinity, seen by some as everlasting beauty, to others rather is benevolent power. For some, an image of divinity is a statue, a graceful, static form to look at. For others, divinity is rather found calling out from fire—ever lively in its formlesssness, but having power to transform; what calls is not something to look at but to listen to, its word recorded in a book for those to read who, lively though perishable, are made in the image of the one whose glory is recounted by the shining in the sky." Harvey Flaumenhaft, "Quest for Order," *Humanities*, January/February 1992, 31.

24. Modern science should have no real difficulty with this conclusion. The sempiternal heavenly bodies may outlast and outshine us and move in beautiful elliptical paths; or, if you prefer a modern equivalent, matter-energy may be virtually indestructible. But only we, not they, can know these facts. Not until there are human beings does the universe become conscious of itself—a remarkable achievement that should surely inspire awe and wonder, even in atheists. I was once present when the Nobel Laureate physicist, James Cronin, was asked by a skeptical high school student whether he believed in miracles. "Yes," said Cronin, as the student's jaw dropped, "that there should be physics is a miracle."

25. Abraham Joshua Heschel, *Who Is Man?* (Palo Alto: Stanford University Press, 1965), 115.

26. Taken from my essay, "The Permanent Limitations of Biology," in *Life, Liberty, and the Defense of Dignity: The Challenge for Bioethics* (New York: Encounter Books, 2002), 288–92.

27. Descartes, *Rules for the Direction of the Mind,* in *The Philosophical Works of Descartes*, ed. Elizabeth S. Haldane and G. R. T. Ross (Cambridge: Cambridge University Press, 1981), 37, emphasis added.

28. Compare the relation of color and shape (*schema*) suggested by Socrates in Plato's *Meno* (75B6): "Shape is that which, alone among all things, always accompanies color." Appealing to our primary experience of the visible world, this account integrates shape and color as the two most evident and always related aspects of any visible body, whose shaped surface we come to see only because of color differences between it and its surroundings. To put it crudely, Socrates' philosophizing deepens lived experience; Descartes' turns its back on lived experience.

7

A Response to Leon R. Kass

David Gelernter

Most of Leon Kass's assertions seem to me exactly right and enormously significant. But they do raise an important and implicit question, beyond the question Kass addresses: Why exactly do we find ourselves in the midst of a quarrel between science and religion now?

Kass refers to "the harmonizers of science and religion," their successes and failures; but who are these "harmonizers"? Certainly they don't include practicing Christians or Jews. If a Jew runs into a disagreement between science and his understanding of Judaism or the Bible, no conflict results. Insofar as he *is* a Jew, he's made his choice: if God and man disagree, he chooses God. Case closed. In this respect science is no different from life in general. The Jew and Christian acknowledge—natural-law theorizing to the side—that unaided reason is an insufficient basis for understanding the world. When Abraham Lincoln said about the Bible that "but for it we could not know right from wrong," he was making the same kind of statement a Jew or Christian makes when he says that, if science proclaims miracles impossible and my religion says they happened, I believe they happened.

So who are these people seeking to "harmonize" science and religion? Kass isn't imagining this urge to harmonize; it's clear that we do face a crisis of scientism today, with religion on the defensive. Yet the urge to harmonize is especially surprising when we compare the situation now to what it was half a century ago, around 1950. By 1950 religion had long since gotten over Darwin and modern geology. The main problems it faced were the Holocaust, of course, but also the "classical problems" of modern man, especially the psychological ones—anxiety, guilt, powerlessness, and so on. But despite these gigantic problems—and the Holocaust is certainly no more solved for theologians today than it was in 1950—religion in 1950 was a going concern, not particularly worried about the threat of scientism. That was an age of celebrity theologians. Such thinkers as Tillich, Niebuhr, and Karl Barth were well known; Martin Buber was among the best known and most widely read of modern philosophers. Judaism's most important thinkers at the time—Eliezer Berkovits and Joseph Dov Soloveitchik, in fact the two leading Jewish philosophers of the twentieth century—worried about many things, but not especially about science. Soloveitchik in fact carefully pointed out (in *The Lonely Man of Faith*) that creative scientists— that is, boldly original, path-breaking scientists—were doing God's work; God had told man to imitate Him, to be holy as He is holy—and God the creator expects man to imitate Him by being creative.[1] Soloveitchik was all in favor of science, and his worldview is still the worldview of so-called modern Orthodox Judaism today.

So who are these "harmonizers"? Their existence is surprising because, as I say, religion back in 1950 was not particularly concerned with the threat of scientism—although in 1950, science itself was a much stronger cultural force than it is today. Fifty years ago science was at the peak of its prestige. Einstein and Freud were names spoken with reverence. The prestige of science continued to increase during the 1960s, when Americans were fascinated by the space race and everyday conversation touched on the Atlas-Mercury vehicle, the LEM, trans-lunar injection—"You are go for TLI" is a phrase I'll bet a substantial majority of Americans recognized. Today computing technology and the Internet dominate our lives. But there is no widespread knowledge of how computers work or what software is, or how the Internet works—or even who built it and owns it. It used to be that our very smartest students would consider careers in physics, engineering, and other sciences; "rocket scientist" meant "brilliant." Today most of the smartest students (at Yale, anyway) want to make their millions and relax as soon as possible. "Arbitrage" and "venture capitalist" have the sex appeal that "theoretical physics" and "rocket science" used to.

In short, science has lost and not gained ground with the public since 1950. It's still the case, moreover, that today religion seems to be far more important than science to most American lives. At life's biggest moments— when someone is born or comes of age or marries or dies—Americans are far more likely to look for a priest, minister, or rabbi than a biochemist. Science has yet to provide intellectual or spiritual tools that matter to our daily lives. For all our talk about science and its method, my own bet is that the average life is no more "logical," no less ad hoc, than it was three hundred years ago.

So why is religion suddenly called on the carpet to answer charges about the unrealism of Genesis or miracles in light of modern science—charges that had been talked to death and more or less disposed of by 1900? These are old accusations, not new ones. Partly we sense the ominous approach of biotechnology in the hands of brilliant idiots—those people about whom Kass aptly says: "One hardly knows which is the more impressive, the height of [their] arrogance or the depth of [their] shallowness."

But I believe there's a more fundamental problem, too. Science has lost ground with the public since 1950, but religion has lost even more. In fact since the late 1960s, since the coup in which intellectuals took over the universities and universities stuck their fingers into every corner of American life, nearly all traditional sources of spiritual strength in the average American life have been threatened or snuffed out.

A study earlier this year suggested that American teenagers were spectacularly ignorant of the Bible and that most American children were getting remarkably little religious education. Anyone who works in education is aware of this trend. Communities of practicing Jews and Christians are as strong as ever or stronger; but outside those communities, religious knowledge is evaporating.

And other traditional sources of spiritual strength are in tough shape also. The year 1950 was a great time for art; since then, the mainstream art world has thrown over all spiritual responsibilities and snickers at truth and beauty. (This situation is starting to turn around—but only starting to.) In 1950 some Americans drew spiritual strength from idealistic left-wing politics, but today the spiritual promise of socialism and Marxism is dead. In 1950 some people drew strength from patriotism, but in many parts of the country—thank goodness not all—patriotism is now obsolete, and schoolchildren laugh at the very idea. I have heard that laughter, and it is not pretty.

So we are revisiting the nineteenth-century question of harmonizing religion and science, it seems to me, in large part because spiritual life is in such deep trouble. The number of people who are spiritually up for grabs has never been greater. If children aren't being taught religion and the Bible, it's true that they aren't learning math and science either; but science and especially technology pervade American culture in a way religion hasn't for a long time. Young people are at least vaguely aware of science and its worldview—and, increasingly, know almost nothing about religion.

In mentioning these spiritual troubles, I'm aware that they aren't new, either. Not long ago I was reading an architectural treatise that attacks neo-classicism as a style for public buildings, calling it "a monstrous absurdity, which has originated in the blind admiration of modern times for every-thing Pagan, to the prejudice and overthrow of Christian art and propriety." I'm quoting Augustus Pugin's famous tract on the neogothic, published in 1841.[2] Of course religion has been in trouble for a long time.

But this fact, too, has meaning for today's crisis. It suggests that thirty or forty or fifty years from now, we'll look back at today as a golden age of American religion. Unless we take the situation in hand and do something about the spiritual crisis that is such a disaster for young people—now growing up, in many parts of the country, largely without religion, without patriotism, without ideals, without art; without spiritual values of any kind; in a world where the only sacred trust is to have a good career—we'll be guilty not only of ignoring a crisis but of failing to make the most of an opportunity. In America's cultural establishment, only careers are holy. Young people know it and resent it; but don't know what to do about it. Those who still remember what "spiritual life" means have a responsibility to young people—a responsibility that we tend, on the whole, to ignore.

I'd like to mention a few specific points in Kass's argument, and con-clude by swinging back to this general issue.

Kass mentions that defects in scientific theory don't entitle us to conclude that "the biblical account of special creation must be correct." But what does "correct" mean? This is a real question, not a postmodern game. Is Hamlet "correct"? Is it "true"? It is true, but not historically. There are other ways of being true. There are other ways of being correct—a point with which Kass actually agrees.

He mentions the "trans-national and trans-religious appeal" of science. He's surely right about this appeal. But of course Christianity had global appeal too, and still does—consider its importance today in some parts of Africa and (even more) in China. That a religion created by a small, battered Mediterranean people two thousand years ago should have catalyzed the settlement of Europeans in America in the seventeenth century, and should galvanize dissenters in China today, strikes me as pretty close to a miracle. (Or two miracles, depending on how you count.)

And on the topic of miracles: Kass calls it a "limping rejoinder" to science's challenge to miracles "to say that an omnipotent God could still perform miracles" if he felt like it, but simply chooses not to—in order to make science possible, or for some other reason.

This rejoinder might be limping, but it has also been inherent in normative Jewish theology since Talmudic times, long before modern science emerged. It is inherent in the sense that, to normative Jewish theology, God's relationship to man and the natural world isn't static or fixed. It develops and changes. And there has been a huge discontinuity in God's relationship to the world, marked by the destruction of the Second Temple; a discontinuity with implications for the meaning of miracles and for every other aspect of religious life.

Hence the plaintive prayer we say on the New Year holiday, Rosh Hashanah, that calls on God to "*m'loch al kol ha'aretz bi'kvodecha*," please rule over the whole earth in your glory. Once, God ruled; no longer. The big change was foreshadowed in biblical times. With the last prophets in the Bible, the Talmud says, "the holy spirit ceased in Israel." The real break comes with the end of the Second Temple; now, says the Talmud, God has nothing in His universe but "the four *amot* of *halakha* alone"—four *amot* being the size of one human being; the phrase means: God has nothing on earth but the religious lives of those who follow the Torah. God no longer rules—otherwise we wouldn't say prayers asking that He resume ruling. Man instead of God has become responsible for interpreting the Torah: the Talmud says this explicitly. And it tells us not to expect miracles; in fact, if we hear a heavenly voice—a *bat kol*—addressing us from on high, we are specifically told to ignore it. Add this up and you get the normative Jewish view: with the destruction of the Second Temple, God has withdrawn out of history, into the human mind. He no longer rules; He no longer talks to prophets or works miracles. He only talks to man from inside, in a "still, small voice"—the Bible's way of saying an inner voice. In Judaism's view, this seeming retreat of God has allowed mankind to grow up.

Jews aren't necessarily happy with this reality—in many ways it's sad to grow up; but they've seen the handwriting on the wall for a very long time. Of course, just as science can't say whether fossils are real or were deliberately planted by God to test or deceive us, religion can't say whether miracles are real or were deliberately planted in human memory by God to test or deceive us—or teach us something.

Kass says that "the enterprise of science as a whole is animated by noble human purpose." Not in my experience. It seems to me—this is purely a subjective impression—that science is animated by a mixture of curiosity and a healthy type of aggression, the intellectual aggression that makes certain children insist on pulling machines apart to see how they work, that isn't content just to look at things—that insists on seeing into them. It seems to me that science and engineering are consequences of man's psychological (not moral or spiritual) makeup. It's the same with art—artists make art because they're unhappy when they don't (in some cases, brutally unhappy). The noble purpose is a wonderful thing, but it's an after-the-fact explanation.

Kass writes that "anyone can doubt or deny creation or immortality . . . but no one can deny" the Pythagorean Theorem, which is fundamentally true. But can anyone deny that "man does not live by bread alone"? Or that "thou shalt not murder"? Certainly; many people have. But to Jews and Christians, those who deny that "man does not live by bread alone" are exactly as wrong as those who deny the Pythagorean Theorem.

I've claimed we're facing a spiritual crisis; that ultimately this crisis is what Leon Kass's argument is all about. How will the crisis resolve? My guess is that the resolution will start on college campuses, in a traditional American way. We're past due for the next Great Awakening. My guess is that, within a generation or two, we'll see a full-scale religious revival in America.

Most likely it will start with a small group of young or youngish people—a group of evangelists representing Protestantism, Catholicism, and Judaism—preaching on American campuses; they will make speeches having to do with spiritual questions and describe the answers offered by the Bible and by these three great religious communities. Audiences will be small at first; but young people want to hear this sort of talk, and they will grow. I imagine such speakers might say something like this: Forget your career and think about your family. Forget your rights and think about your duties. Forget your bank account and think about your country. Forget yourself and think about your God. Teachers and professors, guidance counselors and deans, tell students the exact opposite. But young people know when they're being lied to. They need only for someone to tell them the truth.

If I were a foundation or philanthropist, that's what I would spend my money on. Young people are in trouble spiritually, and they know it. We are the ones who failed them—we adult Americans who teach in the schools and run the culture. We were given a great tradition, a good heritage; we have failed to pass it on. We have an obligation to correct that mistake, or at least to start, or to try—before it's too late.

To end with a brief but more positive comment: in my talk, if not in Kass's less overheated one, science and religion seem like opponents or even enemies. But they don't need to be. You see them in perfect balance in the right kind of art.

One of the most celebrated works of Nikolaus Pevsner, the great historian of art and architecture, is an essay published in 1945 called *The Leaves of Southwell*.[3] Southwell is one of the smallest of the many extraordinary medieval cathedrals of England. It's been celebrated, certainly since Pevsner published this essay, for the superb decorative carvings in its chapter house, dating from the late thirteenth century. The artists covered the stone capitals of the columns and many other surfaces with remarkably lifelike carvings of leaves and flowers from the English countryside—maple, oak, vine, hawthorn, buttercup, and rose. Pevsner points out that during these same decades in the late thirteenth century when the artists were at work, scientifically inclined philosophers, especially Albertus Magnus, were providing the first accurate descriptions of nature based on field observations since antiquity.

Those carvings are remarkably accomplished art, and they embody a new scientific spirit that encourages the direct observation of nature. So they are, in a sense, a synthesis of science and art. But not only that. "Is not the balance of Southwell something deeper too than a balance of nature and style . . . ?" Pevsner writes at the close of his essay.

> Is it not also a balance of God and the World, the invisible and the visible? Could these leaves of the English countryside, with all their freshness, move us so deeply if they were not carved in that spirit which filled the saints and poets and thinkers of the thirteenth century, the spirit of religious respect for the loveliness of created nature? The inexhaustible delight in live form that can be touched with worshipping fingers and felt with all senses is ennobled—consciously in the . . . science of Albert,

unconsciously in the carving of the buttercups and thorn leaves and maple leaves of Southwell—by the conviction that so much beauty can exist only because God is in every man and beast, in every herb and stone.

Religion after all ennobles science, ennobles art, and brings them together in the service of God.

Notes

1. Joseph D. Soloveitchik, *The Lonely Man of Faith* (New York: Jason Aronson, 1997).

2. Augustus Welby Northmore Pugin, *The True Principles of Pointed or Christian Architecture* (London: Academy, 1973).

3. Nikolaus Pevsner, *The Leaves of Southwell* (London: King Penguin Books, 1945), 66–67.

8

Commentary

Stephen M. Barr

I am the only the physical scientist at this gathering, which puts me in an odd position. I find Leon Kass's argument extremely provocative. In fact, I found so much to disagree with in the first half of it that I filled reams and reams of paper with criticisms. But when I got to the second half, I realized that, actually, his main point—brilliantly presented—is one that I am entirely in agreement with.

The main battleground in the war between our traditional culture and scientism (although maybe a better term would be "reductionist materialism") does concern the nature of man: what are we? And that battle has intensified in recent years for a number of reasons. One reason is the aggressive attacks on religion by such materialists as Dawkins, Dennett, Crick, and many others.

Another reason involves advances in neuroscience, molecular biology, cybernetics, and so on, which give greater plausibility in the minds of many people to the proposition that human beings are nothing but complex physical systems. All reductionists ultimately want to reduce reality to physics, the most fundamental branch of science. But the laws of physics simply cannot explain such things as consciousness, subjective experience, what philosophers call "*qualia*"—what "red" looks like to us, or "blue," or what the smell of lilacs is like. Physics cannot explain free will, and it cannot explain reason itself. Therefore, the strategy of the reductionist is what is called "eliminativism"; that which cannot be reduced to physics ultimately is argued to be unreal. It is eliminated.

Thus free will is called an illusion by people like Francis Crick and E.O. Wilson. Wilson says, "The hidden preparation of mental activity gives the illusion of free will."[1] The trouble—or perhaps it is the good news—is that we know we have subjective experience and consciousness. We know we have free will; we have experienced the power to choose. And we know we have reason. These are direct, empirical facts, as much empirical facts as anything discovered in the laboratory. I love this line from Kass's chapter: "Life's self-revelatory testimony with regard to its own vital activity is more immediate, compelling, and trustworthy than all the abstracted explanations that evaporate meaningful lived experience by identifying it with some correlated bodily event."

This was also said, I think, very incisively by Dr. Johnson, who was being pestered by Boswell. Boswell was trying to convince Dr. Johnson that he had no free will, not on materialist grounds but on Calvinistic grounds. Finally, in exasperation, Dr. Johnson said, "If a man should give me arguments that I do not see, though I could not answer them, should I believe that I do not see?"[2] That is the point: we know that we have free will in the same way we know that we see. And we do not need a theory to tell us either one.

I find another of Kass's arguments very powerful, and that is that materialism is a self-defeating philosophy because it cannot ultimately account for, or defend the notion of, truth. This was also the view of a great mathematician, a mathematical physicist in the twentieth century, Hermann Weyl, who said, "[There must be] freedom in the theoretical acts of affirmation and negation. When I reason that two plus two equals four, this actual judgment is not forced upon me through blind natural causality (a view which would eliminate thinking as an act for which one can be held answerable), but something purely spiritual enters in."[3] Reason necessarily involves freedom. If our judgments are determined by chemical reactions in our brain and are not, therefore, free, then we are not using reason.

So reason depends on freedom, and freedom depends on reason, and neither can be accounted for by any scientistic reductionism of everything to physics, because physics deals with quantity, numbers that you calculate with equations, numbers that you measure in the laboratory. There is no way that subjective experience can come out of those equations.

There are a couple of other things concerning this battle that Leon Kass did not mention that can give us hope. One, I think, is the predictable failure of artificial intelligence. If the materialists are correct, then it should be possible in principle to build machines that have free will and that can understand. And I do not think this is going to happen. I think if one is not a reductionist materialist, one believes that this is never going to happen. As the decades roll by, and the promises the AI community has been making for at least fifty years do not materialize—as the machine that can understand and will freely does not emerge—the credibility of the reductionist program is going to be seriously undermined.

Thus time is on our side. I am not afraid of the developments in neuroscience and cybernetics and so forth. I do not think these fields are going to come up with the goods.

There is another thing that can give us hope, though it is perhaps on a plane that will appeal only to some theorists: there are actually arguments against materialist reductionism that come from physics itself and from mathematical logic. I have in mind arguments from quantum theory, which go back to certain arguments made by John von Neumann, elaborated later by London and Bauer, and accepted and stated rather forcefully by some of the leading physicists of the twentieth century, like Eugene Wigner and Sir Rudolf Peierls. This argument is that if you take the traditional understanding of quantum mechanics seriously, it implies that the human mind cannot be completely understood in terms of physics. Obviously we cannot get into the details here, but this is an argument that has never been refuted and has to be taken very seriously. There is as well an argument from the mathematical logic side, based on Goedel's Theorem, which according to some eminent people like Sir Roger Penrose, the mathematician, implies that no computer based on algorithms can possibly reproduce all human intellectual faculties.

One other ace up our sleeve is the existence of a strong Platonic streak in the mathematical community, which is to some extent shared by people who are in the more mathematical branches of science like physics. What science has increasingly discovered is that at the foundation of the physical world is not just some stuff, not just slime, dust, or particles. At the basis of the physical world are very profound, intricate, beautiful, subtle mathematical structures. The structure of superstring theory, for example, is so deep mathematically that, even though it has been worked on for more than twenty years by the greatest mathematicians and mathematical physicists in the world, the surface of the theory has barely been scratched.

This suggests, then, that at the root of physical reality are ideas. Hermann Weyl said in 1932: "We have penetrated so far into physical nature that we have obtained a vision of the flawless harmony which is in conformity with sublime reason."[4] Reason is at the root of the physical world. The great astrophysicist Sir James Jeans wrote in the 1930s that "the universe begins to look more like a great thought than like a machine."

So there is this countervailing tendency. Yes, some biologists and other scientists seem to be getting more and more aggressively materialistic. But on the other hand, there are arguments coming out of physics and cosmology which are moving in the other direction. I would just mention here the Big Bang Theory itself, the apparent fine-tunings of the laws of nature that give the look of having been arranged to make the evolution of life possible, and, again, the mathematical orderliness of the physical world.

I do not know whether Leon Kass would call this harmonizing. But there has undoubtedly been a movement among physical scientists, including people like John Polkinghorne, John Barrow, Owen Gingerich, and (in a small way) myself, as well as biologists such as Francis Collins, toward making arguments that favor a more traditional religious view of the world based on the discoveries coming out of physics and cosmology.

Now I want to get a little more negative. One thing I found a bit disturbing about Leon Kass's argument was the theme of conflict between science and religion, the suggestion of a permanent tension and apparent contradictions between them. According to Kass, religion and science, divine revelation and human reason, have disparate teachings and are not easily harmonized, although "wishful-thinking harmonizers" would like the conflict simply to go away. Kass questions whether being a believer in Darwinism during the week and Christianity on Sunday is rationally defensible and free of contradiction.

To be blunt, none of this makes sense to me. I just do not know what he is talking about. As Kass rightly says, "The primary point of contact and contest between science and religion happens to be about truth." Precisely. If you are saying there is a conflict, you are saying that there are truths asserted by religion and truths asserted by science that are in logical conflict with each other.

Now, I can speak only as a Catholic. I ask myself: are there doctrines of Catholicism—authoritative, binding teachings—which are logically in conflict with well-established scientific facts and theories? I do not know of any, and I have been thinking about such questions for over forty years. I do not think there is a conflict. Now, if you believe in a literal interpretation of Genesis, there is a conflict. If you believe that rain dances cause rain, there is a conflict. Certain religions are in conflict with science, but at least Catholicism is not, and neither is Judaism.

What there has been is not conflict, but estrangement. That is the problem. In the Middle Ages, there was a philosophical system, Aristotelianism, which was a common language between science and theology. When Aristotelianism broke down, that common language was lost and theology and science drifted apart. Because they speak separate languages, they cannot communicate very easily with each other. Thus what is needed is not harmonizing. And in fact that is not what people are doing. What people are doing is trying to build bridges so that scientists and theologians can talk to each other—they are not trying to harmonize, but to show that these things are, in fact, already in harmony.

We must reclaim the history of science. Unfortunately, many scientists and scientifically minded people are socialized into the idea that there is a conflict and that there has historically been a conflict between science and religion. That is almost entirely a myth. I will not go into detail trying to rebut this myth. But one finds hints of it in Leon Kass's essay where he talks about the Christian culture against which science emerged.

Nothing could be further from the truth than this myth. Almost every great scientist of the seventeenth century, the century of the Scientific Revolution, was deeply devout, including Tycho Brahe, Kepler, Boyle, and Newton. And that was true even through much of the nineteenth century. The two greatest physicists in the nineteenth century, Faraday and Maxwell, were not only devout but unusually so, even by the standards of their day.

It is simply not true that modern science built itself in opposition to religion. I do not understand the idea that miracles make genuine science impossible. That statement has been falsified by history, because almost every one of the great founders of modern science from the seventeenth century until the mid-nineteenth century believed in miracles. Not only did that not make it impossible for them to do science; they created modern science.

We have to reclaim the story of science and show that conflict between science and religion is a myth, created largely by anticlerical and atheistic propaganda.

Notes

1. E.O. Wilson, *Consilience: The Unity of Knowledge* (New York: Alfred A. Knopf, 1998), 119.

2. James Boswell, *Life of Johnson*, ed. G.B. Hill, revised by L.F. Powell (Oxford: Oxford University Press, 1934), 2:82.

3. Hermann Weyl, *The Open World: Three Lectures on the Metaphysical Implications of Science* (New Haven, CT: Yale University Press, 1932), 31–32.

4. Weyl, *The Open World*, 28–29.

PART IV

Religion and the Law

9

Religious Freedom and the Truth of the Human Person

Douglas W. Kmiec

In reflecting upon his own nature, man encounters the desire to get beyond the limits of the human condition. He desires to transcend himself. The sentiment has been often expressed. Saint Augustine writes that our hearts are restless until they rest in God.[1] Likewise, C.S. Lewis is explicit that without God, human existence is unfulfilled and empty. "The human soul was made to enjoy some object that is never fully given—nay, cannot even be imagined as given—in our present mode of subjective and . . . temporal experience."[2] In 2007, Pope Benedict XVI issued the encyclical *Spe Salvi* (Saved by Hope), thoughtfully illustrating the very same transcendent hope of man.[3]

On the deck of the *Arabella* in 1630, John Winthrop gave clear expression to man's natural dependency upon God, instructing listeners that man could follow one of two paths.[4] In covenant with God, the new land could be settled as a shining "city upon a hill."[5] Without God, America would become known as a place of sinners—"a story and a by-word through the world."[6] The incorporation document of America—the Declaration of Independence—chose the covenant Winthrop urged by memorializing a corporate or sovereign presupposition of a Supreme Being. The Declaration affirms as self-evident truth man's created nature, his equality before God, and his intrinsic (inalienable) human rights which are derived from God, not government. The government and Constitution to follow were expressly understood to implement and to secure this conception.

Superintending Religion—A Constitutional Power Not Granted

The Constitution is thus akin to bylaws and in that sense is necessarily sub-ordinate to the Declaration, understood as corporate charter.[7] The Constitution fills out operational detail and nuance. In supplying no enumerated power touching upon religious belief or practice, and by expressly protecting individual freedom with respect to both ("Congress shall make no law respecting an establishment of religion, or prohibiting the free exercise thereof") the Constitution subtracts nothing from the presupposition of God in the Declaration. Indeed, it adds a second proposition, freedom; it is up to individual citizens to affirm or deny that premise in their own lives. In this way, the American government came to be established as a reflection of human nature.[8] The Founders understood the essential aspect of man's created nature to be his dependence upon and yearning for God. It was the awesome task of human freedom to accept or reject God.

That man was free to reject in his personal life the presupposition of God did not mean, of course, that man was somehow empowered to diminish or erase the corporate supposition affirmed in the Declaration.[9] The continuing importance of the corporate presupposition can be gleaned from manifold sources. Consider, for example, the admonition of our first president in mid-September 1796:

> Of all the dispositions and habits, which lead to political prosperity, Religion and Morality are indispensable supports. In vain would that man claim the tribute of Patriotism, who should labor to subvert these great Pillars of human happiness, these firmest props of the duties of Men and citizens The mere Politician, equally with the pious man, ought to respect and to cherish them. A volume could not trace all their connections with private and public felicity. Let it simply be asked where is the security for property, for reputation, for life, if the sense of religious obligation *desert* the oaths, which are the instruments of investigation in Courts of Justice? And let us with caution indulge the supposition, that morality can be maintained without religion. Whatever may be conceded to the influence of refined education on minds of peculiar structure, reason and

experience both forbid us to expect, that National morality can prevail in exclusion of religious principle.[10]

In 1835, the French observer Alexis de Tocqueville reveals that the first generation of Americans followed Washington's prudential guidance. Tocqueville writes:

> The short space of threescore years can never content the imagination of man; nor can the imperfect joys of this world satisfy his heart. Man alone, of all created beings, displays a natural contempt of existence, and yet a boundless desire to exist; he scorns life, but he dreads annihilation. These different feelings incessantly urge his soul to the contemplation of a future state, and religion directs his musings thither. Religion, then, is simply another form of hope, and it is no less natural to the human heart than hope itself. Men cannot abandon their religious faith without a kind of aberration of intellect and a sort of violent distortion of their true nature; they are invincibly brought back to more pious sentiments. Unbelief is an accident, and faith is the only permanent state of mankind.[11]

For a century and a half, America honored the presupposition of the Declaration and Tocqueville's insight that faith was the permanent state of mankind. Indeed, it is even possible to make this claim of America today.[12] As discussed below, the modern interpretation of the religion clauses pushes in a different direction. The judiciary in our time, with the exception of one fleeting reference, has ignored the presupposition of a Supreme Being,[13] and it has transformed a guarantee of freedom to believe and practice into an engine of religious exclusion.

In introducing what would become the First Amendment, James Madison made plain that the purpose of the religion clauses was to avoid legal coercion in the form of a national church, or of legal penalties or disabilities imposed on someone choosing a faith other than a nationally favored one. By its terms, these clauses applied only to the national government. Indeed, the phraseology of the amendment was intended to insulate from national interference various state establishments.

Modern Misconstruction

The establishment clause of the First Amendment has in modern times been misinterpreted and misapplied. Instead of a focus on legal coercion, since the late 1940s, this protection against federal imposition has become an instrument by which a wholly secular national and state environment might be achieved.[14] In this shift, neutrality was redefined—not as between faiths, but between faith and no faith. In 1947, in *Everson v. Board of Education*,[15] the Supreme Court in the guise of neutrality articulated the exclusionary view that government may not aid religion generally—a truly extraordinary proposition for a nation informed by the "Laws of Nature and of Nature's God." While subsequent to *Everson* the establishment clause case law has taken numerous other twists and turns, it proceeded primarily in an exclusionary progression. By way of overview, the establishment clause has been interpreted in *Everson* and later in *Lemon v. Kurtzman*[16] as prohibiting (1) any public support for religion in purpose or effect; (2) any government action that might be perceived by a hypothetical observer as an endorsement of religion generally; and (3) the inclusion of religious bodies in governmental programs that provide direct subsidies or in-kind benefits.

The exclusionary nature of the judicially revised establishment clause has been powerfully advanced by an idiosyncratic exception to the Court's usual denial of standing for generalized taxpayer grievances.[17] Except for the establishment clause, taxpayers lack standing to litigate without a particularized and concrete injury-in-fact. Were it otherwise, the federal courts would regularly be drawn into second-guessing the merits of competing public policies, rather than the resolution of "cases or controversies." Modern interpretation of the establishment clause is thus troubled by an unanticipated application of the clause to national and state government alike, an embedded bias toward secularity disguised as neutrality, and an open courthouse door that invites unwarranted judicial, rather than political, resolution.

The incorporation of the establishment clause against the states, while perhaps the most obvious break with original understanding, is also the one needing least attention. Respect was given to state establishments at the founding as an aspect of a federalist bargain rather than acceptance of the coercion such establishments represented. Insofar as a state establishment would likely run afoul of the free exercise clause today,[18] it is an academic exercise without policy merit to advocate the undoing of the judicial incorporation of the establishment clause against the states. There is no constituency for state establishment, nor should there be.

What does have merit is returning to the original meaning of the word "establishment" as it now applies to both the national and state governments. The Framers understood an establishment "necessarily [to] involve actual legal coercion."[19] *Lee v. Weisman*[20] edged the Court back in this direction, even as Justice Kennedy defined coercion in that context more broadly than history suggests appropriate. As Justice Scalia points out, "The coercion that was a hallmark of historical establishments of religion was coercion of religious orthodoxy and of financial support *by force of law and threat of penalty*."[21] Moreover, while not at issue here, the financial support interdicted by the establishment clause was not for religion generally or a public program that included religious providers,[22] but rather the compulsory patronage of certain religious services and the mandatory payment of taxes supporting ministers.

A New Court—A New Day

The retirement of Justice O'Connor and the addition of Chief Justice John Roberts and Justice Samuel Alito create a favorable climate for correction of the Court's establishment clause jurisprudence. Acknowledged by many as the influential center of the new Court, Justice Kennedy has long questioned the O'Connor view, which substituted "no endorsement" for the original meaning of the establishment clause. In its most recent application in the Ten Commandments cases,[23] the O'Connor approach yielded an outcome that found such display to be unacceptable in a courthouse in Kentucky, but just fine on the statehouse lawn in Texas. Such inconsistency led Justice Kennedy to describe the no endorsement theory as "flawed in its fundamentals and unworkable in practice,"[24] productive of "bizarre result."

The no endorsement theory was always something of a non sequitur, even by Justice O'Connor's own description. O'Connor had originated the idea not from original meaning, historical practice, or precedent, but from what she termed "a clarification of our Establishment Clause doctrine." Writing a concurring opinion in *Lynch v. Donnelly*, a crèche display case from Rhode Island, O'Connor postulated that the establishment clause "prohibits government from making adherence to a religion relevant in any way to a person's standing in the political community."[25] By itself, this is a proposition reasonably sustainable, as it is bolstered not only by the original no legal coercion standard of the religion clauses but also by the prohibition against religious test oaths. But Justice O'Connor deduced something far broader; namely, the proposition that the government violates the Constitution if it either "endorses or disapproves of religion."[26] By this, O'Connor put her theory in direct conflict with George Washington's farewell insight about the importance of religion to the nation's prosperity, as well as the Declaration's presupposition of a Creator and man's natural yearning for the transcendent. O'Connor thus made a founding precept into a constitutional transgression.

In 1776, as now, some of our fellow citizens did dissent from the religious beliefs of the majority. The speech clause in the First Amendment affirms this right of dissent.[27] What neither the speech nor religion clauses envisioned was that dissenting voices had the equivalent of a heckler's veto to weaken or erase the basis upon which the nation was incorporated. Yes, a person's legal standing could not be made to turn on belief or practice, but an endorsement of religion without imposed legal consequence is simply not belief or practice. Failure to see the difference invites a level of judicial micromanagement of human freedom—including the trivial aspects of the decor of holiday displays—that is seldom justifiable in any area of the law, let alone an area like religion, where, as Hamilton observed, the federal government was without competence.[28]

Justice O'Connor resisted an originalist interpretation of the establishment clause on the theory that it would render free exercise protection redundant. O'Connor derived this redundancy concern from the school prayer cases and some scholarly comment,[29] which had asserted (incorrectly) that legal coercion was unnecessary to find an impermissible establishment. Legal coercion should be put back at the heart of both clauses to construe them correctly. The clauses simply protect freedom from coerced belief or practice in two separate ways—by an immunity from legally coerced prescription (establishment) and legally coerced prohibition (free exercise). Religious liberty is sacrificed either when one is forced to worship at a church not of his choosing or stopped from worshipping in a chosen manner.[30] One misconstruction of a clause does not justify another, however—especially when it yields the unintended exclusion of a central aspect of human nature. Interpreting the establishment clause to demand secularity was the first judicial fabrication. The no endorsement theory is the second. The no endorsement view took on the semblance of necessity because it was thought necessary to exclude voluntary prayer from school or religious schools from public programs. The newly composed Roberts Court may pierce this facade. Justice Kennedy helpfully began the work of reconnecting establishment with legal coercion in *Lee v. Weisman*.[31] In addition, it is part of the legacy of the late William Rehnquist that there is a greater acceptance of nonpreferential assistance to all schools, especially through vouchers,[32] thereby removing another precedential incentive for an overly exclusionary no endorsement policy.

The no endorsement theory should be likewise abandoned. Justice O'Connor's explanations of how it could be reconciled with the religious suppositions of the Declaration of Independence are highly strained, or worse, dismissive of the meaning of these references to faith. O'Connor concedes the prevalence of practices such as legislative prayers or the opening of Court sessions with "God save the United States and this honorable Court," but instead of acknowledging their obvious religious import, she reduces them to the significance of a gavel banging a proceeding into session. In her words, religious references merely "solemnize" a public occasion. Instead of Winthrop's covenant with God, these recitals express confidence only "in the future," not in a loving Creator.[33] Yet under the no endorsement theory, references to God even for ceremonial purpose could make an atheist observer uncomfortable. Justice O'Connor mitigates this by suggesting that such an observer would know from context that such references in a secular world were without significant meaning. Writes O'Connor in *Allegheny*: "the history and ubiquity" of a practice are relevant because they provide part of the context in which a reasonable observer evaluates whether a challenged governmental practice conveys a message of endorsement of religion.[34] In short, by this sleight of (or back of the) hand, words like "God save the United States and this honorable Court" do not, "despite their religious roots, convey a message of endorsement of particular religious beliefs."[35] As Justice Kennedy insightfully responds, the effort at rationalization may nominally save precedent, but only at the cost of "an unjustified hostility toward religion."[36]

The no endorsement rationale does allow government to lift burdens it has imposed on religion, but this merely illustrates that Justice O'Connor's handiwork overlaps with the free exercise clause. If properly applied, the free exercise clause would itself supply needed exemption from government imposition. But the free exercise clause, too, has been diluted. Ironically, as discussed below, it is Justice O'Connor who comes to the defense of the original understanding of free exercise against Justice Scalia's curious diminution of that provision. As Justice O'Connor would correctly argue in the free exercise context, belief is absolutely protected, while religiously inspired conduct is only qualifiedly so, subject to an inquiry into whether there is a compelling health and safety (public order) need to displace a religious practice, but not subject to an evaluation of the centrality of the religious conduct to the believer. While the no endorsement theory affirms that it is not an impermissible establishment to lift government burden, it nevertheless is one-sided. The no endorsement theory is more attentive to the sensitivities of hypothetical observers than religious believers. The no endorsement test, for example, takes no account of the message sent by, say, the removal of a religious display from a public square, implicitly assuming it has little religious meaning.

What would be the consequence of refocusing the establishment clause on legal coercion? Quite simply, it would disable the exclusionary impulse mistakenly accepted since *Everson*. With that anti-religion bias removed, public religious displays or acknowledgments which today are ensnared in Justice O'Connor's no endorsement theory would be unobjectionable. With a return to the original meaning of the establishment clause, Ten Commandments displays, the historical Latin Cross on Mount Soledad, and Menorahs and crèches displayed in public settings during the holiday season would be fully constitutional. None of these symbolic efforts imposes constitutional injury, for none compels belief or action under law. Returning to the original meaning thus simplifies constitutional adjudication, but it also importantly avoids the extraordinary costs and divisiveness associated with legal efforts that make even the most minor mention of religion into complex federal litigation. Such litigation has led to unsatisfactory, uneven, and unwarranted results. Unsatisfactory because the outcomes often required draining religious symbols of their meaning; uneven, since the no endorsement test is largely subjective; and unwarranted, since there is understandable hesitation to expunge the significance of religious reference in light of the corporate presupposition of a Creator. Few principled lines could be drawn. As Justice Thomas remarked in his concurrence in the judgment in *Newdow*, "this Court's jurisprudence leaves courts, governments, and believers and nonbelievers alike confused."[37] The confusion need not be perpetuated.

To the secularist, however, doctrinal confusion is preferable to the restoration of religious reference. Such reference is antithetical to what may really be behind the modern exclusionary impulse: namely, the refounding of America upon a conception of human nature that emphasizes desire and emotion—and, of course, personal gratification—more than the self-evident truth of created equality. But if reason is made subordinate to desire, the prospects for religious freedom—indeed, any freedom—are dim. As Professor Robert George has asked, what ultimately is the source of human rights if it is neither God nor reason?[38] There may be none, other than an autonomy principle that nominally honors consent, but is then in tension with a secularist conception of man as the sum of desires prompted largely by external stimuli beyond his conscious freedom. This, of course, contrasts sharply with the corporate presupposition of the divine origin of man in the Declaration, with its affirmation of man's intrinsic value (as the possessor of inalienable right) and his reasoned pursuit of happiness.

Far more than Christmas displays are thus in play when religious freedom mutates into a secularist orthodoxy. After all, the "more perfect union" of the Constitution is fashioned to implement ("fulfill the promise" as one Chief Justice remarked[39]) the Declaration. It is intended to facilitate man's flourishing in a community of other men. Human flourishing in the natural law tradition of the Declaration is necessarily bound up with the basic human goods of life, knowledge, family, friendship, and religion.[40] Augustine opined that one can always tell the nature of a people by the objects of their love.[41] Insofar as these basic human goods can be said to be the product of reasoned deduction from the incorporating presupposition in the Declaration, what would be objects of our love if we were to aggressively separate from them? If the fulfillment of material and bodily desire is the essence of the American philosophy in the twenty-first century, have we substituted the shopping mall for the historically significant premise of the Independence Mall? An originalist course correction can avert this, but how do we get there? The journey back may depend as much on a historically faithful account of religious freedom as on observance of the structural limitations on judicial power.

Taxpayer Standing

Returning to original understanding should reduce the number of claims artificially and unnecessarily blocking reference to religion in the public square. Oftentimes these claims are presented to federal courts by taxpayers without specific factual injury, except that of difference of opinion, which does not usually justify treating something as a federal case. As a general matter, taxpayers lack standing to litigate because their grievances are too diffuse. In law review commentary before his appointment to the high court, John Roberts wrote of the importance of standing to the maintenance of a restrained judicial role and the separation of powers:

> One way federal courts ensure that they have a "real, earnest, and vital controversy" before them is by testing the plaintiff's standing to bring suit. The plaintiff must allege at the pleading stage, and later prove, an injury that is fairly traceable to the defendant's challenged conduct and that is likely to be redressed by the relief sought. If the plaintiff cannot do so, the court must dismiss the case as beyond its power to decide—no matter when in the litigation the flaw is discovered or arises. A dismissal on the basis of standing prevents the court from reaching and deciding the merits of the case, whether for the plaintiff or the defendant. Standing is thus properly regarded as a doctrine of judicial self-restraint.[42]

Chief Justice Roberts reaffirmed this thinking in *DaimlerChrysler Corp. v. Cuno*[43] for a virtually unanimous Court. Referencing the Court's decision finding no standing in an atheist father who lacked educational custody of his daughter to object to the words "under God" in the pledge of allegiance,[44] Roberts observed that standing is the "core component" of a bona fide case-or-controversy.

DaimlerChysler presented a challenge to certain Ohio tax credits by state taxpayers who speculated that their tax burden might be greater because of those credits. The challenge was rebuffed, with the Court noting that "this Court has denied *federal* taxpayers standing under Article III to object to a particular expenditure of federal funds simply because they are taxpayers."[45] The interest of a taxpayer is simply too minute and indeterminable, and there is no assurance that invalidating a tax will affect the tax bill of any given taxpayer.

Coterminous with the advent of the exclusionary misinterpretation of the establishment clause, however, the Court fabricated in *Flast v. Cohen*[46] an exception allowing taxpayer standing to raise such objection in that discrete context. *Flast* held that because "the Establishment Clause . . . specifically limit[s] the taxing and spending power conferred by Art. I, § 8," a taxpayer therefore has "standing consistent with Article III to invoke federal judicial power when he alleges that congressional action under the taxing and spending clause is in derogation of" the establishment clause.[47] The thinking behind *Flast* was overbroad since, as discussed below, Congress may not use its spending power in a manner that finances a violation of individual rights generally, not merely of the establishment clause.

Sensing the absence of a principled line of distinction among rights, the claimants in *DaimlerChrysler* sought to expand the exception to include dormant commerce clause limitations on congressional power, but the chief justice persuaded the entire Court to resist. Were it otherwise, there would be no precedential way of distinguishing other constitutional provisions. Such a broad application of *Flast*'s exception would be contrary to *Flast*'s own promise that it would not transform federal courts into forums for taxpayers' "generalized grievances."

The Roberts Court's decision in *DaimlerChrysler* to refuse to expand taxpayer standing is significant, and again, potentially favorable for a fuller public acknowledgment of religion. Moreover, the Chief Justice's discussion of the *Flast* exception in *DaimlerChrysler* points back to original understanding. "The *Flast* Court," wrote Roberts, "discerned in the history of the Establishment Clause the specific evils feared by" its drafters.[48] The main thrust of the Roberts reference is thus best understood as reinforcing Madison's proper remonstrance against paying clergy with public money. "Whatever rights plaintiffs have under the Commerce Clause, they are fundamentally unlike the right not 'to contribute three pence . . . for the support of any one [religious] establishment.'"[49] The rigorous standing aspect of Roberts' jurisprudence thus should work in tandem with the general no-coercion direction of the Kennedy[50] view of the establishment clause.[51]

That the Chief Justice's emphasis upon standing as a bulwark of the separation of powers and judicial restraint should bring greater order to previous tension in this area is illustrated by a pair of Seventh Circuit decisions, the second of which drew the review of the Roberts' Court. In the earlier case, *American Civil Liberties Union v. City of St. Charles*,[52] the appellate court found plaintiffs objecting to the display of a cross on public property at Christmastime to have suffered sufficient injury premised upon an allegation of being "led to alter their behavior—to detour . . . around the streets they ordinarily use," in order to avoid having to see the cross.[53] "The curtailment of their use of public rights of way" was held to be injury enough to support their suit.[54]

In the second Seventh Circuit ruling, *Freedom from Religion Foundation, Inc. v. Chao*,[55] taxpayers challenged the use of money appropriated by Congress under Article I, Section 8, to fund conferences that various executive-branch agencies hold to promote President Bush's Office of Faith-Based and Community Initiatives. This is a program that the president created by a series of executive orders to strengthen community groups assisting people in need. The plaintiffs claimed that the conferences are designed to promote religious community organizations over secular ones, and, based on the mistaken no endorsement test, that they favor religion, even as they show no denominational favoritism nor employ legal coercion. Controversially, a divided panel of the Seventh Circuit found standing for taxpayers to object on a much broader basis than even *Flast* itself. *Chao* broadens *Flast* to allow challenge of any executive action supported by a general appropriation. Dissenting Judge Kenneth Ripple explained at length why this is a troubling expansion of a controversial precedent. The Supreme Court, Judge Ripple demonstrated, has not deviated from the proposition that to merit taxpayer standing a plaintiff must bring an attack against a disbursement of public funds made in the exercise of *Congress*' taxing and spending power. A program originating in the executive branch arguably does not suffice.[56]

The majority in *Chao* asserted that *Flast* was expanded in *Bowen v. Kendrick*.[57] *Bowen* involved a taxpayer challenge to the Adolescent Family Life Act (AFLA), a congressional spending program whose administration was delegated to the secretary of Health and Human Services. Rejecting the secretary's argument that funds were distributed by an executive branch agency rather than by Congress, the Court observed that "the AFLA is at heart a program of disbursement of funds pursuant to Congress' taxing and spending powers, and appellees' claims call into question how the funds authorized by Congress are being disbursed pursuant to the AFLA's statutory mandate."[58] That executive officials had been delegated the actual authority to write the checks did not matter.[59] While executive administration of the funding did not vitiate standing in *Bowen*, it does not truly answer the issue in *Chao*. The key element for *Flast* purposes was that the executive had been directed to spend within the contours of a particular program—a program that implicated the establishment clause. As Judge Ripple in dissent in *Chao* observed: "The touchstone of the *Flast* inquiry, according to *Bowen*, was whether the Secretary had been 'given authority under the challenged statute to administer the spending program that *Congress had created.*'"[60] In *Chao*, Congress did not create a program; it merely supplied general budget authority for the support of the executive in all of its functions. To permit taxpayer standing in such circumstances would be to render the court a general complaint department for executive initiative. The executive can do nothing without general budget appropriations from Congress, and the approach of the *Chao* majority seemingly permitted an individual citizen to challenge any action of the executive with which he disagrees. Yet neither *Bowen* nor any other case countenances judicial intrusion into the affairs of the executive at the request of an individual who can assert no specific connection between his status as a taxpayer and the executive decision. Because this position is contrary to high Court precedent and the decisions of sister circuits,[61] *Chao* was a tempting target for review and reversal, and, restyled as *Hein v. Freedom from Religion Foundation*,[62] reversed it was.

In *Hein*, the Supreme Court decided that taxpayers had no standing to challenge the executive expenditures that allegedly violated the establishment clause. Justice Alito wrote that the line of precedent following *Flast* had never extended that case beyond its facts. He emphasized its "narrow application" and held that "the link between congressional action and constitutional violation that supported taxpayer standing in *Flast* is missing here."[63] Further, the Court rejected the Freedom from Religion Foundation's argument that a distinction between executive and congressional expenditures was arbitrary. The Court noted that the *Flast* exception to the general standing rule was specifically in relation to Congress' taxing and spending power, and that an executive expenditure from general funds was too attenuated from that to confer standing. Such an extension "would surely create difficult and uncomfortable line-drawing problems."[64] If an egregious violation were committed, as the Foundation speculated, Congress could step in, or a plaintiff with a more definite harm could bring suit. Finally, the Court concluded that it was not necessary to address the continuing validity of *Flast*, since "a precedent is not always expanded to the limit of its logic."[65]

Justice Kennedy, who joined the opinion in full, wrote separately to affirm the continuing validity of *Flast*, but also to emphasize why the separation of powers does not permit its extension. Extending *Flast* would make the exception "boundless," and would call into question the freedom of the Executive to experiment with creative responses, even religious ones, to governmental concerns.[66] There cannot be "constant supervision," wrote Justice Kennedy of executive operations and dialogues, or the Court would end up in the inappropriate role of "speech editors" or executive "event planners."[67] The "courts must be reluctant to expand their authority by requiring intrusive and unremitting judicial management of the way the Executive Branch performs its duties."[68] Of course, Justice Kennedy noted that merely because the Court would not be watching did not mean that the "Legislative and Executive Branches are . . . excused from making constitutional determinations in the regular course of their duties. Government officials must make a conscious decision to obey the Constitution whether or not their acts can be challenged in a court of law."[69]

In a concurrence in the judgment (joined by Justice Thomas), Justice Scalia wrote that "if this Court is to decide cases by rule of law rather than show of hands, we must surrender to logic and choose sides" between taking *Flast* to its logical conclusion and overruling it.[70] He distinguished between "psychic injury" and "wallet injury" for the purpose of taxpayer challenges.[71] Wallet injuries, he expounded, were a concrete type of injury, but psychic injuries too attenuated from the expenditure to be traceable and redressable.

The Roberts Court's respect for precedent—and the hesitation of Justice Kennedy—kept it from tossing *Flast* altogether. Nevertheless, as Justice Scalia's dissent illustrated, the *Flast* exception has little analytic justification. It is essentially judicially manufactured standing to vindicate mistaken exclusionary efforts. Where the establishment clause is offended by the imposition of legal coercion, there are plaintiffs enough to vindicate its important protection. The *Flast* exception has no more legitimacy than the no endorsement inquiry. Any mental anxiety is little different from the discomfort felt by other taxpayers who dislike, say, the government's environmental or tax policies.[72]

Judge Easterbrook, in his Seventh Circuit opinion dissenting from the denial of *en banc* review in *Chao*, illustrated at length how the *Flast* exception lacks even internal consistency, pointing out that the distinction between legislative and executive action is entirely formalistic. Likewise, suits have been dismissed that challenge expenditure associated with religious proclamations or speeches, which on its own terms is illogical, except to the extent that it moderates the effect of the underlying illogic of the exclusionary view of the establishment clause. As Easterbrook relates with relish, "Perhaps Michael Newdow should have invoked his tax return, rather than his status as a father, to challenge the inclusion of 'under God' in the Pledge of Allegiance. What is the price tag in both money and the opportunity cost of time to print many million copies of that phrase and read it daily in thousands of classrooms? As it was, however, the Supreme Court deemed his suit non-justiciable."[73] Judge Easterbrook is right that "this arbitrariness is built into the doctrine."[74] In writing for the plurality, Justice Alito conceded that Justice Scalia's analysis (which mirrors that of Easterbrook) was not "'[in]sane,' inconsistent with the 'rule of law,' or 'utterly meaningless'"; it was only "wrong" in light of the newly composed Court's commitment to "resolving the 'Cases' and 'Controversies' before [it and deciding] only the case at hand."[75] Those in the legal academy have no equivalent jurisdictional limitation, and for this reason, many will find Justice Scalia's position to be sound, and inevitable.

Free Exercise

The free exercise clause is also in need of originalist rehabilitation. Here, the dynamic of the new Court will be especially challenged since the source of error is the intellectually formidable Antonin Scalia. Given the discussion immediately above, Justice Scalia's thinking in the free exercise context seems anomalous. The free exercise clause is best grasped as the complement of the establishment clause. Personal faith cannot be prescribed under the establishment clause, and it cannot be prohibited under the free exercise clause. Again, the proper focus is on whether the law coerces—that is, does it, whether intentionally or effectively, prohibit personal belief or practice?

It is only since 1990 and the Supreme Court's 5-4 decision in *Employment Division v. Smith*[76] that coerced prohibition has not been the focus of the free exercise clause. Instead of that focus, the Court for the last decade and a half has been blinded by form. If a law is neutral in form and generally applicable, it matters not whether in application it prohibits a religious practice. In articulating this theory of free exercise, the *Smith* Court conceded that belief was absolutely protected, but that "the 'exercise of religion' often involves not only belief and profession but the performance of (or abstention from) physical acts: assembling with others for a worship service, participating in sacramental use of bread and wine, proselytizing, abstaining from certain foods or certain modes of transportation." *Smith* conceded that such actions are protected under the Constitution if specifically targeted; for example, when they are engaged in for religious reasons, or only because of the religious belief that they display. But that is a rare—almost nonexistent—case.

What is more common and what received virtually no protection by the narrow *Smith* majority was an individual's religious practice when it was prohibited by a generally applicable law. The *Smith* majority claimed this to be the law since *Reynolds v. United States* (1878),[77] where the Court rejected the claim that criminal laws against polygamy could not be constitutionally applied to those whose religion advanced the practice. This was an accurate account of the *Reynolds* result, but not its reasoning. The refusal to protect polygamy in *Reynolds* was premised upon the articulation of a compelling interest—namely, the traditional family. Ample social science was placed in the record that polygamy was apt to breed undesirable patriarchal side effects, including an attitude of civic subservience or disengagement. The Court's radical turn in *Smith* was to make all religious practice proscribable without such compelling justification—indeed, without justification at all, short of irrationality.

In *Smith* the Court rejected the compelling-interest standard based on a prediction of anarchy. The prediction was overstated in its own terms. The

Court conceded that the government often prevailed in free exercise cases—though, of course, that was not uniformly so. On several occasions, for example, the Court invalidated state unemployment compensation rules that conditioned the availability of benefits upon an applicant's willingness to work under conditions forbidden by his religion. Justice Scalia nevertheless manufactured a new rule that vastly under-protects religious practice—even going so far as to label such practice a constitutional anomaly. He argued:

> The "compelling government interest" requirement seems benign, because it is familiar from other fields. But using it as the standard that must be met before the government may accord different treatment on the basis of race, or before the government may regulate the content of speech, is not remotely comparable to using it for the purpose asserted here. What it produces in those other fields—equality of treatment and an unrestricted flow of contending speech—are constitutional norms; what it would produce here—a private right to ignore generally applicable laws—is a constitutional anomaly.[78]

A private right to avoid generally applicable laws would be anomalous, but claims of religious liberty are seldom, if ever, that one-sided. For one thing, most religions situate believers squarely within community, not above it. Men and women are admonished to love their neighbor, not separate from them. In addition, as John Winthrop acknowledged, men and women are created with different talents, and these differences prompt interdependence, not an abstract libertarian "right to live alone." Apart from misstating human nature, *Smith* also failed to honestly deal with the public order exception that had always been an implicit part of the constitutional claim of free exercise. Again, under established First Amendment jurisprudence, the freedom to act, unlike the freedom to believe, is not absolute. Instead, the Court—at least till *Smith*—respected both the First Amendment's express textual mandate and the governmental interest in regulation of conduct; it required the government to justify any prohibition of religiously motivated conduct by a compelling interest and by means narrowly tailored to achieve that interest. This justification is often expressed as the public order exception.

In "The Origins and Historical Understanding of Free Exercise of Religion," Professor (now Judge) Michael McConnell summarizes the historical understanding of the public order exception which gives lie to the *Smith* Court's specter of anarchy:

> State constitutions provide the most direct evidence of the original understanding [of the Free Exercise Clause], for it is reasonable to infer that those who drafted and adopted the first amendment assumed the term "free exercise of religion" meant what it had meant in their states. The wording of the state provisions thus casts light on the meaning of the first amendment.
>
> New York's 1777 Constitution was typical:
>
> [T]he free exercise and enjoyment of religious profession and worship, without discrimination or preference, shall forever hereafter be allowed, within this State, to all mankind: Provided, That the liberty of conscience, hereby granted, shall not be so construed as to excuse acts of licentiousness, or justify practices inconsistent with the peace or safety of this State.
>
> Likewise, New Hampshire's provision stated:
>
> Every individual has a natural and unalienable right to worship GOD according to the dictates of his own conscience, and reason; and no subject shall be hurt, molested, or restrained in his person, liberty or estate for worshipping GOD, in the manner and season most agreeable to the dictates of his own conscience, . . . provided he doth not disturb the public peace, or disturb others, in their religious worship.
>
> As a final example, Georgia's religious liberty clause read: "All persons whatever shall have the free exercise of their religion; provided it be not repugnant to the peace and safety of the State.". . . In addition to these state provisions, article I of the Northwest Ordinance of 1787, enacted contemporaneously with the drafting of the Constitution and re-enacted by the First Congress, provided: "No person, demeaning himself in a peaceable and orderly manner, shall ever be molested on account of his mode of worship, or religious sentiments, in the said territory."

. . . The most common feature of the state provisions was the government's right to protect public peace and safety. As Madison expressed it late in life, the free exercise right should prevail "in every case where it does not trespass on private rights or the public peace." This indicates that a believer has no license to invade the private rights of others or to disturb public peace and order, no matter how conscientious the belief or how trivial the private right on the other side.[79]

No one should question the right of the government to maintain public order. The threat posed by the murderous practices of radical Islam are sufficient to make the point. But neither Islam with its millions of adherents (who do not share the transformation of jihad as personal conversion into jihad as a holy war) nor less well-known minority faiths ought to be treated as presumptively invisible to the Constitution. By contrast, the ruling in *Smith* gives government prohibition, not faith or religious practice, the presumption of validity. It is as if the First Amendment stated that "Congress shall make no law . . . prohibiting the free reign of governmental intrusion against religious practices." With only a rational basis needed to justify any generally applicable and neutrally phrased prohibition, religious practice lost its preferred position. Because these suppressions of religious conduct often—though not always—occur individually, they may seem trivial—except of course to the believer singled out for disfavor, whether "a devout librarian fired for refusing to work on Sunday" or a modest church community denied a zoning permit or "a student rebuked for saying 'God bless you' to a classmate who sneezed."[80] The *Smith* Court left it to the popular will to supply legislative exemption to general laws that substantially burden religion. But when religious practices challenge social norms, as many do, will the legislature respond? As is suggested by contemporary refusals to exempt Catholic employers from supplying contraceptive insurance coverage for their employees (or to supply only an exemption that effectively would require forfeiting a large part of the charitable work of the church contrary to its social justice mission),[81] the likely answer is in the negative. As a *Harvard Law Review* analysis of a recent case observed: "Twenty-one states have passed contraception coverage statutes. . . . Denying any exemptions . . . square[s] more neatly with *Smith*. . . . Far from resolving a contentious matter, the case instead relegated the legality of compulsory contraceptive coverage laws to the same morass in which much of First Amendment jurisprudence currently resides."[82]

The ill consequence of *Smith* was mitigated a few years later by Justice Kennedy in *Church of the Lukumi*.[83] Kennedy refused to accept facial neutrality as sufficient to insulate a municipal ordinance that effectively targeted for prohibition animal sacrifice undertaken for religious reasons. Kennedy rejected the contention advanced by the city that the Court's inquiry must end with the text of the laws at issue: "Facial neutrality is not determinative. The free exercise clause, like the establishment clause, extends beyond facial discrimination. The clause forbids subtle departures from neutrality," and "covert suppression of particular religious beliefs." Official action that targets religious conduct for distinctive treatment cannot be shielded by mere compliance with the requirement of facial neutrality. The free exercise clause protects against governmental hostility which is masked, as well as overt. "The Court must survey meticulously the circumstances of governmental categories to eliminate, as it were, religious gerrymanders."[84]

The Kennedy approach was utilized by Justice Alito while on the appellate bench to invalidate a police department ordinance that allowed medical, but not religious, exceptions for beards.[85] What is especially interesting to note is Alito's extended discussion of pre-*Smith* case law. He highlights in particular that a plurality had flirted with the idea of applying heightened scrutiny to neutral, generally applicable laws that affirmatively compel or prohibit conduct.[86] Under this structure, rational basis review would have been confined to benefit denials. One senses that Alito would have found this judicial approach far more sensitive to religious freedom than the across-the-board leveling of religious practice that *Smith* represented. Alito himself characterizes the 1990 opinion in *Smith* as changing the legal landscape "dramatically."

The Alito Third Circuit opinion does not include a call to overturn *Smith*. That would be out of character for any appellate judge, and especially for the judicially restrained Justice Alito. That said, the thoughtful manner in which Justice Alito examined the religious claim suggests a proper sensitivity to matters of religious practice. That sensitivity may well be attracted to the calls by other members of the Court to reexamine *Smith*. As Justice Souter pointed out, *Smith* is a notably weak precedent, having emerged without full briefing of the surprising turn it took and having taken that turn without overruling the more protective free exercise clause interpretations that *Smith* fails to follow. Citing numerous sources, Souter argues that

> the Clauses' development in the First Congress, from its origins in the post-Revolution state constitutions and pre-Revolution colonial charters, and from the philosophy of rights to which the Framers adhered, [show] that the Clause was originally understood to preserve a right to engage in activities necessary to fulfill one's duty to one's God, unless those activities threatened the rights of others or the serious needs of the State. If, as this scholarship suggests, the free exercise clause's original "purpose [was] to secure religious liberty in the individual by prohibiting any invasions thereof by civil authority," then there would be powerful reason to interpret the Clause to accord with its natural reading, as applying to all laws prohibiting religious exercise in fact, not just those aimed at its prohibition, and to hold the neutrality needed to implement such a purpose to be the substantive neutrality of our pre-*Smith* cases, not the formal neutrality sufficient for constitutionality under *Smith*.[87]

That reexamination would appear even more likely in light of the compatible unanimous statutory ruling issued by the Chief Justice in *Gonzales v. O Centro Espirita Beneficente Uniao Do Vegetal*.[88] *O Centro* dealt with an obscure religious sect which employed a minor amount of hallucinogenic tea in its liturgy. The tea was a Schedule I drug under the Controlled Substances Act, and under *Smith*, the government's interest in a uniform drug law would have been sufficient to sustain its interdiction. The sect prevailed, however, in light of Congress's passage of the Religious Freedom Restoration Act, or RFRA.[89] RFRA was invalidated in its application against the states since Congress lacked power under section 5 of the Fourteenth Amendment to redefine the meaning of the free exercise clause[90]—even if that meant returning it closer to its original roots. But the federal government with respect to its own actions could elect to protect religious conduct more generously and more consistently with the founding idea. By this reasoning, Chief Justice

Roberts led a unanimous Court to both require a compelling interest to sustain the prohibition of religious tea usage and advance that interest by the more tailored means.

The government was unable to meet its burden. It was not that controlling illicit drug use was not significant; it was that the pre-*Smith*/RFRA standard requires that compelling need be justified "to the person." Given the *de minimis* amounts of the prohibited substance involved in *O Centro*, that was not possible to demonstrate. Moreover, the Chief Justice had little sympathy for the idea expressed in *Smith* that sensitively evaluating claims for exemption would lead to anarchy. This, said the Court, was little more than a slippery slope concern. "The Government's argument echoes the classic rejoinder of bureaucrats throughout history: If I make an exception for you, I'll have to make one for everybody, so no exceptions." But RFRA operates by mandating specific consideration, under the compelling interest test, of exceptions to "rule[s] of general applicability." Congress determined that the legislated test "is a workable test for striking sensible balances between religious liberty and competing prior governmental interests."[91] This determination finds support, noted the Chief Justice, in the pre-*Smith* case law. The prospect seems bright under the new Court for returning to an understanding of religion, and the religion clauses, as not anomalous.

Concluding Thoughts

First, religion is the source of American order that predates the Constitution or any other instrument of law. Those coming to this unknown and unexplored place nearly four centuries ago entered into a pact or covenant that claimed insight about God and man. The God of America was not uninterested in the fate of his creatures, but he was superior in intelligence and would favor those who "choose life" by "obeyeing His voyce" and "cleaveing to Him." Man was also formed with different capability so "that every man might have need of others and from hence they might be all knitt more nearly together. . . . " The call to "form a more perfect union" was immanent in the human soul and was far more than a political strategy to overcome a weak and unworkable league of friendship among separate sovereign entities—though practically it was that, too. One goes wrong rather quickly if the transcendent presupposition (embodied in our national incorporation in the Declaration of Independence) is ignored, or worse, subverted with an autonomy principle—too puny upon which to form a nation—of doing no harm and asserting a right to be left alone.

Second, man's grasp of God, of his own nature, and of the universe is imperfect. Imperfect knowledge gives rise to imperfect action in public or personal life. The original Constitution being a reflection of human nature, it seeks to be true to the corporate supposition of God's existence and our creation, while out of the humility of imperfect knowledge it divides and enumerates power. A principal enumeration is the express denial to the national government of the power of religious establishment and the protection of freedom to believe or practice religion, or not, as individual conscience dictates. The individual freedom to deny God for oneself does not include the power to deny the corporate presupposition of God and the importance of religion to the nation's prosperity and well-being.

Third, beginning in the late 1940s, Supreme Court establishment clause jurisprudence mistakenly substituted secularity for neutrality. The modern conception of neutrality between religion and no religion cannot be reconciled with the corporate presupposition of religion's salience. This irreconcilability manifests itself in constitutional misconstruction, where the no establishment protection becomes a guarantee of religious exclusion or "no endorsement." A similar failure, which underestimated the importance of faith a decade and a half ago, inverted the constitutional protection of free exercise, such that the prohibition of religious practice (not its protection) is privileged. Thus, on the pretext of avoiding the constitutional anomaly of every person potentially being a law unto himself, approval was given to the anomalous remaking of a guarantee of individual right into its repression so long as it is accomplished in generally applicable form.

The Supreme Court by reason of change in composition is poised to correct its errors of misconstruction. In the establishment context, Justice Kennedy has long been illustrating the weakness and subjectivity of the no endorsement theory propounded by (the now retired) Justice O'Connor. In matters of free exercise, Justice Alito comes to the high bench with demonstrated appellate understanding of the intended scope of this constitutional protection. The Chief Justice has already primed a favorable revival of free exercise with a unanimous statutory opinion of like import. Critically, reasonable speculation can count to five with respect to the refocusing of both the establishment and free exercise clauses on the avoidance of legal coercion in matters of religion.

These anticipated favorable developments have already minimized—and perhaps in a subsequent case will eliminate altogether—the illogical creation of an exception to the rule against taxpayer standing. A bona fide injury in fact is a prerequisite to Article III involvement, and the Roberts Court has reaffirmed this basic proposition. Beyond the formal confines of the courthouse, the corrections discussed may also bring clarity to the relevance of religion in the context of judicial confirmation or other public office.

Both John Roberts and Samuel Alito were cross-examined about their Catholicism when they faced the Senate Judiciary Committee. On one level the prohibition of test oaths and the general guarantee of free exercise suggest that these inquiries bordered on an improper religious "litmus test" perhaps spitefully employed. Yet paradoxically, it seemed that some political figures who objected to the inquiries into John Roberts's or Sam Alito's faith sought in the unembarrassed blink of the analytical eye to deploy Harriet Miers's faith as a positive credential. The relevance or irrelevance of faith to judicial office requires more careful treatment than space permits here. However, as a general matter, if judges do not presume to legislate like lawmakers, judges are not morally responsible for the laws the polity enacts or fails to enact. (There are a select number of places where a judicial opinion might be argued to be a material or formal cooperation with an intrinsic, moral evil enacted into statutory law).

Having said that, of course, the tendency of justices to exercise will rather than judgment at least explains why both nominator and senator are tempted to explore the faith of nominees. Yet, the history recounted briefly in this chapter suggests there may be even more to it. Even were judges paragons of restraint never veering from the limits of the judicial office, the premise of this chapter—differentiating corporate presupposition of the Divine from the personal freedom to disbelieve—suggests that at least with respect to the former it may be hardly intemperate to inquire whether a prospective judge can pledge allegiance under God. Writes Tocqueville:

In the United States, if a politician attacks a sect, this may not prevent the partisans of that very sect from supporting him; but if he attacks all the sects together, everyone abandons him, and he remains alone.[92]

History has been contended for by two unsatisfactory views: one that would impose religious belief by legal coercion and one that would use law to deny the public expression of belief. The first camp—the imposers—is frighteningly exemplified in the larger world by radical Islam. They are reminiscent—in religious attitude but not in deed—of Puritan extremists who sought to persecute those who did not see faith the Puritan way.[93] But this is not what presently confounds religious liberty in America. The second camp—the deniers, or, more commonly, the secularists—are nominally less threatening (because they do not plant roadside bombs), but in reality, the secularists set man on a path of his own self-denial and self-destruction. Both positions dehumanize or deny the intrinsic, created nature of the human person, and the way back is to honor religious belief in the fullest sense of the American founding—both as a corporate premise for the republic and as a necessary aspect of human freedom.

Notes

1. Saint Augustine, *The Confessions of Saint Augustine*, ed. E.B. Pusey (Modern Library, 1999).

2. C. S. Lewis, preface to *The Pilgrim's Regress* (Grand Rapids, MI: Eerdmans, 1992). For a more contemporary expression of this important insight, see Kevin Seamus Hasson, *The Right to Be Wrong: Ending the Culture War Over Religion in America* (New York: Encounter Books, 2005). Mr. Hasson is the founder of the Becket Fund for Religious Liberty and is one of the first contemporary authors to grasp the special relation between faith and human nature.

3. Pope Benedict XVI argues in *Spe Salvi* (November 30, 2007) that without God and the hope of salvation, life is tedious and potentially burdensome, even if it is marked by material affluence and technical progress. The distinguishing mark of Christians is "not that they know the details of what awaits them, but they know in general terms that their life will not end in emptiness." Hope is not, then, something for the future alone, a sort of wishful thinking about what might be; it offers meaning for life today. Benedict argues that the insight of hope is not only for Christians, since others, while not sharing in the faith, intuitively grasp that hope comes from within the person—the realm of faith and conscience. Benedict cautions man against finding false hope in social systems "founded on political ideologies, economic models and social theories and which come from outside the person." Available at http://www.vatican.va/holy_father/benedict_xvi/encyclicals/documents/hf_ben-xvi_enc_20071130_spe-salvi_en.html (accessed December 19, 2007).

4. John Winthrop, "A Model of Christian Charity" (1630) in *A Documentary History of American Life*, ed. Jack P. Greene (New York: McGraw-Hill, 1966), 66–69.

5. Ibid.

6. Ibid.

7. The late Robert C. Cannada of Jackson, Mississippi, devoted a good portion of his professional life to highlighting the importance of the relationship between the Declaration and the Constitution in just this sense in conversation with the leaders of the law, from Robert Bork to Edwin Meese. See Robert C. Cannada, Address to the 1998 National Lawyers Association Convention, http://www.nla.org/library/conv9803/address_of_robert_cannada.html (accessed December 19, 2007). This approach is also the one subscribed to by Justice Clarence Thomas. See Scott Douglas Gerber, *First Principles: The Jurisprudence of Justice Clarence Thomas* (New York: New York University Press, 1999).

8. Douglas W. Kmiec, "The Human Nature of Freedom and Identity—We Hold More Than Random Thoughts," *Harvard Journal of Law and Public Policy* 29 (2005): 33.

9. There is no better volume tracing and drawing out these points and the interrelationship of the Declaration and the Constitution than Michael Novak's book *On Two Wings: Humble Faith and Common Sense at the American Founding* (San Francisco: Encounter Books, 2002).

10. Jared Sparks, *The Writings of George Washington* 227 (1837).

11. Alexis De Tocqueville, *Democracy in America*, ed. Phillip Bradley (New York: Alfred A. Knopf, 1945), 309–10.

12. The evidence is easily confirmed in the polls repeatedly showing belief in God in America to exceed 90 percent. See, for instance, David Masci and Gregory A. Smith, "God is Alive and Well in America," Pew Forum on Religion & Public Life, April 4, 2006, which notes: "The existence of God is one of the few things almost all Americans consistently agree on. Recent polling by the Pew Research Center for the People & the Press and the Pew Forum on Religion & Public Life found that 96% of the public says they believe in God or some form of Supreme Being, roughly the same number as in a 1965 survey. In addition, the role of faith and religion is a regular focus of public comment."

13. In *Zorach v. Clauson*, the Supreme Court gave specific recognition to the proposition that "we are a religious people whose institutions presuppose a Supreme Being." 343 U.S. 306, 313 (1952).

14. Kathleen Sullivan, "Religion and Liberal Democracy," *University of Chicago Law Review* 59 (1992): 195, 197–214 (negative bar against establishment of religion implies affirmative establishment of secular public order), cited with approval by Justice Ginsburg in her dissenting opinion in *Capitol Square v. Pinette*, 515 U.S. 753 (1995).

15. *Everson v. Board of Education*, 330 U.S. 1 (1947).

16. *Lemon v. Kurtzman*, 403 U.S. 602 (1971).

17. See the discussion of *Flast v. Cohen*, 392 U.S. 83 (1968), infra.

18. See *Cutter v. Wilkinson*, 544 U. S. 709, n. 3 (2005) (Thomas, J., concurring).

19. *Elk Grove Unified School District v. Newdow*, 542 U.S. 1, 52 (2004) (Thomas, J., concurring).

20. *Lee v. Weisman*, 505 U.S. 577 (1992).

21. Ibid., 640 (Scalia, J., dissenting).

22. Cf. *Mitchell v. Helms*, 530 U.S. 793 (2000)

23. *Van Orden v. Perry*, 545 U.S. 677 (2005); *McCreary County v. ACLU*, 545 U.S. 844 (2005).

24. *County of Allegheny v. ACLU*, 492 U.S. 573 (1989).

25. Ibid., 687; *Lynch v. Donnelly*, 104 S.Ct., at 1366 (1984).

26. *County of Allegheny v. ACLU*, 688.

27. As a matter of logic and consistency, a nonbeliever would not rely on the protection of free exercise.

28. Alexander Hamilton, John Jay, and James Madison, *The Federalist: A Commentary on the Constitution of the United States*, ed. Robert Scigliano (New York: Modern Library, 2001), *Federalist* 84. In this regard, Justice O'Connor's "no endorsement" test approves a holiday display of a crèche when part of a larger exhibit with secular objects, but not when it is alone or with an insufficient secular message. This has led some to view the test as promoting outcomes based more on interior decorating than constitutional principle.

29. See *Abington School District v. Schempp,* 374 U.S. 203, 233 (1963): "The distinction between the two clauses is apparent—a violation of the free exercise clause is predicated on coercion while the Establishment Clause violation need not be so attended." See also Douglas Laycock, "'Nonpreferential' Aid to Religion: A False Claim About Original Intent," *William and Mary Law Review* 27 (1986): "If coercion is also an element of the establishment clause, establishment adds nothing to free exercise" (922).

30. Jurisprudentially, any modern redundancy is the likely consequence of not correctly perceiving the establishment clause as simply a federalist protection of state establishments.

31. *Lee v. Weisman,* 577 (finding impermissible coercion in the context of a middle school graduation, where the prayer originated with the state officer [the school principal], the person selected to pray was designated by the state officer, and the prayer was then authored subject to the direction of the state officer).

32. *Zelman v. Simmons-Harris,* 536 U.S. 639 (2002).

33. *Lynch v. Donnelly,* 693 (concurring opinion).

34. *County of Allegheny v. ACLU,* 630 (O'Connor, J., concurring).

35. Ibid., 631 (O'Connor, J., concurring).

36. Ibid., 655 (Kennedy, J., concurring and dissenting).

37. See *Elk Grove Unified School District v. Newdow,* 45, n. 1 (Thomas, J., concurring in judgment) (collecting cases). The following religious references have been successfully challenged: a sign noting that a public building would be closed for Good Friday, *Granzeier v. Middleton,* 955 F. Supp. 741, 743 & n. 2, 746–47 (E.D. Ky. 1997), aff'd on other grounds, 173 F. 3d 568, 576 (6th Cir. 1999); a cross in the Mojave Desert honoring war dead, *Buono v. Norton,* 212 F. Supp. 2d 1202, 1204–5, 1215–17 (C.D. Cal. 2002); and numerous municipal seals, e.g., *Robinson v. Edmond,* 68 F. 3d 1226 (10th Cir.1995); *Murray v. Austin,* 947 F. 2d 147 (5th Cir. 1991); *Friedman v. Board of Cty. Comm'rs of Bernalillo Cty.,* 781 F. 2d 777 (10th Cir. 1985) (en banc).

38. Robert P. George, "A Clash of Orthodoxies," *First Things* 95 (August/September 1999): 33–40. "If reason is purely instrumental and can't tell us what to want but only how to get to what we want, how can we say that people have a fundamental right to freedom of speech? Freedom of the press? Freedom of religion? Privacy? Where do those fundamental rights come from? What is their basis? Why respect someone else's rights?"

39. The full quotation is: "'The Declaration of Independence was the promise; the Constitution was the fulfillment.'" Charles Alan Wright, "In Memoriam: William Burger: A Younger Friend Remembers," *Texas Law Review* 74 (1995): 213, 219.

40. See John Finnis, *Natural Law and Natural Rights* (Oxford: Oxford University Press,1980) for a somewhat differently stated exposition of incommensurate, basic human goods.

41. St. Augustine writes: "If one should say, 'A people is the association of a multitude of rational beings united by a common agreement on the objects of their love,' then it follows that to observe the character of a particular people, we must examine the objects of its love. And yet, whatever those objects, if it is the association of a multitude not of animals but of rational beings, and is united by a common agreement about the objects of its love, then there is no absurdity in applying to it the title of a 'people.' And, obviously, the better the objects of this agreement, the better the people, the worse the objects of this love, the worse the people." St. Augustine, *The City of God*, 19.24.

42. John G. Roberts, "Article III Limits on Statutory Standing," *Duke Law Journal* 42 (1993): 1219.

43. *DaimlerChrysler Corp. v. Cuno*, 126 S. Ct. 1854 (2006).

44. See *Elk Grove Unified School Dist. v. Newdow*, 1.

45. *DaimlerChrysler Corp. v. Cuno*, 1862.

46. *Flast v. Cohen*, 83 (sustaining a taxpayer challenge in federal court to an alleged violation of the establishment clause). Congress had appropriated money for grants of financial assistance to private as well as public schools, and the plaintiffs complained that insofar as some of the grants had been made to parochial schools, the statute violated the establishment clause.

47. *Flast v. Cohen*, 105–6.

48. *DaimlerChrysler Corp. v. Cuno*, 1865.

49. Ibid. Roberts is quoting *Writings of James Madison*, ed. Gaillard Hunt (New York: G.P. Putnam Sons, 1901), 2:186.

50. A view likely shared in the main by Justices Scalia, Thomas, Alito, and Roberts.

51. It may also be assisted by a recent congressional effort to remove "attorney fee" incentives to filing lawsuits based solely on a desire to suppress public religious reference. See H.R. 2679, the Public Expression of Religion Act, passed by the House precluding the award of attorney's fees under 42 U.S.C. 1988 for causes of action premised upon the establishment clause.

52. *American Civil Liberties Union v. City of St. Charles*, 794 F.2d 265, 267–69 (7th Cir. 1986).

53. Ibid., 268.

54. Ibid.

55. *Freedom from Religion Foundation, Inc. v. Chao*, 433 F.3d 989, 993 (7th Cir. 2006).

56. See *Valley Forge Christian College v. Americans United for Separation of Church and State, Inc.*, 454 U.S. at 479 (1982): "*Flast* limited taxpayer standing to challenges directed only at exercises of congressional power" (internal quotation marks and alterations omitted); *Schlesinger v. Reservists Committee to Stop the War*, 418 U.S. at 228 (denying standing because the taxpayer plaintiffs "did not challenge an enactment under Art. I, § 8, but rather the action of the Executive Branch").

57. *Bowen v. Kendrick*, 487 U.S. 589 (1988).

58. Ibid., 619–20.

59. Ibid., 619: "We do not think . . . that appellees' claim that AFLA funds are being used improperly by individual grantees is any less a challenge to congressional taxing and spending power simply because the funding authorized by Congress has flowed through and been administered by the Secretary."

60. Ibid., emphasis added.

61. For example, the Court of Appeals for the District of Columbia Circuit, when asked by municipal taxpayers to prohibit the District of Columbia from expending public funds to oppose citizens' initiatives, observed that the "[Supreme] Court has never recognized federal taxpayer standing outside [of *Flast's*] narrow facts, and it has refused to extend *Flast* to exercises of executive power." *District of Columbia Common Cause v. District of Columbia*, 858 F.2d 1, 3–4 (D.C. Cir. 1988) (citations omitted). Similarly, in *In re United States Catholic Conference*, 885 F.2d 1020 (2d Cir. 1989), the Court of Appeals for the Second Circuit denied taxpayer standing to pro-choice supporters who alleged that the IRS, by granting tax-exempt status to the Catholic Church, had violated the no establishment clause. The court reasoned:

> Plaintiffs in the instant case do not challenge Congress' exercise of its taxing and spending power as embodied in § 501(c)(3) of the [Tax] Code; they do not contend that the Code favors the Church. . . . Instead, they argue that the IRS, in allegedly closing its eyes to violations by the Church, is disregarding the Code's mandate and the Constitution. The complaint centers on an alleged decision made solely by the executive branch that in plaintiffs' view directly contravenes Congress' aim. The instant case is therefore distinguishable from [*Bowen v. Kendrick*]. In that case, there was "a sufficient nexus between the taxpayer's standing as a taxpayer and the congressional exercise of taxing and spending power, notwithstanding the role the Secretary plays in administering the statute." *Kendrick,* 108 S. Ct. at 2580. Here, there is no nexus between plaintiffs' allegations and Congress' exercise of its taxing and spending power. Hence, *Kendrick* does not alter the requirements of taxpayer standing to allow the instant plaintiffs to challenge how the IRS administers the Code. (Ibid., 1028)

In short, the Second Circuit squarely held that the alleged *executive branch misapplication* of a statutory tax exemption enacted by Congress under its taxing and spending power is, under prevailing Supreme Court precedent, insufficient to support taxpayer standing. Like an arguably illegal executive expenditure (like the one alleged in *Chao*), the misapplication of a tax exemption has an impact upon the congressional policy decision embodied in the statute. It is not, however, an attack on Congress' exercise of the taxing and spending power. As these cases demonstrate, other circuits have refused to interpret *Bowen* as affording taxpayer standing based simply upon a showing that a statute enabled the executive branch to violate the establishment clause. This circuit ought to follow the same course and, in the process, adhere to the principles set forth in the Supreme Court's case law.

62. *Hein v. Freedom from Religion Foundation*, 127 S. Ct. 2553 (2007).

63. Ibid., 41, 32.

64. Ibid., 47–48.

65. Ibid., 50.

66. Ibid., 53 (Kennedy, J., concurring).

67. Ibid., 54.

68. Ibid.

69. Ibid., 56.

70. Ibid., 56 (Scalia, J., concurring).

71. Ibid., 57.

72. See *Lujan v. Defenders of Wildlife*, 504 U.S. 555 (1992); *Allen v. Wright*, 468 U.S. 737, (1984); *Simon v. Eastern Kentucky Welfare Rights Organization*, 426 U.S. 26 (1976); *United States v. Richardson*, 418 U.S. 166 (1974); *Schlesinger v. Reservists Committee to Stop the War*. Compare *Metro-North Commuter R.R. v. Buckley*, 521 U.S. 424 (1997).

73. See *Elk Grove Unified School District v. Newdow*, 1.

74. Ibid. (Easterbrook, J., concurring).

75. *Hein v. Freedom From Religion Foundation, Inc.*, 2572.

76. *Employment Division, Dep't of Human Res. of Oregon v. Smith*, 494 U.S. 872 (1990).

77. *Reynolds v. United States*, 98 U.S. 145 (1878).

78. *Employment Division v. Smith*, 885–86 (citations omitted).

79. Michael McConnell, "The Origins and Historical Understanding of Free Exercise of Religion," *Harvard Law Review* 103 (1990): 1409, 1456–58, 1464.

80. Diana B. Henriques, "In the Congressional Hopper: A Long Wish List of Special Benefits and Exemptions," *New York Times*, October 11, 2006, A1, citing the work and concerns of the Becket Fund for Religious Freedom. This multipart series, as its headline suggests, had the most definite slant of illustrating how religious groups have succeeded in some contexts in securing legislative exemption. After *Smith*, of course, religious practice is remitted to legislative assembly to try to recover what the Constitution had previously guaranteed.

81. *Catholic Charities of Sacramento, Inc. v. Superior Court*, 85 P.3d 67 (Cal. 2004) (rejecting no establishment and free exercise challenge to the state compulsory contraceptive coverage law). The narrow religious exemption would have forced Catholic Charities to refuse assistance to non-Catholics in order to be exempt from the law.

82. Recent Case, "Constitutional Law— First Amendment," *Harvard Law Review* 117 (2004): 2761, 2767.

83. *Church of the Lukumi Babalu Aye Inc. v. City of Hialeah*, 508 U.S. 520 (1993).

84. Ibid., 534 (citations omitted).

85. *Fraternal Order of Police Newark Lodge No. 12 v. Newark*, 170 F.3d 359 (3d Cir. 1999).

86. *Bowen v. Roy*, 476 U.S. 693, 708 (1986).

87. *Church of the Lukumi Babalu Aye, Inc. v. City of Hialeah*, 575–76 (citation omitted) (Souter, J., concurring).

88. *Gonzales v. O Centro Espirita Beneficente Uniao Do Vegetal*, 546 U.S. 418 (2006).

89. U.S.C. 2000bb-1(b).

90. *City of Boerne v. Flores*, 521 U.S. 507 (1997) (invalidating RFRA as applied to States to be beyond Congress' legislative authority under § 5 of the Fourteenth Amendment).

91. *Gonzales v. O Centro Espirita Beneficente Uniao Do Vegetal*, 436 (citation omitted).

92. De Tocqueville, *Democracy in America*, 280.

93. As described by the Library of Congress in an online exhibit titled *Religion and the Founding of the American Republic*:

> Although they were victims of religious persecution in Europe, the Puritans supported the Old World theory that sanctioned it, the need for uniformity of religion in the state. Once in control in New England, they sought to break "the very neck of Schism and vile opinions." The "business" of the first settlers, a Puritan minister recalled in 1681, "was not Toleration"; but "[they] were professed enemies of it." Puritans expelled dissenters from their colonies, a fate that in 1636 befell Roger Williams and in 1638 Anne Hutchinson, America's first major female religious leader. Those who defied the Puritans by persistently returning to their jurisdictions risked capital punishment, a penalty imposed on four Quakers between 1659 and 1661. Reflecting on the seventeenth century's intolerance, Thomas Jefferson was unwilling to concede to Virginians any moral superiority to the Puritans. Beginning in 1659 Virginia enacted anti-Quaker laws, including the death penalty for refractory Quakers. Jefferson surmised that "if no capital execution took place here, as did in New England, it was not owing to the moderation of the church, or the spirit of the legislature."

Library of Congress, "America as a Religious Refuge: The Seventeenth Century," part 2, "Persecution in America," *Religion and the Founding of the American Republic*, http://www.loc.gov/exhibits/religion/rel01-2.html (accessed November 26, 2007).

10

A Response to Douglas W. Kmiec

Michael Greve

I greatly enjoyed Douglas Kmiec's account of the constitutional basis for religious freedom, and I agree with much of it. My comments focus mainly on a few areas of disagreement.

As an initial matter, I am uncomfortable with Kmiec's heavy emphasis on the presuppositions of the Declaration of Independence and its continuity with the Constitution. I do not think it is quite right to say that the Constitution is a working out of the "operational details" of government, or a set of "bylaws" to the "charter" of the Declaration. I am inclined to think of the Constitution itself as a governing charter. Moreover, that charter has striking features that render a straight-line narrative from the Declaration to the Constitution somewhat problematic. For example, I am hardly the first to observe that the Constitution's Preamble makes no mention whatever of a creator, or deity, or God. That omission has to be intentional, because it must have struck people in the founding era as very discordant. (Even today, almost all state constitutions contain a reference to a Supreme Being in some form.) I do not want to make too much of this observation. Obviously, the relation between the Declaration and the Constitution is a very complicated story. Kmiec's version of that story, or something close to it, may be plausible. But for purposes of constitutional law, I would not want to base any argument on such a case unless I had to.

Hence, my question: How much work are the Declaration and its presupposition actually supposed to do in this account? To what extent are they necessary to arrive at principles and positions that one cannot get from the text, structure, and history of the First Amendment? I have put my concern in the form of a question because these difficult matters are above my pay grade. I am more confident in commenting on the issues of law and legal strategy that Kmiec discusses: taxpayer standing, the coercion test, and free exercise claims.

On taxpayer standing, I agree entirely with Kmiec's analysis: *Flast v. Cohen* will be dramatically narrowed, and that is all to the good.[1] One has to fear that similar cases then will migrate to the states, many of which have much less stringent standing requirements. Still, a sharp reduction of taxpayer cases at least at the federal level is worth having.

It is quite plausible that a coercion test in establishment cases is much preferable to "endorsement" or "entanglement" or some other *Lemon* test du jour. It is also plausible that there might be a Supreme Court majority for such a move. I suspect, however, that the matter is more complicated. For example, I should think that a motto of "In Jesus We Trust" on U.S. currency, while not coercive, would be unconstitutional. So a coercion test would have to be supplemented with some additional test or tests—perhaps nonsectarianism (meaning neutrality among religions), or rootedness in our political traditions. I want to know what those tests would be.

A still harder problem is that "coercion" is not self-explanatory. Kmiec notes the point, but arguably understates the difficulty. Obviously, mere exposure to a crèche on public property is *not* coercion. Thus, a coercion test would dispose of the holiday display or "interior decorating" cases, to paraphrase two of my favorite jurists.[2] But those cases, I assume, would disappear in any event under tightened standing rules. What, then, of closer cases, such as school prayer? Forced participation is obviously coercion. But what about the exposure of captive audiences to religious ceremonies? Does the possible stigma of being the lone nonparticipant count as an injury? Can religious public ceremonies create a "hostile environment" (which in many other contexts, such as employment discrimination, we now recognize as a form of coercion)? Is "coercion" limited to public acts backed by threat of penalty (as Justice Scalia has argued), or does it extend to subtle social pressures (as Justice Kennedy would have it)?[3]

Even justices who are persuaded that *Lemon* and its prongs make no sense may be very reluctant to substitute a superficially attractive principle with uncertain reach and implications. Thus, any serious effort to nudge the Court toward a coercion test would require three fairly complicated maneuvers. First, legal scholars would have to elaborate a workable coercion test in some detail. Second, repeat litigators in this sector would have to think about, and then engineer, the proper sequence of cases. The wrong, "bridge too far" case at the wrong time could doom the entire effort. Third, litigators would then have to perform the most important task of Supreme Court advocacy, which is to explain to the justices what they *actually* mean when they say what they say. ("Rightly understood, Justice Kennedy's coercion theory stands for the following propositions . . .")

To illustrate the importance and the difficulty of these conditions: I understand Kmiec's discussion to imply that the principle of nondiscrimination against religion, or against the exclusion of religious speakers or organizations from public programs, is now firmly established. That is by and large true, despite the inexcusably sloppy *Davey v. Locke* decision. The reason why that is so is precisely that the two-plus–decade campaign to entrench the neutrality principle satisfied the three conditions just sketched. It had a legal mastermind (Michael McConnell) who worked through the theory and who then participated in the next steps—a sensible (if not error-free) sequencing of cases, such that access-to-facilities cases (*Widmar v. Vincent, Lamb's Chapel*) came before the tougher financial support cases (*Rosenberger*); and a sequence of briefs and arguments to the effect that "neutrality" meant what Justice O'Connor, rightly understood, had always meant (whether or not she realized it). Advocates of a coercion test would have to replicate that sustained effort, without Judge McConnell's assistance. I do not doubt the feasibility of such an effort, but I would not underestimate its difficulty.

Finally, on free exercise and accommodation, Kmiec harshly criticizes *Employment Division v. Smith*, but I believe that the case was probably rightly decided. It has a very important institutional justification, which I take to be Justice Scalia's principal concern. Scalia does not trust the Court with any kind of compelling interest test in any area. Such a test leaves too much to judicial discretion and manipulation. The neutrality rule of *Smith*, by contrast, seeks to minimize the courts' role in policing religious accommodation. That orientation, I think, is continuous with an effort to curb taxpayer standing. One way or the other, you end up with less judicial "superintendence," as Kmiec rightly puts it.

Kmiec himself admits that the free exercise clause cannot be a license to disturb the public order. But what is wrong in most of the litigated accommodation cases is our absurd notion of public order, not the neutrality rule of

Smith. The true threat to public order is not a few dope-smoking Indians; it is the war on drugs and especially the Bush Justice Department. In the middle of what is supposed to be a war against global terror, the federal government spends its resources on tracking down gravely ill pot-smokers in Santa Clara County. *Gonzales v. Raich* (2005), the appalling Supreme Court case that arose over those facts, illustrates the problems that arise long before religion enters the picture.

Religion did enter the picture in the *O Centro* decision, briefly discussed by Kmiec. A handful of Indians consumed drug-laced tea as part of their religious ceremonies. How the federal government tracked them down I have no idea. The Justice Department then argued that the Religious Freedom Restoration Act—the statutory equivalent of the compelling interest test Kmiec defends as a constitutional matter—did not require an accommodation in this case. It had its head handed to it on a platter in a Tenth Circuit opinion by Judge McConnell. There is only one plausible explanation for the department's subsequent decision to drum the case into the Supreme Court: fanaticism. Happily and predictably, the justices followed Judge McConnell's road map and rejected the government's over-the-top position.

When one confronts an overbearing government and its demagogic policies, one is always tempted to plead for exemptions—for religion, the afflicted, small business, whatever. On balance, however, I think the better way is to go the other route—learn to live with Justice Scalia's free exercise clause, argue over the wisdom and consequences of religious exemption statutes in the political arena, and perhaps even rethink our sometimes extravagant notions of public order.

Neutrality strikes me as preferable to a demanding, constitutional compelling-interest test, especially in light of the threat of radical Islam. Sooner or later, we will have public school teachers in head scarves and *burkas*. What will we do? Religious accommodation of the Amish, Seventh Day Adventists, and practitioners of marginal Indian religions is one thing. By and large, these religions understand that accommodation is a two-way bargain, which demands from the accommodated a respect not simply for public order but for the institutions and traditions of a liberal society. Militant Islam utterly lacks that respect. It is thus far more likely to press the point, and entirely unlikely to observe the bargain.

Even under a mere neutrality norm, we will have great trouble explaining that a teacher's head veil is destructive of public school governance in a way that a small crucifix is not. I do not worry about our ability to draw neutral distinctions in these situations. I do worry that our distinctions will have little purchase with the ACLU, let alone the affected communities. A constitutional accommodation mandate would infinitely exacerbate our problems.

Notes

1. Taxpayer standing has since been limited, albeit not as sharply as I (and, I assume, Doug Kmiec) would prefer. See *Hein v. Freedom From Religion Foundation*, 127 S.Ct. 2553 (2007).

2. "Our Establishment Clause jurisprudence on holiday displays . . . has come to 'requir[e] scrutiny more commonly associated with interior decorators than with the judiciary.'" *Lee v. Weisman*, 505 U.S. 577, 636 (1992) (Scalia, J. dissenting) (quoting *American Jewish Congress v. Chicago*, 827 F. 2d 120, 129) (7th Cir. 1987) (Easterbrook, J. dissenting).

3. See the opinions in *Lee v. Weisman*.

11

Commentary

Kevin J. "Seamus" Hasson

Douglas Kmiec focuses on the verb "presuppose" in what everyone supposes is a Justice Douglas throw-away line in *Zorach v. Clauson*: that we are religious people whose Constitution presupposes a Supreme Being. I've often thought that Justice Douglas somehow got struck by lightning that day and chose precisely the perfect verb: the government doesn't decide that there's a Supreme Being, it doesn't choose to believe that there's a Supreme Being, it presupposes that there's a Supreme Being who was there before it was, and that is momentous for a number of reasons.

I think Kmiec is right to suggest a role for the language of the Declaration of Independence in shaping our understanding of the Constitution. It is true that the Constitution does not mention God explicitly, but it is not true that it is therefore a radical break with the Declaration. The Constitution is written in an environment that presupposes the state constitutions, and presupposes that the state constitutions are the places where religion will be worked out. You can see that in the juxtaposition of the oaths clause and the no religious test clause in the original and amended Sixth Article. The oaths clause was an accommodation for Quakers, and allowed one to declare one's fealty to the United States by affirmation as well as by oath. The very next clause says, "But no religious test shall ever be required for any office or trust into these United States."

So the oaths clause applies to both federal and state officials. The no religious test clause applies only to federal officials. Why would that be? It would be because eleven of the original thirteen states had religious tests for public office, and wanted to keep them. That juxtaposition shows the context of the state constitutions in which the federal Constitution is written.

In effect, the preamble obliquely refers to God when it talks about securing the blessings of liberty. Blessings don't appear by metaphysical spontaneous combustion. In the eighteenth century, blessings were known—more than they are today—to come from a blesser.

If it is true, and I believe it is, that our institutions do presuppose a Supreme Being, then how coercive is it to require our citizens to recite that presupposition in, for example, the Pledge of Allegiance? Is it coercive to require that the pledge be recited, and allow an opt-out only for somebody who objects, or is it so coercive that the Pledge of Allegiance itself must not be recited?

That's the case that the Ninth Circuit is now dealing with and that will, I think, make its way to the Supreme Court. If, in fact, it is not coercive to allow only an opt-out, then is it also not coercive to allow only an opt-out for the Romper Room prayer that the Supreme Court struck down forty years ago? "God is great, God is good, let us thank him for our food." That prayer was struck down in such a way that not only did the individual child who objected—or whose parents objected—not have to recite it, but nobody else could recite it in the child's presence. If that prayer is coercive then why isn't the Pledge of Allegiance coercive? Correspondingly, if the Pledge of Allegiance isn't that coercive, then why should the Romper Room prayer be that coercive?

Finally, I want to reflect upon the equal protection note that Kmiec struck near the end. I wonder if a way to present this point in the court of public opinion, and to litigate it in court, might be to compare race and ethnicity with religion. It could be argued, that is, that we celebrate race and ethnicity and cultural origins in America in ways that we have the common sense to know are not harmful. Why is it that when it comes to doing the parallel thing with religion, we panic?

So, for example, race and ethnicity, under the Fourteenth Amendment's due process clause, and the equal protection component of the Fifth Amendment's due process clause, require the same sort of standard for compelling state interest as the establishment clause requires for government distinctions based on religion. Nevertheless, March 17 passes in peace every year, and the same people who sue to stop nativity scenes don't try to block St. Patrick's Day parades. Aren't these parades an ethnic power grab? February passes in peace without Anglo-Americans trying to block African

American History Month. Isn't that a racist power grab? Everyone knows it's simply a cultural expression of ethnicity. Why should it be that nativity scenes are harbingers of St. Bartholomew's Day when African American History Month and St. Patrick's Day are not the foretaste of ethnic cleansing?

We know better. We should know better across the board and be able to see that celebrations of religion and ethnicity are comparable, and comparably harmless. And as a strictly legal matter, pushing the establishment clause in the direction of the equal protection clause would give us the opportunity to examine the ways in which the government distinguishes among believers. I wonder if this might add a strategic and tactical element to Kmiec's otherwise excellent analysis.

PART V

Religion and Art

12

The Vocation of Art

Roger Kimball

After one has abandoned a belief in god, poetry is that essence
which takes its place as life's redemption.
> — Wallace Stevens, "Adagia"

Beauty is the battlefield where God and the devil war for the soul
of man.
> — Fyodor Dostoyevsky, *The Brothers Karamazov*

Today we live in a world where the symbolic life . . . is progres-
sively eliminated—the technician is master. In a manner of
speaking the priest and the artist are already in the catacombs,
but separate catacombs—for the technician divides to rule. No
integrated, widespread, religious art, properly so-called, can be
looked for outside enormous changes in the character and orientation and nature of our civilization . . .
> — David Jones, "Religion and the Muses"

Sometimes the simplest questions are the hardest to answer. Take the question, "Why do we care so much about art?" *That* we care is graven in the
stones of our museums, theaters, and concert halls, embossed on the pages
of novels and volumes of poetry, enshrined in the deference—financial,
social, spiritual—that the institutions of art command in our society. But
why? Art satisfies no practical need; it is not useful in the sense in which a
law court or a hospital, a farm or a machinist's shop, is useful. And yet we
invest art and the institutions that represent it with enormous privilege and
prestige. Why? Why is something apparently useless accorded such honor?

179

One reason, of course, is that utility is not our only criterion of value. We care about many things that are not in any normal sense useful. Indeed, for many of the things we care about most, the question of use seems peculiarly out of place, a kind of existential category mistake. But we still can ask: What is it about art, about aesthetic experience, that recommends itself so powerfully to our regard?

A lot of ink has been spilled trying to answer that question.[1] The word "aesthetics" was not coined (and the discipline it names was not born) until the middle of the eighteenth century, but a fascination with beauty is perennial. Beauty, wrote the philosopher Jacques Maritain, would "like to believe that paradise is not lost. It has the savor of the terrestrial paradise, because it restores, for a moment, the peace and the simultaneous delight of the intellect and the senses."[2] From Plato on down, philosophers and artists—and philosopher-artists—have eulogized beauty as providing intimations of spiritual wholeness and lost unity.

This is one reason that, of all branches of philosophy, aesthetics tends to be the most oleaginous. Especially in times when traditional religious commitments are in retreat, many people look to art for spiritual dividends previously sought elsewhere. This burdens art, and intellectual talk about art, with intoxicating expectations. The expectations are consistently disappointed, but the intoxication remains. The result is the hothouse rhetoric of Romanticism, full of infinite longings, sublime impatience, impetuous raids on an ever-retreating, capital-A Absolute.

One problem with this tendency to invest art with unanchored religious sentiment is that it makes it difficult to keep art's native satisfactions in focus. The difficulty is compounded because aesthetic delight involves a feeling of wholeness that is easy to mistake for religious exaltation. Art *does* offer balm for the spirit, but it is not a religious balm. Exactly what sort of balm is it? Therein lies a tale . . .

Aesthetic Judgment and Beauty

"Tantalizing" is not a word most people associate with the work of Immanuel Kant. But the first half of his *Critique of Judgement*, which deals with the nature of aesthetic judgment, is full of tantalizing observations about the nature of aesthetic experience. Kant saw that the appeal of aesthetic experience was strikingly different from the appeal of sensory pleasure, on the one hand, and the satisfaction we take in the good, moral, or practical, on the other.

For one thing, with both sensory pleasure and the good, our satisfaction is inextricably bound up with *interest*, which is to say with the existence of whatever it is that is causing the pleasure. When we are hungry, a virtual dinner will not do: we want the meat and potatoes. It is the same with the good: a virtual morality is not moral.

Things are different with aesthetic pleasure. There is something peculiarly *disengaged* about aesthetic pleasure. When it comes to our moral and sensory life, we are constantly reminded that we are creatures of lack: we are hungry and wish to eat, we see the good and know that we fall short. But when we judge something to be beautiful, Kant says, the pleasure we take in that judgment is ideally an "entirely disinterested satisfaction."[3]

The great oddity about aesthetic judgment is that it provides satisfaction without the penalty exacted by desire. This accounts both for its power and for its limitation. The power comes from the feeling of wholeness and integrity that a disinterested satisfaction involves. Pleasure without desire is pleasure unburdened by lack. The limitation comes from the fact that, unburdened by lack, aesthetic pleasure is also unmoored from reality. Precisely because it is disinterested, there is something deeply subjective about aesthetic pleasure: what we enjoy is not an object but our state of mind. Kant spoke in this context of "the free play of the imagination and the understanding"—it is "free" because it is unconstrained by interest or desire.[4]

It is a curious fact that in his reflections on the nature of aesthetic judgment Kant is only incidentally interested in art. The examples of "pure beauty" he provides are notoriously trivial: sea shells, wallpaper, musical fantasies, architectural ornamentation. But Kant was not attempting to provide lessons in art appreciation. He was attempting to explain the mechanics of taste. It is not surprising that the *Critique of Judgement* became an important theoretical document for those interested in abstract art: in Kant's view, the purest beauty was also the most formal, the most abstract.

There is, however, another side to Kant's discussion of beauty. This has to do with the moral dimension of aesthetic judgment. If the pleasure we take in the beautiful is subjective, Kant argued, it is nonetheless not subjective in the same way that sensory pleasure is subjective. You like your steak well done, I like mine rare: that is a mere subjective preference. But when it comes to the beautiful, Kant observes, we expect broad agreement. And this is because we have faith that the operation of taste—that "free play of the imagination and understanding"—provides a common ground of judgment. We cannot *prove* that a given object is beautiful, because the point at issue is not the object but the state of mind it occasions. Nevertheless, Kant says, "We woo the agreement of everyone else, because we have for it a ground that is common to all."[5] Which is to say that if judgments about the beautiful are in one sense subjective, in another sense they are universal because they exhibit our common humanity. The feeling of freedom and wholeness that aesthetic experience imparts is thus not *merely* private but reminds us of our vocation as moral beings. In this context, Kant famously spoke of beauty as being "the symbol of morality" because in aesthetic pleasure "the mind is made conscious of a certain ennoblement and elevation."[6]

Art without Beauty

But wait a moment: "Ennoblement"? "Elevation"? What are we talking about here? It is worth pausing to consider the tremendous irony that attends our culture's continuing investment in art—emotional, financial, and social investment—given the oppositional and "transgressive" character of much of the contemporary art world. We continue to behave as if art were something special, something important, something spiritually refreshing. But when we canvas the roster of "name" artists today, what do we find?

Well, doubtless we find a great many things. But it is striking how much of what we find exists in the febrile bubble of "cutting-edge" notoriety. It is a curious situation. Traditionally, the goal or end of fine art was to make beautiful objects. Beauty itself came with a lot of Platonic and Christian metaphysical baggage, some of it indifferent or even, *nota bene*, positively hostile to art. But art without beauty was, if not exactly a contradiction in terms, at least a description of *failed art*. How different things are today!

But if large precincts of the art world have jettisoned the traditional link between art and beauty, they have done nothing to disown the social prerogatives of art. Indeed, we suffer today from a peculiar form of moral anesthesia: an anesthesia based on the delusion that by calling something "art" we thereby purchase for it a blanket exemption from moral criticism—as if being art automatically rendered all moral considerations beside the point.

George Orwell gave classic expression to this point in "Benefit of Clergy: Some Notes on Salvador Dalí." Acknowledging the deficiency of the philistine response to Dalí's work—categorical rejection along with denial that Dalí possessed any talent whatever—Orwell goes on to note that the response of the cultural elites was just as impoverished. Essentially, the elite response to Dalí was the response of *l'art pour l'art*, of extreme aestheticism. "The artist," Orwell writes,

> is to be exempt from the moral laws that are binding on ordinary people. Just pronounce the magic word "Art," and everything is O.K. Rotting corpses with snails crawling over them are O.K.; kicking little girls in the head is O.K.; even a film like *L'Age d'Or* [which shows among other things detailed shots of a woman defecating] is O.K.[7]

A juror in the obscenity trial in Cincinnati over Robert Mapplethorpe's notorious photographs of the S&M homosexual underworld memorably summed up the paralyzed attitude Orwell described. Acknowledging that he did not like Mapplethorpe's rebarbative photographs, the juror nonetheless concluded that "if people say it's art, then I have to go along with it."[8]

"If people say it's art, then I have to go along with it." It is worth pausing to digest that comment. It is also worth confronting it with a question: Why do so many people feel that if something is regarded as art, they "have to go along with it," no matter how offensive it might be? Part of the answer has to do with the confusion of art with "free speech."[9] Another part of the answer has to do with the evolution and what we might call the institutionalization of the avant-garde and its posture of defiance.

You know the drill: black-tie dinners at major museums, *tout le monde* in attendance, celebrating the latest art-world freak: maybe it's the Chapman brothers with their pubescent female mannequins festooned with erect penises; maybe it's Mike Kelley with his mutilated dolls, or Jeff Koons with his pornographic sculptures depicting him and his now-former wife having sex, or Cindy Sherman with her narcissistic feminism, or Jenny Holzer with her political slogans. The list is endless. And so is the tedium. Today in the art world, anything goes but almost nothing happens. As with any collusion of snobbery and artistic nullity, such spectacles have their amusing aspects, as Tom Wolfe, for example, has brilliantly shown. In the end, though, the aftermath of the avant-garde has been the opposite of amusing. It has been a cultural disaster. For one thing, by universalizing the spirit of opposition, it has threatened to transform the practice of art into a purely negative enterprise. In large precincts of the art world today, art is oppositional or it is nothing. Celebrity replaces aesthetic achievement as the goal of art.[10]

It is a situation that tempts one to sympathize with Leo Tolstoy's views on art. In a famous passage of *What is Art?*, Tolstoy wrote, "Art, in our society, has been so perverted that not only has bad art come to be considered good, but even the very perception of what art really is has been lost."[11] Poor Tolstoy. He thought things were bad in the 1890s. What if he were around today? Imagine him strolling through the Chelsea galleries in New York or taking in the latest offerings at Tate Modern. Matthew Barney. Damien Hirst. The Chapman brothers. Tracey Emin. What a menagerie! Tolstoy would not, I suspect, have thought much of Andy Warhol as an artist, but he would have admired his candor. "Art," Warhol observed in 1987, "is what you can get away with."[12] Too true, Andy, too true!

Consider, to take just one example, the case of Damien Hirst, who in the prevailing scale of awfulness clocks in at about 50 percent, not nearly as disgusting as some but still reliably repellent. Hirst made his reputation exhibiting stuffed or bisected animal carcasses preserved in formaldehyde. One of his earliest triumphs was a stuffed shark, which he presented to the public under the title "The Physical Impossibility of Death in the Mind of Someone Living." Hirst did not capture the shark. He did not kill it, or stuff it, or make the glass container in which it floats. But he did come up with the pretentious title, which in the present circumstances was enough to spark his ascent to art stardom.

In his most recent collection of essays, the British satirist Craig Brown quotes from an interview with Mr. Hirst:

Interviewer: "What is art?"
Damien Hirst: "It's a fucking poor excuse for life, innit, eh?! Art-schmart, God-schmod, Jesus-schmeesus. I have proved it

to myself that art is about life and the art world's about money. And I'm the only one who fucking knows that."
Interviewer: "What is good art?"
Hirst: "Great art is when you just walk round the corner and go, 'Fucking hell! What's that!'"[13]

"What's that?" indeed. A few years ago the BBC reported on a terrible mishap at the Eyestorm Gallery in London: "A cleaner at a London gallery cleared away an installation by artist Damien Hirst having mistaken it for rubbish. Emmanuel Asare came across a pile of beer bottles, coffee cups and overflowing ashtrays and cleared them away."[14] I remember thinking at the time that Mr. Asare's bold act of art criticism qualified him for a senior post at a major London paper. As far as I know, however, no paper took the initiative. Meanwhile, Mr. Asare's good work has been undone, since the gallery owners—spurred, possibly, by the "six-figure-sum" that Hirst's work was expected to fetch—instantly set about putting his opus back together. Thank goodness they had "records of how it had looked."

There are two things to bear in mind about Damien Hirst. The first is that his work is not a freakish exception in the contemporary art world but is, on the contrary, wholly typical of what is adulated as important art today. The second point is that this sort of thing, far from being novel, has been around for the better part of a century. In 1914, Marcel Duchamp dusted off a commercial bottle rack and offered it, tongue firmly in cheek, to the public as art. The public (at least the taste-making part of it) swooned with delighted outrage. In 1917, Duchamp upped the ante. He scrawled the name "R. Mutt" on a urinal, baptized it "Fountain," and said (in effect) "How about it?" What a delicious scandal ensured! How original! How innovative! But also how destructive of the essential protocols and metabolism of art.

But not, it soon became clear, as destructive as Duchamp had wished. "I threw the bottle rack and the urinal into their faces as a challenge," Duchamp noted contemptuously some years later, "and now they admire them for their aesthetic beauty."[15] Duchamp had wished not to extend but to short-circuit, to destroy, the whole category of art and aesthetic delectation. Instead, his antics polluted and trivialized it. These days, a great premium is placed on novelty in the art world. If something can't be heralded as "new," it is out of the running in the celebrity sweepstakes of contemporary art. But here's the irony: almost everything championed as innovative in contemporary art is essentially a tired repetition of gestures inaugurated by Duchamp and his immediate successors. Damien Hirst? Been there. Tracy Emin? Done that. Jeff Koons, Barbara Kruger? Ditto, ditto. As the sage of Ecclesiastes put it, there is nothing new under the sun.

The Dangers of Beauty

It is worth pointing out, however, that not all the news from the world of art (which is not quite the same thing as the art world) is bad. There is plenty of vigorous, appealing, accomplished art being produced today. It just tends not to be the art you see paraded about at the Chelsea galleries or the Whitney. It's not the sort of thing you find celebrated in the pages of *The New York Times* or featured in the trendier precincts of the art world. The serious art of today tends to be a quiet affair. It takes place not at Tate Modern or the Museum of Modern Art, not in the Chelsea or TriBeCa galleries, but off to one side, out of the limelight.

But this would have done nothing to cheer Tolstoy. Indeed, even though it is easy to concur with his judgment that art in our society has been "perverted," his own view of "what art really is" must give us pause. Tolstoy was very strict about the feelings he thought it proper for art to convey. In his view, the "upper classes" of his own society, "as a result of unbelief," favored art that was "reduced to the conveying of the feelings of vanity, the tedium of living, and, above all, sexual lust."[16] Art was for Tolstoy "a spiritual organ of human life,"[17] which sounds plenty reassuring. But his conception of what counts as legitimately "spiritual" is so narrow that it excludes not only the Damien Hirsts of the world but also most of the world's great artists. Of the literature of his own time, for example, he seems to have approved some simple folk tales and fables about peasants but little else. Anything that traded in mystery or symbolism he abominated. Baudelaire ("crude egotism erected into a theory") does not pass muster, nor does Verlaine ("flabby licentiousness") or Mallarmé ("devoid of meaning").[18]

This is not the place for a full inventory of the odd opinions expressed in *What is Art?*—the contention, for example, that in the future, artists will be so devoted to their work that they "will not even understand how it is possible for an artist, whose joy consists in the widest dissemination of his works, to give these works only in exchange for a certain payment."[19] But it is worth pausing to consider the breathtaking extent of Tolstoy's bill of indictment. Beethoven's Opus 101 is "only an unsuccessful attempt at art" while the Ninth Symphony "without any doubt" belongs to the category of bad art. Dante fails to make the grade, and so does Kipling. Tolstoy tells us about how he sat through a production of *Hamlet* and shudders at the recollection of "that special suffering produced by false simulacra of artistic works."[20] In a remarkable passage that repeats Plato's strictures on art in *The Republic*, Tolstoy writes:

> If the question were put as to which would be better for our Christian world, to lose all that is now regarded as art, including *all* that is good in it, together with false art, or to continue to encourage or allow the art that exists now, I think that any reasonable and moral person would again decide the question the way it was decided by Plato for his republic and by all Church Christian and Muhammadan teachers of mankind—that is, he would say: "Better that there be no art than that the depraved art, or simulacrum of it, which exists now should continue."[21]

"Fortunately," he adds, we do not have to ask that question. Nevertheless, Tolstoy's allegiance is clear. For him, art is either a handmaiden to a certain species of moral pedagogy or it is corrupt.

As Richard Pevear notes, Tolstoy regarded the categories "poet" and "sinner" as "mutually exclusive." "He wanted to purify art of all non-good feelings, all false and enslaving mysteries, all that is ambiguous, irrational, antinomic."[22] Tolstoy describes the task facing the art of the future as "enormous." "Preposterous" might be closer to the mark. "Genuine art," he says, will be "guided by religion with the help of science" to "make it so that men's peaceful life together, which is now maintained by external measures—courts, police, charitable institutions, workplace inspections, and so on—should be achieved by the free and joyous activity of men. Art should eliminate violence."[23] And why not rickets, the trade deficit, and world poverty into the bargain?

The problem—one problem—with Tolstoy's animadversion is that he threatens to throw out the proverbial baby with the bathwater. And yet it is worth reminding ourselves that Tolstoy's wary attitude about art is far from exceptional. We tend to place a metaphysical plus sign in front of art, linking it with religion as a beneficent expression of human creativity. But the traditional attitude toward art and beauty has been characterized as much by suspicion as by celebration. There has been a recurrent worry that the attractions of beauty will lead us to forsake *the* good for the sake of *a* good. "The eyes delight in beautiful shapes of different sorts and bright and attractive colors," writes Augustine in a typical passage, warning against the temptations of visual pleasure. "I would not have these things take possession of my soul. Let God possess it, he who made them all. He made them all *very good*, but it is he who is my Good, not they."[24]

Like beauty, art also causes uneasiness. The Platonic-Christian tradition, investing beauty with ontological significance, looks to beauty for a revelation of the unity and proportion of what really is. In this sense, our apprehension of beauty betokens a recognition of and submission to a reality that transcends us. But the alliance between art and illusion also mobilizes beauty, enlisting it in its charming fabrications. As Jacques Maritain put it, art establishes "a world apart, closed, limited, absolute," an *autonomous* world that, at least for a moment, relieves man of the "ennui of living and willing."[25] And while this is certainly not true of all art, it is easy to see Maritain's point. Instead of directing our attention beyond sensible beauty toward its supersensible source, art works to fascinate us with beauty's apparently self-sufficient presence, even drawing, if necessary, on the prestige of its association with the supersensible to strengthen its effect. It counterfeits being in lieu of revealing it. Considered thus, as an end in itself, apart from God or being, beauty appears first of all as a usurper, furnishing not a *foretaste* of beatitude but a humanly contrived substitute. From this point of view, as Iris Murdoch explains in her book about Plato, "art is dangerous chiefly because it apes the spiritual and subtly disguises and trivializes it."[26] This helps explain why Western thinking about art and beauty has tended to oscillate between adulation and deep suspicion. It marks a tension that finds dramatic expression in Mitya Karamazov's lament that beauty is the battlefield where God and the devil contend with each other for the heart of man.[27]

The tension goes deep. When deploring the terrible state of the art world today—Tolstoy's word "perverted" is not too strong—we often look back to the Renaissance as a golden age when art and religion were in harmony and all was right with the world. But for many traditional thinkers, the Renaissance was the start of the trouble. Thus Maritain, claiming that "with the sixteenth century the lie installed itself into painting," charges that "the Renaissance was to drive the artist mad, and to make of him the most miserable of men . . . by revealing to him his own peculiar grandeur, and by letting loose on him the wild beast Beauty which Faith had kept enchanted and led after it, docile."[28]

If Maritain is right, already with the shattering of the Medieval cosmos and the flowering of Renaissance humanism, "prodigal Art aspired to become the ultimate end of man, his Bread and Wine, the consubstantial mirror of beatific Beauty."[29] We can begin to give substance to Maritain's claim by considering how the rivalry between art and religion reveals itself in the usurpation of Christian categories by art. Three motifs come immediately into view: The image of the artist as a second god and, correspondingly, the apotheosis of human creativity; the idea of the artwork as constituting a second world, an alternative to God's creation; and the exploitation of aesthetic experience as a surrogate redemption or beatitude.[30]

The Artist as God?

In itself, the analogy between the artist and God, drawing on the orthodox account of man as *imago Dei*, is quite traditional and needn't suggest rivalry or usurpation. Thus Thomas naturally has recourse to the figure of the artist and the idea of artistic creativity in his explanation of God's creativity: "God's knowledge is the cause of things. For God's knowledge is to all creatures what the artist's (*artifex*) knowledge is to things made by his art. Now the artist's knowledge is the cause of things made by his art."[31] But, again, if artistic fabrication is analogous to divine creativity and justifies our speaking of the artist as a "creator," then it is equally important to remember what separates divine from human creativity. Because (as Thomas writes) "to create is to make something from nothing," creativity "can be the proper action of God alone."[32] God creates; man *recreates* by shaping the created.

But already in Plato the image of the artist, that "truly clever and wonderful being,"[33] is attended by an aura of illegitimacy and pridefulness. In forging (I use the word advisedly) replicas of all that exists, "including himself, and thereto the earth and heaven and the gods, and all things in heaven and in Hades under the earth," the artist, in Plato's view, in effect puts himself in the place of the gods, or even above the gods, since they now become his creations. For Plato, the artist's activity is best understood as a kind of ontological legerdemain in which the mere *appearance* of things is substituted for the reality. Thus Socrates' celebrated analysis of artistry as an elaborate play with mirrors in the *Republic*. And so it is that Plato repeatedly implies a link between artistry and wizardry or magic, describing the artist, for example, as an enchanter or conjurer or *sophiste*, an adept or diviner of sorts who, like the ordinary sophist with whom he shares the name, seduces the unwary from reality or truth "by means of words that cheat the ear, exhibiting images of all things in a shadow play of discourse."[34]

Granted, a moment's reflection may lead one to wonder whether there isn't a bit of mirror-play in Plato's easy comparison of art with mirror-play. For one thing, it is by no means clear that the process of imitation (an intentional activity) is identical with the phenomenon of reflection (an optical effect). Nor, as Hamlet's rather different use of the analogy between art and a mirror suggests, is it clear that mirror images need be understood as purveying simply the bare reproduction of some antecedently available datum. If art "holds the mirror up to nature," as the prince says, it serves first and foremost to reveal something that otherwise remains hidden.

Still, Plato's comparison is telling, especially if we direct our attention away from the narrowly epistemological issues that impinge on the concept of mimesis toward the larger question of the meaning of art for life. ("It is no ordinary matter we are discussing," Socrates tells Glaucon in Book 1 of *The Republic*, "but the right conduct of life.") Behind Plato's criticism of art for being akin to mirror-play is a criticism of the artist's ambition to circumvent reality with his enchanting but insubstantial constructions.

This connection becomes even more explicit in Alberti's discussion of the origin and value of painting. According to Alberti, painting—understood essentially as the skillful fixing of images seen as if reflected in a mirror—contains a "divine force" that lets one forget the passing of time and can make the absent seem present, the dead alive.[35] Thus the accomplished artist "sets himself up almost as a god," feels himself to be "another god." In this context, it is not without interest that Alberti credits Narcissus with the invention of painting. As Alphonso Procacinni notes à propos Alberti, "This mirror relationship—artist—art—is what constitutes the self-contained and autonomous value of the new art theory. The narcissistic pattern is clearly and consciously inherent in the strategy."[36]

"The story of Narcissus," Alberti tells us, "is most to the point," for "what else can you call painting but a similar embracing with art of what is presented on the surface of the water in the fountain?" Just as Narcissus, having turned away from the world and from Echo's love, sought to embrace the glittering, inaccessible image projected on the pond, so the painter, turning away from the immediately given, seeks to embrace the measured image with which he reconstructs the visible world. Painting for Alberti does not so much reveal as remake reality. It represents man's triumph over otherness in the construction of a world that, resisting the indifferent voracity of time, gives its creator a sense of godlike sovereignty.

How seriously should we take this rhetoric that figures the artist as a second god? No doubt it is in part hyperbole. But, like most hyperbole, talk of the artist as a second god is exorbitant language striving to express an exorbitant claim. Here, the claim originates in man's burgeoning consciousness of himself as a free and creative being. As the philosopher Hans Blumenberg observed, "the discovery of the capacity for creativity is part of the self-articulation of modern consciousness, however much it may have been connected with the formulas (used initially with a pious intent) of the *alter deus* and *deus in terris* [second god, earthly god], which had served at first as hyperbolical paraphrases of the biblical idea that God made man in his own image."[37]

We have to wait for Romanticism and the flowering of the cult of genius for the completion of this discovery. But the apotheosis of artistic creativity begins long before the nineteenth century. Already with the rise of fixed-point perspective, which Alberti's *On Painting* (published in Latin in 1435, in Italian in 1436) first systematized and made generally available, the artist enters into a new consciousness of his freedom and creativity. Space is geometrized, reconstructed according to a matrix provided by the subject. "The discovery of one-point or central perspective in the first quarter of the fifteenth century," Procacinni notes, "offers a fascinating model for the formulation of an aesthetic theory whose very identity insists on committing what from an Augustinian perspective would be termed an idolatrous act of pointing back to itself and seeking self-justification."[38]

Though he repeatedly claims to take his distinctions "from nature," Alberti in fact presents us with a view of art in which nature is systematically subordinated to the demands of the human spirit.[39] As Erwin Panofsky pointed out, the achievement of fixed-point perspective marked not only the elevation of art to a science (the prospect of which so enthused Renaissance artists) but also "an objectification of the subjective," a subjection of the visible world to the rule of mathematics.[40]

Again, Panofsky is on target when he notes that

> this strange fascination which perspective had for the Renaissance mind cannot be accounted for exclusively by a craving for verisimilitude. . . . There was a curious inward correspondence between perspective and what may be called the general mental attitude of the Renaissance: the process of projecting an object on a plane in such a way that the resulting image is determined by the distance and location of a "point of view" symbolized, as it were, the *Weltanschauung* of a period which had inserted an historical distance—quite comparable to the perspective one— between itself and the classical past, and had assigned to the mind of man a place "in the center of the universe" just as perspective assigned to the eye a place in the center of its graphic representation.[41]

In this sense, the perfection of one-point perspective betokens not only the mastery of a particular artistic technique but implies also a new attitude toward the world. Increasingly, nature is transformed from a book in which man's destiny is figuratively writ to material for the artist's and technician's play.

The Artist and the Demonic

As the widespread passion for tricks of perspective and optical illusions during the Renaissance suggests, imitation in an important sense begins to take precedence over reality. "The technique," observes Procacinni, "is to invent a fiction that claims to be nonfiction."[42] Here, too, the common association of the artist with the magician or thaumaturge is noteworthy.[43] To quote from Panofsky once more, perspective, "transforming *reality* into *appearance*, seems to reduce the divine to a mere content of human consciousness."[44] More than ever, art becomes a self-conscious play with illusion, a deliberate deception, a game. Embracing perspective, man embraces illusion. To demand truth in the face of such illusion is to question the legitimacy not only of perspectival rendering but of the entire spiritual milieu that gave birth to it.

Consider Protagoras: The subjectivistic tenor of the modern age that so vexed Maritain ("with the sixteenth century the lie installed itself into painting") is strikingly crystallized in the figure of the ancient sophist who had had the singular distinction of drawing the sharp criticism of both Plato and Aristotle.[45] It is perhaps not fortuitous that Protagoras should enjoy something of a renaissance in the Renaissance in the hands of writers like Alberti and Nicholas of Cusa.[46] Not only does his rehabilitation—which amounts to an assertion of the reduction of ontology to anthropology—suggest something of the deep historical and conceptual connections between the discovery of modern science and the (characteristically modern) formulation of fixed-point perspective in the arts,[47] but Protagoras also furnished us with what is surely the most stunningly appropriate motto for the ambitions of the modern age: "Man is the measure of all things."

The closer one moves toward the present time, the more blatant and unabashed is the association of the artist with God. Thus Alexander Baumgarten compares the poet to a god and likens his creation to "a world": "Hence by analogy whatever is evident to the philosophers regarding the real world, the same ought to be thought of a poem."[48]

And Shaftesbury, whose enormous influence on eighteenth-century aesthetics does not seem widely appreciated today, asserts that in the employment of his imagination the artist becomes "a second god, a just Prometheus under Jove."[49] The good Earl speaks of a "*just* Prometheus," ignoring the oxymoron. But the facts (if not the implications) of the statement are recognized by Ernst Cassirer in his gloss on Shaftesbury's paean: "the difference between man and God disappears," he writes, "when we consider man not simply with respect to his original immanent forming powers, not as something created, but as a creator. . . . Here man's real Promethean nature comes to light."[50]

"Man's real Promethean nature": if the artist in the modern age emerges as a "second god," his lordship, based on an assertion of human autonomy, tends to shut itself off from reality in order to clear a space for art's ensorcelling fabrications. As such, the artist tends to draw close to the demonic, which Kierkegaard astutely defines as freedom "shutting itself up" apart from the good.[51] ("Myself am Hell," Milton's Satan declares in a moment of startling self-insight.)[52] If, as Valéry put it, "the artist's whole business is to make something out of nothing,"[53] then, unable to meet this demand, he will find himself wandering alone among the shadows cast by the world he forsook in order to salvage his freedom and creativity. Divinization gives way to demonization.[54] The impulse behind this development has its roots in the demand for freedom in a world where freedom is increasingly eclipsed. Hugo Friedrich's assessment of modern poetry can stand as a more general diagnosis. "Poetry," he writes,

> is haunted by the suffering from lack of freedom in an age domi-
> nated by planning, clocks, collective constraint, an age in which
> the "second industrial revolution" has reduced man to a mini-
> mum. He has been dethroned by his own machines, the prod-
> ucts of his own power. The theory of cosmic explosion and the
> reckoning with billions of light-years have depreciated him to an
> insignificant accident.[55]

Such threats to man's freedom beget an "excessive passion for freedom" that turns against the strictures of reality in order to salvage some remnant of transcendence, even (especially?) an empty transcendence. Here one recalls the observation of Dostoyevsky's "underground man" that if reason should manage to calculate everything in advance so that no mystery remained, man would seek refuge for freedom in madness. Friedrich refers to this movement as "the dialectic of modernity" and argues that though "the relationship of twentieth-century poetry to the world is many-faceted, yet the result is always the same: a devaluation of the real world." For almost by definition, empirical reality, since it inevitably stands in the way of the unfettered expression of man's freedom, is experienced as the inadequate, the insufficient.[56]

The notion that beauty "has the savor of the terrestrial paradise" is one way of expressing beauty's power to deliver man from the strictures of time and empirical reality. As such, it implies an analogy between beauty and beatitude. An analogy operates by positing an element of similarity between things that in other important respects are dissimilar. In order to grasp the analogy *as* an analogy, we must do justice both to what joins and what distinguishes the terms of the analogy. The element of difference is thus no less essential in preserving the analogy than the element of similarity is in establishing it. Understood as a foretaste of beatitude, beauty maintains its status as analogue by affirming its place in an integrated ontological order. As the radiance *of* being, beauty subordinates itself to what it reveals; the genitive here expresses something like a hierarchy, a rank-order. But emancipated from that order, beauty threatens to displace the totality it once illumined, conjuring in its stead a rival order of its own. As the "difference" that an analogy depends on dissolves, the prime analogate becomes phantom-like, inaccessible. "Paradise," "being," "beatitude," "God"—to what extent does our culture (never mind one's own theological commitments) still in good faith entertain such terms as more than rootless similitudes? And if the place they have traditionally occupied has become empty, is it surprising that aesthetic experience with its power to arrest and enrapture should step in to fill the vacancy?

We do not need Nietzsche to tell us that the disintegration of the Platonic-Christian world view, begun already in the late Middle Ages with nominalistic and voluntaristic speculations on the infinity and omnipotence of the Christian God,[57] is today a cultural given. Nor is it news that the shape of modernity—a shape that emerged in large part out of man's faith in the power of human reason and technology to remake the world in his own image—has made it increasingly difficult to hold on to the analogy between beauty and beatitude in any but a disconcertingly analogous way. Again, the traditional view ties beauty to being and truth, investing it with ontological significance. But modernity, the beneficiary of Descartes' relocation of truth to the subject (*Cogito, ergo sum*), implies the *autonomy* of the aesthetic sphere and hence the isolation of beauty from being or truth. For to the extent that human reason is made the measure of reality, beauty forfeits its ontological claim and becomes merely *aesthetic*, that is to say, merely a matter of *feeling*.[58]

Art and the Transcendent

I mention all this because I believe there is an important difference between asking whether great art can be created "absent a belief in the transcendent power of truth, beauty, and goodness" (this is the phrase used by organizers of the conference out of which this volume grew) and asking about the chances of "a renewed religious seriousness within the fine arts." At the end of his book *Human Accomplishment*, Charles Murray argues that "religion is indispensable in igniting great accomplishment in the arts."[59] Murray goes on to note that he is using the term "religion" at once loosely and stringently:

> Going to church every Sunday is not the definition I have in mind, nor even a theology in its traditional sense. Confucianism and classical Greek thought were both essentially secular, and look at the cultures they produced. But both schools of thought were tantamount to religion in that they articulated a human place in the cosmos, laid out a clear understanding of the end—the good—toward which humans aim, and exalted standards of human behavior. And that brings me to the sense in which I use *religion* stringently. Confucianism and Aristotelianism, along with the great religions of the world, are for grownups, requiring mature contemplation of truth, beauty, and the good. Cultures in which the creative elites are not engaged in that kind of mature contemplation don't produce great art.[60]

I have a good deal of sympathy with the intention behind Murray's argument. But my first response to his contention that "religion is indispensable in igniting great accomplishment in the arts" might be summed up by that Saul Steinberg cartoon in which a smallish "yes" is jetting along toward a large "BUT." Murray has done a lot to insulate his argument: by "religion" he doesn't mean church-going or even theology. He is right that classical Greece, though essentially secular (I might say "pagan," but close enough), was a cultural powerhouse: it was "religious" insofar as it devoted serious attention to contemplating "truth, beauty, and the good."

But I wonder. In one sense, Murray seems to be arguing that in order to have serious art you have to take art seriously (hence the bit about "truth, beauty, and the good"). Listing toward tautology, perhaps, but fair enough. The question is whether a culture in which elites engage in "mature contemplation" of "truth, beauty, and the good" is necessarily *religious* in any but an honorific sense. Like Cardinal Newman, I believe that about a great many things to think correctly is to think like Aristotle. Aristotle certainly devoted serious attention to truth, beauty, and the good, but was he or the culture which he advocated religious? I am not so sure.

Noting that our own culture is aggressively secular—the names Darwin, Marx, Freud, and Einstein stand as beacons in humanity's progressive self-disillusionment—Murray suggests that that disillusionment is itself "ephemeral," merely a stage in mankind's spiritual maturation. "It may well be," he observes, "that the period from the Enlightenment through the Twentieth Century will eventually be seen as a kind of adolescence of the species."[61] Who can say? Kant thought that maturity came with the Enlightenment. Enlightenment betokened man's coming of age, his "leaving his self-caused immaturity," where by "immaturity" Kant meant the "incapacity to use one's intelligence without the guidance of another." The primary lack that forestalled Enlightenment was therefore not intellectual but moral: it was, Kant thought, a lack of courage to face up to the way the world really is.[62]

There is plenty to criticize about the Enlightenment (just as, let us remind ourselves, there is plenty to celebrate about it), but my point is merely to question whether the symbiotic relation between great art and religion is as close as Murray suggests. Fra Angelico, a deeply religious painter, was a great artist, but then so was Titian, a conspicuously worldly one. Bach was a pious soul and was possibly the greatest composer who ever lived; but what about Beethoven? If he was religious, he was so in a way different from Bach. Jane Austen was conventionally religious in her personal life, but her novels, although great, are specimens of secular wit and wisdom. Art and religion are both *eulogistic* words: calling something a work of art endows it with a nimbus of value; the same is true of "religious." But is it the same sort of value?

The Catholic Welsh poet David Jones had it right, I believe, when he suggested that "no integrated, widespread, religious art, properly so-called, can be looked for outside enormous changes in the character and orientation and nature of our civilization"[63]—changes, I think, that would be deeply at odds with our commitment to liberal democracy.

Jones agrees that it would be nice if "the best of man's creative powers" were "at the direct service of the sanctuary." But that can happen only "if the epoch itself is characterised by those qualities." "This cannot," Jones argues, "be said of our epoch." It is not, he goes on to note, a matter of will: what is possible to the artist in the way of creating religious art "has little or nothing to do with the will or wishes of this or that artist." Be a painter ever so pious, still "he cannot change himself into an artist of some other culture-sequence."[64] Some things were possible in the Middle Ages which are not realistically possible today.

The real threat to the arts, Jones thought, was the modern world's increasing submission to "technocracy," to a thoroughly instrumental view of life that had no room for what Jones called the "intransitive": that realm of freedom and disinterestedness that were traditionally the province of religious experience, on the one hand, and art and aesthetic experience on the other.

The disjunction is crucial. The priest and the artist, he says, might both be consigned to the catacombs, but they are *separate* catacombs. Art aims at the perfection of a work; religion aims at the perfection of the soul. At bottom, Jones argued, there can no more be a Catholic art than there is "a Catholic science of hydraulics, a Catholic vascular system, or a Catholic equilateral triangle."[65] W. H. Auden made a similar point when he wrote that "there can no more be a 'Christian' art than there can be a Christian science or a Christian diet. There can only be a Christian spirit in which an artist, a scientist, works or does not work."[66]

We live at a time when art is enlisted in all manner of extra-artistic projects, from gender politics to the grim linguistic leftism of neo-Marxists, poststructuralists, gender theorists, and all the other exotic fauna who are congregating in and about the art world and the academy. The subjugation of art—and of cultural life generally—to political ends has been one of the great spiritual tragedies of our age. Among much else, it has made it increasingly difficult to appreciate art on its own terms, as affording its own kinds of insights and satisfactions. This situation has made it imperative for critics who care about art to champion its distinctively aesthetic qualities against attempts to reduce art to a species of propaganda.

At the same time we lose something important when our conception of art does not have room for a spiritual dimension. If *this* is what Murray meant when he suggested that "religion [or at least serious attention to the ends of human life] is indispensable in igniting great accomplishment in the arts,"[67] I would agree. That is to say, if politicizing the aesthetic poses a serious threat to the integrity of art, the isolation of the aesthetic from other dimensions of life represents a different sort of threat. The principle of "art for art's sake," T. S. Eliot observed, is "still valid in so far as it can be taken as an exhortation to the artist to stick to his job; it never was and never can be valid for the spectator, reader, or auditor."[68] The Austrian critic Hans Sedlmayr articulated this point eloquently in the 1950s. The fact is, Sedlmayr wrote,

> that art cannot be assessed by a measure that is purely artistic and nothing else. Indeed such a purely artistic measure, which ignored the human element, the element which alone gives art its justification, would actually not be an artistic measure at all. It would merely be an aesthetic one, and actually the application of purely aesthetic standards is one of the peculiarly inhuman features of the age, for it proclaims by implication the autonomy of the work of art, an autonomy that has no regard to men—the principle of *l'art pour art*.[69]

By the nineteenth century, art had long been free from serving the ideological needs of religion; and yet the spiritual crisis of the age tended to invest art with ever greater existential burdens—burdens that continue, in various ways, to be felt down to this day, as witness Wallace Stevens's contention that "after one has abandoned a belief in God, poetry is that essence which takes its place as life's redemption."[70]

The idea that poetry—that art generally—should serve as a source—perhaps the primary source—of spiritual sustenance in a secular age is a Romantic notion that continues to resonate powerfully. It helps to explain, for example, the special aura that attaches to art and artists, even now—even, that is, at a time when poseurs like Andres Serrano and Bruce Nauman and Gilbert & George are accounted artists by persons one might otherwise have had reason to think were serious people. This Romantic inheritance has also figured, with various permutations, in much avant-garde culture. We have come a long way since Dostoyevsky could declare that, "incredible as it may seem, the day will come when man will quarrel more fiercely about art than about God."[71] Whether that trek has described a journey of progress is perhaps an open question. My own feeling is that Eliot was right when he disparaged the efforts of moral aesthetes like Matthew Arnold and Walter Pater to find in art a substitute for religion, "to preserve emotions without the beliefs with which their history has been involved."

> Nothing in this world or the next is a substitute for anything else; and if you find you must do without something, such as religious faith or philosophic belief, then you must just do without it. I can persuade myself . . . that some of the things that I can hope to get are better worth having than some of the things I cannot get; or I may hope to alter myself so as to want different things; but I cannot persuade myself that it is the same desires that are satisfied, or that I have in effect the same thing under a different name.[72]

This much, I think, is clear: without an allegiance to beauty, art degenerates into a caricature of itself; it is beauty that animates aesthetic experience, making it so seductive; but aesthetic experience itself degenerates into a kind of fetish or idol if it is held up as an end in itself, untested by the rest of life.

In the context of a discussion about religion and the American future, it seems to me that there are as many opportunities for confusion as for enlightenment in linking the ambitions of art and religion. There is much to bemoan about the state of art and culture today. Above all, perhaps, there is a lack of seriousness underwritten by a lack of traditional skill. But in this sense, the emancipation of art from religion is less an impediment than an opportunity. As Auden noted in his reflections on Christianity and art, "We cannot have any liberty without license to abuse it. The secularization of art enables the really gifted artist to develop his talents to the full; it also permits those with little or no talent to produce vast quantities of phony or vulgar trash."[73] The triumph of the latter does nothing to impeach the promise and the achievements of the former. In my Jesuit high school, the priests were wont to dispense various wise sayings, one of which occurred to me when pondering this paper: "Never deny, seldom affirm, always distinguish." Let us leave to one side the question of whether the direction "never deny" is good advice and settle instead on the admonition "always distinguish." Man is the sort of creature whose nature it is to delight in art and aesthetic experience; man may also be by nature (I believe he is) a religious animal, that is to say a creature who becomes who he really is only when acknowledging something that transcends him. These different aspects of humanity will often conspire, but we do them both a disservice if we blur or elide their essential difference. I think of Apelles's advice to the cobbler who began by criticizing the way the great painter delineated a sandal and then went on to criticize other aspects of the painting: *Ne supra crepidam sutor judicaret*, which is Latin for (near enough) "always distinguish."

Notes

1. I draw in this section on some previous writings, in particular "Schiller's 'Education,'" in my book *Lives of the Mind: The Use and Abuse of Intelligence from Hegel to Wodehouse* (Chicago: Ivan R. Dee, 2002), 101–18.

2. Jacques Maritain, *Art and Scholasticism and the Frontiers of Poetry*, trans. Joseph Evans (Notre Dame: University of Notre Dame Press, 1974), 24.

3. Immanuel Kant, *Critique of Judgement*, trans. J. H. Bernard (New York: Hafner, 1972), 5.

4. Ibid., 9.

5. Ibid.,19. Bernard translates this as "We ask for the agreement of everyone else." But Kant writes, more suggestively, "Man wirbt um jedes anderen Beistimmung." The element of rhetorical suasion is key: taste is a suitor of acquiescence, of agreement.

6. Ibid., 59, 42.

7. George Orwell, "Benefit of Clergy: Some Notes on Salvador Dalí," in *The Collected Essays, Journalism and Letters of George Orwell*, vol. 3, *As I Please 1943–1945* (New York: Harcourt, Brace and World, 1968), 160.

8. Quoted in Jonathan Yardley, "Worrisome Picture: Cincinnati Case Shows How Expert Handling Can Beat 'Obscene' Art," *Washington Post,* October 17, 1990, 31.

9. More precisely, it has to do with the confusion of art with a debased idea of free speech that supposes any limits on expression are inimical to freedom. Moral and aesthetic objections cannot always be answered simply by appealing to the First Amendment. The issue was strikingly articulated in the 1920s by John Fletcher Moulton, a British judge, when he observed that "there is a widespread tendency to regard the fact that [one] can do a thing as meaning [one] may do it. There can be no more fatal error than this. Between 'can do' and 'may do' ought to exist the whole realm which recognizes the sway of duty, fairness, sympathy, taste, and all the other things that make life beautiful and society possible." One of the most destructive aspects of our culture has been the evisceration of that middle ground of "duty, fairness, sympathy, taste," etc.— everything that Lord Moulton congregated under the memorable category of "obedience to the unenforceable." ("Law and Manners," *The Atlantic Monthly,* July 1924, 3, 2).

10. See "The Trivialization of Outrage" in my book *Experiments Against Reality: The Fate of Culture in the Postmodern Age* (Chicago: Ivan R. Dee, 2000), 277–304.

11. Leo Tolstoy, *What is Art?*, trans. Richard Pevear and Larissa Volokhonsky (New York: Penguin Books, 1995), chap. 15.

12. Quoted in Jacques Barzun, *From Dawn to Decadence: 500 Years of Western Cultural Life; From 1500 to the Present* (New York: HarperCollins, 2000), 791.

13. Quoted in Damien Hirst and Gordon Burn, "On the Way to Work," in Craig Brown, *The Tony Years* (London: Ebury Press, 2006), 228

14. BBC News, October 19, 2001, http://news.bbc.co.uk/2/hi/entertainment/1608322.stm.

15. Duchamp in Hans Richter, *Dada: Art and Anti-Art* (New York: McGraw-Hill, 1965), 207–8.

16. Tolstoy, *What is Art?* chap. 10.

17. Ibid., chap. 18.

18. Ibid., chap. 20.

19. Ibid., chap. 14.

20. Ibid.

21. Ibid., chap. 17.

22. Richard Pevear, preface to Tolstoy, *What is Art?*.

23. Tolstoy, *What is Art?* chap. 20.

24. Augustine, *Confessions* 10: 34.

25. Maritain, *Art and Scholasticism*, 9.

26. Iris Murdoch, *The Fire and The Sun: Why Plato Banished the Artists* (New York: Oxford University Press, 1977), 65.

27. Fyodor Dostoevsky, *The Brothers Karamazov*, bk. 3, chap. 3.

28. Maritain, *Art and Scholasticism*, 52, 22.

29. Ibid., 36.

30. The rhetoric as well as the intention of all three would seem to support Augustine's claim (*Confessions* 2: 6) that "all those who desert you and set themselves up against you merely copy you in a perverse way." At the same time, though, it is worth observing that the analogy works both ways, thus raising the question of priority. For example, if the artist is figured as a second god, so God is often figured as a kind of artist or craftsman. One thinks, for example, of Plato's Demiurge (*demiourgos* first of all means simply "craftsman"). See also the appendix "God as Maker" in E. R. Curtius's *European Literature and the Latin Middle Ages* (Princeton: Princeton University Press, 1973), 544–46. Curtius writes: "To elucidate the topos *Deus artifex* completely we must go behind it to the myths of the ancient world. There in both East and West, we find numerous concurring accounts according to which the creation of the world and man goes back to the handiwork of God—a god who appears now as weaver, now as needleworker, now as potter, and now as smith," (545).

31. Thomas Aquinas, *Summa Theologicae*, 1, art. 14, ad. 8.

32. Ibid., 1, art. 45, ads. 1, 5. See also M. H. Abrams's discussion in *The Mirror and the Lamp: Romantic Theory and the Classical Tradition* (New York: Oxford University Press, 1981), especially 273ff.

33. Plato, *Republic*, 596.

34. Plato, *Sophist*, 234c. Compare *Symposium*, 203d, where *eros* is described as being "an adept in sorcery, enchantment, and seduction."

35. For this and the following quotations from Alberti, see *On Painting*, trans. John Spencer (New Haven: Yale University Press, 1976), 63–7.

36. Alphonso Procacinni, "Alberti and the 'Framing' of Perspective" *Journal of Aesthetics and Art Criticism* (Fall 1981): 36. I am indebted for this discussion of the

importance of perspective to Karsten Harries's *Infinity and Perspective* (Cambridge, MA: MIT Press, 2001), especially 64–77.

37. Hans Blumenberg, *The Legitimacy of the Modern Age*, trans. Robert M. Wallace (Cambridge, MA: MIT Press, 1983), 109.

38. Procacinni, "Alberti and the 'Framing' of Perspective," 31. For a careful historical overview of the development of perspective in the Italian Renaissance, see John White, *The Birth and Rebirth of Pictorial Space* (London: Faber & Faber, 1972).

39. Thus Anthony Blunt, in *Artistic Theory in Italy: 1450–1600* (New York: Oxford University Press, 1978), refers to the "*weapons* of perspective and anatomy" that Renaissance naturalism enlisted in its conquest of the visible world" (1, my emphasis).

40. Erwin Panofsky, "Perspective as Symbolic Form" (photocopy, Columbia University Libraries, New York, 194?), 15. "This achievement in perspective," Panofsky writes, "is only a concrete expression of what had been put forward at the same time on the part of epistemology and natural philosophy. In the same years during which the space of Giotto and Duccio . . . was overthrown by the gradual formation of central perspective . . . abstract thought definitely and publicly completed the break . . . with Aristotle's view of the world by giving up the idea of a cosmos built around the midpoint of the earth as around an absolute center and closed by the outermost sphere of the heavens as by an absolute limit and by developing the notion of an infinity not only prefigured in God but also actually realized in empirical reality" (14–15). Panofsky made cognate observations elsewhere, e.g., in "Albrecht Dürer and Classical Antiquity," reprinted in *Meaning in the Visual Arts* (New York: Doubleday, 1955), see especially 278ff. On Renaissance art's ambition to be a science, see Rudolf Wittkower, *Architectural Principles in the Age of Humanism* (New York: Norton, 1971), 29 and 101:"The conviction that architecture is a science . . . may be called the basic axiom of Renaissance architects," and Blunt's *Artistic Theory in Italy: 1450–1600*, especially chap. 1, "Alberti," 1–22.

41. Erwin Panofsky, *The Life and Art of Albrecht Dürer* (Princeton: Princeton University Press, 1955), 260–61.

42. Procacinni, "Alberti and the 'Framing' of Perspective," 37.

43. See Jurgis Baltrusaitis, *Anamorphic Art*, trans. W. J. Strachen (New York: H. N. Abrams, 1977).

44. Panofsky, "Perspective as Symbolic Form," 18.

45. See Plato, *Theaetetus,* passim, especially 157ff, and Aristotle, *Metaphysics*, 1009a ff.

46. See *On Painting*, 55, where Alberti mentions Protagoras in the context of his assertion that "all things are known by comparison," the effect of which was to deny the necessity of an absolute measure and invest man's unaided reason with the power to discern truth, and *De Beryllo*, where Cusa questions Aristotle's criticism of Protagoras' dictum that "man is the measure of all things": "aristoteles dicit prothagoram in hoc nihil profundi dixisse, mihi *tamen magna valde dixisse videtur.*"

Nikolaus von Kues, *Werke*, ed. Paul Wilpert (Berlin: Walter De Gruyter, 1967), 2:734. See also *Nicholas of Cusa on Learned Ignorance* (*De Docta Ignorantia*), trans. Jasper Hopkins (Minneapolis: Banning, 1981), 50–51; and Hans Blumenberg, *Die Genesis der kopernikanischen Welt* (Frankfurt am Main: Suhrkamp, 1975), 564, and *The Legitimacy of the Modern Age*, 525ff. Unfortunately, this is a case where history has not cooperated with the dictates of historiography as fully as it might have. For, suggestive though the association of Protagoras with the Renaissance is, little substantial influence can be documented. As Charles Trinkaus argues, interest in Protagoras in the Renaissance was "small or anecdotal." ("Protagoras in the Renaissance: An Exploration," in *Philosophy and Humanism: Essays in Honor of Paul Oskar Kristeller*, ed. Edward Mahoney [New York: Columbia University Press, 1976], 212.) Besides the texts cited above, Trinkaus turns up only a handful of rather offhand references. Still—and this is the point of his article—the conceptual parallel is so striking that he can write that "even if there was no connection between [the Greek sophist movement, which Protagoras may be said to epitomize, and the Italian Renaissance], there ought to have been" (190). It has been left to modernity to fulfill this "ought" and exploit the connection between Protagoras and the Renaissance fully.

47. On which see Karsten Harries, "The Infinite Sphere: Comments on the History of a Metaphor," *Journal of the History of Philosophy* 13 (January 1975): 5–15, especially 7.

48. Alexander Baumgarten, *Reflections on Poetry*, trans. K. Aschenbrenner and W. B. Holther (Berkeley: University of California Press, 1954), 68.

49. Ernst Cassirer, *The Philosophy of the Enlightenment*, trans. Fritz Koelin and James Pettegrove (Princeton: Princeton University Press, 1979), 316; on Shaftesbury, see also 84.

50. Ibid., 316.

51. Søren Kierkegaard, *The Concept of Dread*, trans. Walter Lowrie (Princeton: Princeton University Press, 1970), 107ff. The demonic—for Kierkegaard, "dread of the good"—is freedom willing itself to be unfree by insisting on itself to the denial of its dependence on the good. See also Kierkegaard, "The Despair of Willing Despairingly to be Oneself—Defiance," in *The Sickness Unto Death*, trans. Walter Lowrie (Princeton: Princeton University Press, 1970), 200–8.

52. John Milton, *Paradise Lost*, bk. 4, line 75.

53. Quoted in Milton C. Nahm, *The Artist as Creator: An Essay of Human Freedom* (Baltimore: Johns Hopkins University Press, 1956), 4.

54. On the relation between the artist's striving for autonomy and the demonic, see Hans Sedlmayr's provocative discussion in *Art in Crisis: The Lost Center* (New Brunswick: Transaction Publishers, 2006), especially 158ff. and 173ff.

55. Hugo Friedrich, *The Structure of Modern Poetry*, trans. Joachim Neugroschel (Evanston: Northwestern University Press, 1974), 129.

56. Ibid., 156; cf. 53.

57. See Leszek Kolakowski's discussion in *Religion* (New York: Oxford University Press, 1982), 20ff. "The theory," he writes, "which made logical, mathematical, and moral laws dependent entirely on God's free and arbitrary decree was, historically speaking, an important step in getting rid of God altogether. . . . The nominalistic tendency to devolve responsibility for our logic and ethics on the Creator's arbitrary fiat marked the beginning of his separation from the universe. If there is no way in which the actual fiat can be understood in terms of God's essence, there is simply no way from creatures to God. Consequently, it doesn't matter much, in our thinking and actions, whether He exists or not" (23). See also Hans Blumenberg's *The Legitimacy of the Modern Age*, 150–79, and *Die Genesis der kopernikanischen Welt*, 555–66; and Alexander Koyré's *From the Closed World to the Infinite Universe* (Baltimore: Johns Hopkins University Press, 1974).

58. On this distinction between the "ontological" and "aesthetic" conception of beauty, and the predominance of the latter in the modern age, see Ernesto Grassi's *Die Theorie des Schönen in der Antike* (Koln: DuMont, 1962), and Karsten Harries, "Hegel on the Future of Art," *Review of Metaphysics* 27.4 (June 1974): 677–96. A representative statement of the ontological conception is Hegel's claim that "beauty is only a certain manner of expressing and representing the true"; the aesthetic conception, on the other hand, Harries writes, "stresses the autonomy of the aesthetic sphere and denies any connection between beauty and truth" (681). Following Heidegger, Harries shows how the typically modern conception of truth, heir to Descartes' insistence on the clear and distinct, understands truth on the model of conceptual transparency and thus has to exclude art—indeed, all that is marked by the sensible—from the realm of truth. "There is something about our epoch," he notes, "which makes it difficult for us to take seriously art's claim to serve the truth, viz., our tendency to tie truth to transparency" (684).

59. Charles Murray, *Human Accomplishment: The Pursuit of Excellence in the Arts and Sciences 800 B.C. to 1950* (New York: HarperCollins, 2003), 455.

60. Ibid., 456.

61. Ibid., 457.

62. Immanuel Kant, "What is Enlightenment?" in *The Philosophy of Kant*, ed. Carl J. Friedrich (New York: Modern Library, 1949), 132.

63. David Jones, "Religion and the Muses," in *Epoch and Artist: Selected Writings*, ed. Harman Grisewood (London: Faber and Faber, 1959), 103.

64. Ibid., 97.

65. Jones, "Art and Sacrament," in *Epoch and Artist,* 143.

66. W. H. Auden, "Christianity and Art," in *The Dyer's Hand and Other Essays* (New York: Random House, 1962), 458.

67. Murray, *Human Accomplishment*, 455.

68. T. S. Eliot, "Arnold and Pater," in *Selected Essays of T. S. Eliot* (New York: Harcourt, Brace & World, 1964), 392.

69. Sedlmayr, *Art in Crisis*, 218.

70. Wallace Stevens, "Adagia," in *Opus Posthumous: Poems, Plays, Prose* (New York: Alfred Knopf, 1957), 158.

71. Well, I *think* it was Dostoyevsky, but the citation eludes me.

72. T. S. Eliot, *The Use of Poetry and the Use of Criticism* (Cambridge: Harvard University Press, 1993), 106.

73. Auden, *The Dyer's Hand*, 460.

13

A Response to Roger Kimball

Charles Murray

I shall be more aggressive than Roger Kimball in making the case for a link between religion and great art. But let me begin with two large caveats. I will not argue that every great work of art has a religious element, direct or indirect. I will not argue that every great artist has been a religious person. Rather, I am going to reflect on the conclusion that I reached in the course of poring over the inventories of great art and great artists that I compiled when writing *Human Accomplishment* (a conclusion that Kimball, citing my book, himself quotes at length [p. 196]). In any given culture and era, religion is indispensable for igniting a major stream of great accomplishment in the arts.[1]

Specifically, I will expand on the idea that religiosity, in the sense of systematic and mature reflection on the great themes of life—it can be the religiosity of an Aristotle or Confucius as well as the religiosity of an Aquinas—has to be part of the milieu in which artists work if they are to produce much great art.

Great Art and Life's Purpose

The most encompassing of these great themes of life is the very meaning of life. Here, the role of religiosity involves the energy that the creative elites bring to their work. My argument is that a major stream of human accomplishment is fostered by a culture in which the most talented people believe that life has a purpose and that the function of life is to fulfill that purpose.

Why should it make any difference whether someone thinks life has a purpose? Why shouldn't people who don't think life has a purpose—let us call them *nihilists*—accomplish as much as anyone else? They *can* accomplish a lot, but if we are talking about means and distributions, nihilists as a group have a built-in disadvantage. This has to do in part with the intense and unremitting level of effort that is typically required to do great things. But it has to do also with the nature of the goals that creative people set for themselves.

One of the most overlooked aspects of excellence is the work it takes. Fame can come easily and overnight, but excellence is almost always accompanied by a crushing workload, pursued with single-minded intensity. Psychologists have put specific dimensions to this aspect of accomplishment. One thread of the literature on this subject, inaugurated in the early 1970s by Herbert Simon, argues that expertise in a subject requires a person to assimilate about fifty thousand "chunks" of information about the subject over about ten years of experience—simple expertise, not the mastery that is associated with great accomplishment.[2] Once expertise is achieved, it is followed by thousands of hours of practice, study, labor.[3] As one reviewer of the literature on creative people concluded, "Not only every sample, but every individual within each sample appears to be characterized by persistent dedication to work."[4] The accounts that he surveyed reveal not a few hours a week beyond forty, or a somewhat more focused attitude at work than the average, but levels of effort and focus that are three or four standard deviations above the mean. Whether Edison's estimate of the ratio of perspiration to inspiration (99:1) is correct is open to argument, but his words echo the anonymous poet from ancient Greece who wrote that "before the gates of excellence the high gods have placed sweat."[5]

The willingness to engage in such monomaniacal levels of effort is related to a sense of vocation. By *vocation*, I have in mind the dictionary definition of a function or station in life to which one is called by God. Again, I hedge on the necessity of a traditional belief in God, but there has to be a coherent belief in *something* that invests life with meaning, and God is by far the most readily available source of that conviction. A person with a strong sense of *this is what I have been put on earth to do* is more likely to accomplish great things than someone without it. Ennui, anomie, alienation, and other forms of belief that life is futile and purposeless are at odds with the zest and life-affirming energy needed to produce great art or great science.

Nihilists are also at a disadvantage when it comes to their choice of content. Once again, I am talking about means and distributions for which there are individual exceptions, but most of those exceptions come at the beginning of a nihilistic period. Friedrich Nietzsche wrote about the great themes of philosophy, as did Jean-Paul Sartre. They had to, because they were struggling to bring down an edifice of thinking about the great themes that they thought was wrong. But once the edifice is down, whether in philosophy, literature, art, or music, the choice of content becomes more problematic. People who see a purpose in their lives have a better chance of creating enduring work than people who don't, because the kind of project they work on *does* make a difference to them. To believe life has a purpose carries with it a predisposition to put one's talents in the service of whatever is the best—not the most lucrative, not the most glamorous, but that which represents the highest expression of the object of one's vocation.

This link is to some degree a tautology. We use the phrase *life has a purpose* only when that purpose has a transcendental element, something more important than the here and now. When someone says something like "Sure, my life has a purpose: to make as much money as I can," we recognize that as mocking the word *purpose*. To have a purpose in life is to be compelled to try to live up to that transcendental element.

Great Art and the Transcendental Goods

Just what is this transcendental element? "Platonic ideal" is a figure of speech still in use twenty-three hundred years after Plato died because the concept resonates so powerfully. We need not accept Plato's entire epistemological argument to accept his core point that the world is filled with objects imperfectly embodying ideal qualities. We know they imperfectly embody those qualities because we can envision perfection even if we never encounter it. They are transcendental in that they refer to perfect qualities that lie beyond direct, complete experience, even though they have referents in everyday experience.

In the classic Western tradition, the worth of something that exists in our world can be characterized by the three dimensions known as the true, the beautiful, and the good. The triad did not become iconic in other intellectual traditions as it did in the West, but the same three qualities have been recognized and treated as central in the great civilizations of Asia as well. I hereafter refer to the true, the beautiful, and the good as transcendental goods.[6]

The true and the beautiful are familiar phrases, even if we argue over what they mean. *The good*, however, is not a term in common use these days, so I should spell out how I am using it. The ultimate Good, capitalized when used in that sense, is a way of thinking about and naming God. But I will be focusing on the good without the capitalization, explained by Aristotle in the opening sentence of the *Nicomachean Ethics*: "Every art and every inquiry, and similarly every action and pursuit, is thought to aim at some good; and for this reason the good has rightly been declared to be that at which all things aim."[7] Aristotle was evoking the concept, common to Plato and other Greek thinkers, that every object and creature has an end and an excellence. The end of the eye is sight, and excellence in the eye consists of clear vision. The end of the pruning hook is cutting the branches of a vine, and excellence in a pruning hook consists in being better able to cut off branches than other tools not designed for that purpose.[8] For human beings, the focus of my use of *the good*, the question then becomes, what is the end of human beings and in what lies excellence in achieving that end? A specific answer is not important for understanding my use of *the good*. If a culture has a coherent, well-articulated sense of what constitutes excellence in humanness—what constitutes the ideal of human flourishing—it has a conception of the good as I am using the term.

The good in this sense is distinct from moral codes, but to hold a conception of the good is also to worry about right and wrong. The word *good* rules out certain understandings of excellence in human flourishing. To say, for example, that the end of human beings is to enslave other human beings and excellence consists of enslaving them most ruthlessly makes a mockery of language. But though a conception of the good gives rise to moral codes, it should be remembered that the essence of *the good* is not rules that one struggles to follow, but a vision of the best that humans can be that attracts and draws one onward.

My proposition is that great accomplishment in the arts is anchored in one or more of these three transcendental goods. Art and science can rise to the highest rungs of craft without them, wonderful entertainments can be produced without them, amazing intellectual gymnastics can be performed without them. But, in the same way that a goldsmith needs gold, a culture that fosters great accomplishment needs a coherent sense of the transcendental goods. *Coherent sense* means that the goods are a live presence in the culture, and that great artists and thinkers compete to come closer to the ideal that captivates them.

In discussing these issues with friends and colleagues, I have become aware that introducing words such as *true*, *beautiful*, and *good* into a discussion of historical issues is problematic. Three misconceptions seem difficult to avoid, so I will state them explicitly.

I am not using the good, true, and beautiful in a poetic sense. Their role is not just "inspiration" in the abstract, though it can be that as well. Conceptions of the good, true, and beautiful prevailing at any given time concretely affect how excellence manifests itself.

I am not using the good, the true, and the beautiful in a saccharine sense. Great paintings can portray brutality and ugliness. Great literature can depict human depravity. Truths need not be uplifting.

The effects of a culture's prevailing conceptions of transcendental goods are not limited to believers. To say that a conception of the ideal of beauty was a live presence among artists in the Italian Renaissance does not mean that every single artist spent his days thinking about what the beautiful meant, nor that all artists consciously held such a view. Rather, a culture's prevailing view provides a resource that suffuses the practice of that domain independently of the variation in beliefs among specific people.

In the arts, all three of the transcendental goods have played different roles at different times, interacting in ways that make it difficult to say which is which.

The Beautiful. It goes without saying that beauty has often been the explicit measure of excellence in art. Artists in some eras have denied that any other consideration is even relevant. Exactly what that conception of the beautiful might be is less important than that a coherent conception exists. By way of illustration, suppose you were able to talk to painters from the Tang dynasty, the Italian Renaissance, and France in the 1860s, three different eras and cultures with different conceptions of the beautiful. What links them is that they each *had* a well-articulated conception of the beautiful that the artists of the age saw themselves as trying to realize in their work independently of other considerations.

Contrast that conversation with one you would have with painters in two other eras, medieval Europe and Europe between the world wars. Two more radically different sets of painters are hard to imagine, but they would have this in common: they would both resist the idea of a well-articulated conception of the beautiful as an *independent* goal in their work. The medieval painters would not have been hostile to the concept of beauty, because they would see beauty as pleasing to God. But, for most, pleasing God and glorifying God would have been the point, not the creation of beauty in itself. Most twentieth-century artists working between the world wars would have turned the conversation to the nature of the creative act, the imperative of self-expression, and the ways in which the concept of the beautiful had become an impediment to the progress of art, not a framework for it.[9] That a work might turn out to be beautiful by classical definitions would be only fortuitous.

The True. Truth has also played an explicit role in the arts, with as many different roles for the true as there have been conceptions of the beautiful. In the visual arts, the centuries-long quest to perfect techniques for depicting people and objects was linked to the service of truth; so was the quest to capture the inner truth of a face or event, a quest that led some artists in the nineteenth century to abandon literally accurate depictions. Shakespeare attained his unique stature because of his unmatched ability to use drama to convey deep truths about human personality and the human condition. The novel was expressly seen as a vehicle for truth—in Stendahl's famous words from *Le Rouge et le Noir*, "A novel is a mirror that strolls along a highway. Now it reflects the blue of the skies, now the mud puddles underfoot."[10] In music, the role of the true in the form of compositional logic—often logic of mathematical precision—is popularly associated with the works of J. S. Bach, but has characterized serious musical composition more broadly.

The Good. The good is at least as important as the beautiful in shaping the nature of accomplishment in the visual arts and literature. Sometimes the shaping is a direct product of a moral vision, whether religious or secular. In Giotto's *The Lamentation* and Hugo's *Les Misérables*, completely different as these works are, the role of the moral vision that the artist brought to the work is palpable. The translation of the moral vision onto the canvas or into the written word is often what separates enduring art from entertainment.

Extract its moral vision, and Goya's *The Third of May, 1808* becomes a violent cartoon. Extract its moral vision, and *Huckleberry Finn* becomes *Tom Sawyer.*

But the expression of the artist's moral vision is only one way in which conceptions of the good shape the content of the arts. An artist's conception of excellence in a human life provides a kind of frame within which the varieties of the human experience are translated into art. Good art often explores the edges of the frame, revealing to us the depths to which human beings can fall as well as the heights to which they can rise. But the exploration of the edges of the frame is given structure by the nature of the frame. The depiction of violence in the absence of a conception of the good in human life is mere sensationalism; in its extreme form, a type of pornography. The depiction of violence in the presence of such a conception can be profound and clarifying; in its extreme form, a *Macbeth.*

Thus I hold that a stream of great accomplishment in the arts depends upon a culture's enjoying a well-articulated, widely held conception of the good. I suggest as well that art created in the absence of a well-articulated conception of the good is likely to be arid and ephemeral. To exclude a conception of the good from artistic creations withdraws one of the major dimensions through which great art speaks to us. For an artist to have no understanding of or commitment to the good is a handicap.

The Twentieth Century as Evidence

I close by using the twentieth century as a textbook case for the proposition that artists without a coherent belief in life's purpose and without commitment to coherent visions of the true, beautiful, and good have a hard time producing great art.

The rejection of a meaningful purpose in life was one of the hallmarks of artists in the first half of the twentieth century, exemplified by the French existentialists but part of the artistic milieu in London, New York, Berlin, and Rome as well. By the second half of the twentieth century, artists no longer devoted so much of their effort to moaning over the meaninglessness of life; it had just become part of the received wisdom. One of the chief effects was to destroy any objective basis for selecting the content of one's work. Because life is purposeless, no one kind of project could be intrinsically more important than any other kind. At the extreme, this produced capricious and trivial choices in doing one's work that represented, as Ronald Sukenick put it with regard to the plight of the novelist, "ways of maintaining a considered boredom in the face of the abyss."[11] But even short of the extreme, a broader generalization applies: without a sense of purpose, the creative personality of the twentieth century had no template that constantly forced an assessment of whether he was making the best possible use of his talents.

Turning to conceptions of the true, the beautiful, and the good in the arts, the transition began in the late 1800s and extended through World War I, when many of those who saw themselves engaged in high art consciously turned away from the idea that their function was to realize the beautiful, and then rejected the relevance of the true and the good as valid criteria for judging their work.

The change was least drastic in literature. An avant-garde—James Joyce is the exemplar—rejected the traditional conventions of narrative and tried to do for literature what contemporaries were doing in the visual arts, but a large number of the best writers continued to write novels and poetry in familiar forms that were underwritten by more or less coherent conceptions of the true and the beautiful. For writers, the main casualty of the twentieth century was a unifying conception of the good in the Aristotelian sense and of goodness in a moral sense. Exceptions existed, but the community of European and American writers from World War I to 1950 was for the most part secularized and disillusioned with Western culture. Many had substituted politics for religion as the source of their beliefs about right and wrong. With notable exceptions—Eliot, Yeats, Faulkner, Pound—they came from the left, caught up in the widespread enthusiasm among intellectuals for the young Soviet Union.

The moral vision that came with allegiance to Communist socialism lent itself to two tracks, neither of which had much to do with a transcendental conception of the good. The idealistic objectives of socialism were equality, liberation of the proletariat from grinding poverty and inhuman working conditions, and other admirable goals, but that same socialism held that man has no soul, that there is no God, and that you have to break eggs—meaning kill innocent people for social ends—if you want to make an omelet. There's only so much a writer can do with a moral vision that excludes the soul and rationalizes the slaughter of innocents. Émile Zola,

Maxim Gorky, and a few others had earlier shown that good literature is possible with that moral vision, at least until the revolutionaries actually take power, but the range of themes is restricted and the logic of ideology pushes literature toward what came to be known as socialist realism—simplistic morality tales.

The other track for the left of the 1920s and 1930s was the kind of nihilistic, situational morality that by the end of the first half of the twentieth century had become known as existentialism, fostered primarily by French intellectuals. This option consisted of an explicit denial that the classic conception of *the good* has any meaning. Human beings have no end; having no end, there is no definition of what constitutes excellence in a human life. Nihilist writers could still have their characters struggle with moral decisions, but if there's no real right or wrong out there, objective and regnant, what's the point of the struggle? Their characters could aspire to happiness, but the denial of the good means that whatever happiness they find is likely to be ephemeral. Not surprisingly, the pointlessness of life became a pervasive theme among the serious writers of this era. The portrayal of repugnant acts no longer aimed to clarify the vision of the good, but was used to deny the existence of any such thing, or, more depressingly, was inserted merely for the sake of sensationalism.

The effects of withdrawing the good from serious literature were substantial—I would enter most of the serious novels from the end of World War I onward as evidence for my earlier statement that art in the absence of a well-articulated conception of the good is likely to be arid and ephemeral. But *most* is not the same as *all*—in America, the single exception of Faulkner is of huge consequence, and other countries have their own examples.

The more drastic revolution occurred in the visual arts and music. That painters, sculptors, and composers rejected the traditional ideals that had ruled their arts during the early twentieth century is not a new or controversial proposition.[12] The artists and composers themselves said so, long and loudly. What happened was not merely one more turn in the endless cycle in which artists try to do something different from those who had gone before, but a wholesale throwing off of a legacy that had become unendurably burdensome. "The great geniuses of the past still rule over us from their graves," painter and author Wyndham Lewis lamented. "[T]hey still stalk or scurry about in the present, tripping up the living . . . a brilliant cohort of mortals determined not to die, in possession of the land."[13] And so the artists of the twentieth century did something about it. They killed off the geniuses from the past as best they could. Jacques Barzun describes their three strategies:

> One, to take the past and present and make fun of everything in it by parody, pastiche, ridicule, and desecration, to signify rejection. Two, return to the bare elements of the art and, excluding ideas and ulterior purpose, play variations on those elements simply to show their sensuous power and the pleasure afforded by bare technique. Three, remain serious but find ways to get rid of the past by destroying the very idea of art itself.[14]

Barzun's reference to "excluding ideas and ulterior purposes" is what I have in mind by eliminating transcendental goods. Sometimes, the new way of thinking was expressed bluntly and cynically. "To be able to think freely," André Gide wrote, "one must be certain that what one writes will be of no consequence," adding that "the artist is expected to appear after dinner. His function is not to provide food, but intoxication."[15] Sometimes the proponents of the new art used the old language, but in a way that involved an Orwellian redefinition of words. Here, for example, is Guillaume Apollinaire's use of the word *beauty* in an essay extolling cubism: "The modern school of painting seems to me the most audacious that has ever appeared. It has posed the question of what is beautiful in itself. It wants to visualize beauty disengaged from whatever charm man has for man."[16]

The idea that beauty can have meaning "disengaged from whatever charm man has for man" is audacious, but audacity was not in short supply among the new wave of artists in the twentieth century—nor was contempt for their audiences. Painters and composers not only discarded their role as realizers of the beautiful, they put themselves and their own needs on the loftiest of pedestals. Arnold Schoenberg, who announced the death of tonality and then did all he could to make his prediction come true, wrote that

> those who compose because they want to please others, and have audiences in mind, are not real artists. They are not the kind of men who are driven to say something whether or not

there exists one person who likes it, even if they themselves dislike it . . . They are more or less skillful entertainers who would
renounce composing if they did not find listeners.[17]

Contempt for the audience could not be plainer, nor the godlike role in which
Schoenberg placed the artist.

This is not the place to go into the reasons why visual artists and composers of the high culture became so alienated from the legacy of Western
culture and from their audiences in the early twentieth century, but merely
to note that they did. In this sense, the mainstream of the visual arts and of
concert music in the twentieth century was qualitatively different from the
mainstreams of the preceding five centuries. I say *mainstream* to acknowledge that each of the arts had a channel that was a lineal descendent of pre-
twentieth-century traditions—men such Stravinsky and Kandinsky, who
were aware of the legacy and valued it, but sought, as artists had sought
before, to use the raw materials of great art in new ways for their own time.
But they and other artists in this channel tended to come early in the twentieth century, and their numbers dwindled as time went on. The generalization remains: in large part, the literature, visual art, and concert music of the
twentieth century is what they become when their creators do not tap into
the transcendental goods.

Was any great work created in the twentieth century by our secularized
creative elites? Of course. But according to every indicator of population,
wealth, access to education, and ease of transportation and communication,
the twentieth century had a greater number of talented people available to
create great art than in any preceding century in history, by many orders of
magnitude. I submit that the legacy that will still be part of the cultural
landscape in, say, the year 2300, in the same way that hundreds of writers,
painters, and composers from earlier centuries are still part of our cultural
landscape, will be paltry. Any plausible explanation for their meager record
must take into account the role of secularization.

Notes

1. Charles Murray, *Human Accomplishment: The Pursuit of Excellence in the Arts and Sciences, 800 B.C. to 1950* (New York: HarperCollins, 2003). The text that follows is adapted from material in chapters 19, 20, and 22.

2. Herbert Simon, "Productivity Among American Psychologists: An Explanation," *American Psychologist* 9 (1972): 804–805.

3. For the role of practice, see A. Ericcson and C. Tesch-Romer, "The Role of Deliberate Practice in the Acquisition of Expert Performance," *Psychological Review* 100 (1993): 363–406.

4. See R. Ochse, *Before the Gates of Excellence: The Determinants of Creative Genius* (Cambridge: Cambridge University Press, 1990), 131, summarizing his review of the literature. For another review using other kinds of evidence, see chapter 5 in D. Simonton, *Greatness: Who Makes History and Why* (New York: Guilford Press, 1994).

5. Quoted in Ochse, *Before the Gates*, 132.

6. In metaphysics, the term *transcendentals* is rigorously defined in a way that should not be confused with my more informal use of *transcendental goods*. The tradition began with Aristotle's discussion of the nature of existence—the nature of being—and the group of properties that belong to being *qua* being. In Thomas Aquinas's elaboration, those properties are one, true, good, and beautiful. This list comes from the opening of E. Gilson, *Elements of Christian Philosophy* (New York: Doubleday & Co., 1960), 137–63, which provides an excellent discussion of transcendentals in Catholic philosophy. I am indebted to Michael Novak for drawing this issue to my attention.

7. Aristotle, *Nicomachean Ethics* 1:1094a.

8. These examples are taken from Plato's *Republic* 1: 352–53.

9. The evolution of the role of beauty from the postimpressionists such as Cézanne and Van Gogh into the more radical forms of art in the twentieth century is vividly conveyed by letters and essays written by the artists themselves, collected in H. Chipp, *Theories of Modern Art: A Source Book by Artists and Critics* (Berkeley: University of California Press, 1968).

10. Stendahl, *The Red and the Black* (New York: Modern Library Books, 1953), vii.

11. R. Sukenick, "The Death of the Novel," in *The Death of the Novel and Other Stories* (New York: Dial, 1969), 41.

12. Two excellent recent accounts of the ways in which artists and composers consciously saw themselves as overthrowing the Western tradition on a grand scale are P. Watson, *A Terrible Beauty: A History of the People and Ideas That Shaped the Western Mind* (London: Weidenfeld & Nicolson, 2000), chap. 4; and J. Barzun, *From Dawn to Decadence: 500 Years of Western Cultural Life; 1500 to the Present* (New York: HarperCollins, 2000), 713–71.

13. Quoted in Barzun, *From Dawn to Decadence*, 718.

14. Ibid.

15. Quoted in J. Maritain, *The Responsibility of the Artist* (New York: Charles Scribner's Sons, 1960), 21.

16. Apollinaire, "The Cubist Painters," in *Theories of Modern Art: A Source Book by Artists and Critics*, ed. Herschel B. Chipp (Berkeley: University of California Press, 1968), 228.

17. Quoted in Roger Scruton, "The Eclipse of Listening," in *The Future of the European Past*, ed. Hilton Kramer and Roger Kimball 55–56.

14

Commentary

Joseph Bottum

Roger Kimball's excellent discussion covered a wide variety of points of contact between art and religion. But I do think he missed several key ones.

To begin with, there is the simple fact that the star-making mechanisms in our culture are very much in the hands of the Left, of the cultural elite of the Left. That elite is extremely antireligious and thus will consistently reward those whose work is perceived as attacking religion. It takes a great deal of effort or luck for someone whose work is not hostile to religion to succeed in that environment. To the extent that the cultural Right has any artistic heroes it can call its own, it has almost always—from Saul Bellow to Rick Hart—had to poach them once they have been recognized by the star-making mechanisms of the Left. Right now, there are very few ways—maybe they are increasing, but they are still very few—in which a strong religious believer can gain a footing in art in the first place.

A second point that ought to be mentioned in this discussion is the old general-knowledge question: how much of literature are you going to understand if you do not know the Bible? I was recently looking over Auden's Harvard Phi Beta Kappa poem ("Under Which Lyre") in which he advises that we should not be friends with those "who read the Bible for its prose." But there was at one time the idea that you had to be generally educated. You had to have a certain base of knowledge, and then art could play with that knowledge for comedy and tragedy.

A perfect example is in *A Good Man is Hard to Find*. The old lady has the gun to her head and says, "Jesus. Jesus." The misfit interprets it as a prayer and replies, "Yes'm, . . . Jesus thrown everything off balance." That exact moment is played for comedy by the writer Peter De Vries, the old humor editor for the *New Yorker*, in one of his comic novels. It's *Slouching Towards Kalamazoo*, I think: A family goes off to a revival, leaving the idiot son in charge of the grandfather, who is the village atheist. He is on his deathbed, lecturing the idiot boy about the joys of atheism. A bolt of lightning strikes the oak tree outside the window, which goes up in flames. The grandfather sits up, shouts out, "Jesus Christ!" and falls back dead. The family comes home and asks the idiot boy, "What happened?" He says, "He died with our Savior's name on his lips." The ability to do that sort of thing in art, it seems to me, is something that religion makes possible.

A further point Roger Kimball's piece did not take up is hinted at by Charles Murray when he speaks of art in pursuit of truth. Art is understood to convey knowledge, and one of the reasons art occupies the high cultural position it supposedly occupies is because of a belief that there is some mystical knowledge being conveyed in it. Whether or not it is in fact conveyed by the sort of art we see now is another question. But there has long been a belief that, as Joyce Carey put it in, I believe, *The Horse's Mouth*, "All mystics have been to the same country." The claim here is that the artistic mystic and the religious mystic have been to this place, and they are bringing back some insight.

Surely in terms of the novel, that is true. We read the novel, the classic novel, to see what another life would look like. The novel, in our actual experience as readers, supports the belief that there can be in a work of art a genuine knowledge that is, if not at the level of religion, then nonetheless true and beyond normal reason. In other words, the Arnoldian substitution of art for religion is not so far-fetched.

Lee Harris

Roger Kimball notes how tantalizing Kant's third *Critique* is in its assessment of aesthetics. A key question Kant takes up, one hotly debated in his time, was whether French classicism, with its rigid set of rules that a work of art had to follow in order to be judged worthwhile, should serve as a model of judging art. Kant sought to reach some compromise on that question, and to argue that one of the essential things about art—unlike the moral law, which is definitive—is that in art you can break a rule and still produce great art. You can still create something beautiful.

Now, the tricky thing about this, and the way this finally leads to exhibitions of beer bottles and ashtrays, is that—to take music as an instance—when Haydn wrote a symphony, everyone who listened to that symphony was in on the game. Everyone knew the rules that Haydn was expected to play by. When Haydn did not exactly play by those rules, it was exciting; it was a thrilling thing. Or take Beethoven's Third Symphony. In its first performance, someone apparently stood in the middle of the first movement and said, "When will this thing end?" It was a philistine reaction, of course, but at the same time it was an informed reaction of somebody who said, "This guy is supposed to be playing by rules that I know."

Now, however, think of the man Roger Kimball quotes, who said, "If people say it's art, then I have to go along with it." This happens because today there is no sense of a set of rules that defines the boundaries of art, even if these rules are not always obeyed. A person who looks at a work of art does not really know what to expect. He does not know what rules are supposed to be there in order for it to be called a work of art.

This occurs because artists ran out of rules to break, and began to break the very notion of rules. What is called transgressive art came about as, at some point in the nineteenth century, artists who had broken all the possible aesthetic rules they could began to violate the social taboos, and increasingly to do things to show originality and to startle. What they had to do was start getting more and more insulting and offensive, and then say, let's still call it art.

This is a serious problem for art, and especially in the United States. Here, most people come from a rather plebeian background, in which art is something that we do not necessarily know about or value. Most of us have had to learn about it, not from our parents but from somebody else. So we are prone to accept the idea that art is the preserve of the educated elite, and that we really cannot pass judgment on it. We feel this just as we feel that we cannot pass judgment on a theory of science—a complicated string theory, say. We have to follow the judgment of the experts.

There is a great danger for a whole society when this happens in relation to a religion, to art, and to science. We are being led to a position where we no longer feel that we are capable of forming our own judgment on whether it is a scientific theory; whether it is a work of art or just a bunch of beer cans in the garbage. That is very bad for us, and it's very bad for American art.

Leon R. Kass

Roger Kimball's insightful argument occasions this brief comment on the relation between religion and art, beginning really with a pagan example drawn from my own experience visiting three religious sites in Greece, arranged in chronological order.

If you go to the palace at Knossos, you see that the palace is aligned with the double-humped peak of Mount Ida, sacred to the earth goddess Demeter. The hearth is inside the palace, but what is worshipped is outside.

You next come to the temple of Apollo at Delphi, and the wonderful road toward the temple winds this way and that way. If you are walking this way, you look up at big columns against the background sky and you say, "What a wonderful construction is this temple!" When the road winds the other way, the temple is dwarfed by the horns of Mount Parnassus, the top of which is in the clouds; a little spring gurgles at the bottom, and you can imagine the gods are living and speaking there.

Then you come to the Acropolis and the Temple of Athena at Athens; and what is in fact worshipped there are the Athenians and Pericles and the sculptor Phidias. The place leaves you with a sense that it is calling attention to those who produced it, rather than to those to whom it is dedicated. Art, in these instances, begins as a way to celebrate the divine but turns out to be a celebration of the celebrators.

I wonder whether the beginning of the relation between religion and art in the Christian tradition does not carry in it this same kind of danger: that what begins as an expression of reverence for something beyond us eventually turns out to be the celebration of the artist. You could think about medieval funerary monuments, whose sculptors, while purporting to instruct us about "dust to dust," erect huge statues that glorify themselves. Artists, after all, sign their paintings. Later on, they start to paint portraits of themselves, and eventually you get a theory of the artist, which is no longer expressed in terms of a muse but in terms of creativity.

Once you have come to that point, art becomes an argument for undermining the rules of its own civilization: creativity is not creative if it is bound by anything. It seems to me there is a danger, one that leads directly to this degenerate art, in the bringing of art to bear on what is to begin with subservient and celebratory. In the end, you get an artist who is for himself alone, and the more transgressive he can be, the more free and the more honored.

PART VI

The View from Europe

15

Europe without God and Europeans without Identity

Marcello Pera

Europe, unlike America, is on a collision course with its own history. Often it voices an almost visceral denial of any possible public dimension for Christian values.

—Cardinal Joseph Ratzinger,
Without Roots: The West, Relativism, Christianity, Islam[1]

Modern secularism has such affinities to moral nihilism that even those who wish simply to affirm or reaffirm moral values have little choice but to seek grounding for such values in a religious tradition.

— Irving Kristol,
Neoconservatism: The Autobiography of an Idea[2]

Europe today is trying another of those experiments against its own history that it started with the Enlightenment: that is, to build up a society without God. The old experiment attempted to replace the Judeo-Christian God of the European tradition with the "goddess of Reason," or the god of "Science," "Progress," and so on. According to the new experiment, God is to be replaced by such new different deities as "Democracy," "Liberalism," "Individual Freedom," etc. Although the goal pursued by both the new and old experiments is the same, the tools are different.

The old Enlightenment used the language of universalism: it maintained that there is only one true and universal reason, science, morality, polity, and so on. Today European culture—the "New Enlightenment"—speaks in terms of pluralism: according to it, there are, and there must be, many different cultures, traditions, lifestyles, conceptual frameworks, etc., each with its own rules, standards, criteria, and so on.

Between the two Enlightenments—the old and the new, the modern and the postmodern—lies the so-called "critique of the foundations," which has transformed the former into the latter. The core of this critique is that no universal truth claims concerning reason, reality, and human nature can ever be justified or validated, simply because they are about metaphysical entities that can never be grasped. Therefore, all such claims have to be replaced by their much more modest empirical or pragmatic or historical counterparts. To avoid the recurring illusions and the frequent mistakes of those philosophers who still persist in speaking the old metaphysical language, and to educate the people who might continue to use it, the postmodern Enlightenment provides a philosophically correct manual of translation that gives the old concepts their proper meanings in "Newspeak." Browsing through it, one finds that yesterday's traditional, familiar notions are upside down today: truth is rendered as "enforced consensus," objectivity as "solidarity," scientific theories as "paradigms," facts as "conceptual or social constructs," moral norms as "habits," and so on. It is no wonder that, in the field of human conduct, "the 'real' is what plays an important role in the kind of life one wants to live."[3]

In this way, the old essentialism and absolutism have been updated and turned into relativism and localism. But the goal pursued by the new experiment is exactly the same, because the idea underlying it has not changed: God is dead, anyway. For there can be no place for God whether religion is to be confined "within the boundaries of mere reason" or is to be treated as just a language game left to those who still wish to play it. And the outcome of the new experiment, too, is the same as the old: a tension between religion and politics, a conflict between state and church, a gap between what tradition says and what the Newspeak states, an alienating effect on people's life. Put simply, a spiritual and moral crisis.[4]

Unfortunately, history is a bad teacher: it never lets people sufficiently understand the harmful consequences they are doomed to face when they try to deny or forget it. For today's Europe, totalitarianism, paganism, nihilism, as well as many other "enlightened" ideas or institutions or regimes, never existed, or, if they did, they were just undesirable and unpredictable consequences of a perfect design, if not costs to be paid. The fact that sometimes dreams turn into nightmares is not contemplated or is repressed; if it comes back—by chance, or because the calendar reminds Europeans about some terrible dates in their history—a few canonical ceremonies for the memory, rhetorical speeches for the massacres, and ritual dry tears for the victims are considered to be enough to avoid repeating the past and setting one's conscience to rest. In spite of everything, the temptation of the European experiment—transferring Heaven to Earth—is still so deep and strong, and any antidote to it apparently so meager, that Europeans continue to capitulate to it. No matter if generations upon generations of sons continue to lament— if they do—the crimes, that is to say the broken dreams, of their fathers.

An incredible contradiction is playing out in Europe today. On the one hand, while genuflecting in the many memorial cemeteries scattered across their lands, Europeans—in particular European intellectuals—reflect on the perversity of the Enlightenment experiment of dropping God out of their lives; on the other hand, while preaching from academic chairs, political pulpits, the popular media, and scholarly books, they continue to spread the idea of the splendor of the godless society. Due to this contradiction, Europe is becoming schizophrenic, and this is why it is lacking an identity: not because it could not have one, but because it deliberately wants to get rid of the one it used to have.

What I will present here stems from this sad analysis and these dark feelings. In a nutshell, my view is that European societies and nations are not merging, and the European Union—let alone the United States of Europe—is not growing because it *cannot*. It lacks, because it rejects it, that sort of cement—a creed, a faith, a trust, a religion—thanks to which groups of inhabitants become a single people and a single nation. To support this view, I shall introduce and maintain three theses.

First, the unification of Europe as contemplated in the now dead-and-buried European Constitution, is based on a conceptual and political paradox; second, the European paradox stems from the secularization of European states and societies; and third, European secularization is connected to the relativism that dominates European culture. As these theses may be taken as premises of one single argument, my conclusion is that since relativism weakens the state and corrodes society, today not only the European Constitution as a juridical document and the European Union as a political body are at risk, but so, too, is Europe itself as the oldest pillar of Western civilization. My view is that a return to the Judeo-Christian tradition, to be lived by believers as a new mission, and by nonbelievers as a civil custom, could be a good antidote to the crisis in Europe—provided it is not too late already, of course.

The European Paradox

Those whose intent was the unification of Europe were forced to make necessity the mother of their invention. The need derived from the fact that following first *economic* unification (the 1992 Maastricht Treaty and the 1997 Amsterdam Treaty) and then *monetary* unification (the 1988 introduction of the Euro), a step forward towards *political* unification had to be taken. This was done through the Charter of Rights (Nice 2000) and especially through the European Constitution (Rome 2004). Since the Charter of Rights was incorporated in the Constitution as its second part, I will refer to this text as the European Charter or simply the Charter. And since both the body charged to draft the Charter of Rights and the body that drafted the Constitution liked to call themselves the "Convention"—clearly after the name of the most famous American Convention—I will call their members the European Fathers or simply the Fathers.

It is easy to see the dramatic problem the Fathers were facing. A European *demos* does not exist, because in Europe there are as many peoples and nations as there are member states; a European *ethnos* does not exist either, because the history of Europe is one of ethnic mixing; nor does a single European *ethos* exist, because each nation, in spite of its many similarities and affinities to the others, has its own specific history, culture, tradition. As far as a European *telos*, things are even worse, because in the absence of a single unified people or nation, the very self-perception that feeds the idea of one's own identity or mission or goal cannot see the light and grow. Given this situation, how can a European charter be drafted? And how can it give form to a European patriotism, without which no charter can live and become the flesh of a single European society?

Since the necessity was pressing and the invention attractive, the Fathers made two moves. They decided to bypass the *real* and to look towards an *ideal*. For them the reality to avoid was precisely that of the particular, specific histories, cultures, and traditions of the European countries, which over the centuries had given rise to nationalisms, conflicts, and wars. The ideal to look to in order to avoid this past was identified in a set of fundamental values called collectively "the European area of justice," "the European common space of human rights," and so forth. As the Charter states in listing them all, "The Union is founded on the values of respect for human dignity, freedom, democracy, equality, the rule of law and respect for human rights, including the rights of persons belonging to minorities."[5]

By writing down the fundamental values and the fundamental human rights stemming from them—a sort of new Tablets from which Europe should draw inspiration and to which it should pay homage—the Fathers appeared to have achieved several objectives at the same time: unify the peoples of Europe under the same principles; make them all part of a single political community; replace the old and recent forms of nationalism with a new kind of patriotism, which jurists, political scientists, and philosophers, notably Jürgen Habermas, had already labeled "constitutional patriotism";[6] realize the Kantian dream of a republic made up of political and moral actors; and guarantee the other Kantian idea of a "perpetual peace." After years of hard work, necessity seemed to have finally and happily given birth to the desired invention.

Historically, the dream of political unification of Europe lasted until the French and Dutch referendums (May 29, 2005, and June 1, 2005, respectively). But conceptually, the whole enterprise was doomed to failure from the onset. The fact is that in the process, *too much* was invented. Fundamental human rights have a nature: by definition they are rights that belong to each and all without regard to individual histories or geographical location. In the same vein, Kantian ideas have a logic: in a Kantian republic there can be no limits to individual citizenship and state membership. If this logic and this nature are to be applied to the European political body then several consequences follow: first, the European Charter is *cosmopolitan*, because the fundamental human rights refer to each and every human being; second, European citizenship is *universal*, because those very rights cannot have any geographical boundary; third, European identity is *juridical*, because it stems from, and is forged by, the adhesion to the Charter and does not preexist it.

This was decidedly too much even for the most optimistic of the Fathers. While necessity called them to draft a *European* Charter, namely for Europeans, their invention produced a *universal* Charter, namely applicable to all rational and moral beings. And this raises a paradox, which we may call the European paradox. It says: Europeans give themselves a Charter but the Charter does not identify Europeans. In other words, the European identity is not specifically European. In yet other terms, Europeans are not Europeans, namely citizens of the *historical European world*, but rather cosmopolitan, namely citizens of an *abstract juridical cosmos*. This is my first thesis.

The European Design

In order to set out my second thesis—that the paradox of the European Charter is the result of the secularization of Europe—we have to take a deeper look at the kind of validation argument that was and still is generally used to support the Charter. I believe that it is a typical case of constructivism. The unification of Europe that has been pursued is a kind of political cold fusion; that is, a mere juxtaposition of different and diverging histories without the right fuel to ignite them.

As I have said, to draft the Charter the European Fathers deliberately chose not to look at the history of Europe and its present situation, but to a theory of Europe and its future goals, or to a European design and its intrinsic merits. Moreover, the Fathers held that this theory should be validated not through recognized and shared *pre*-political events or *pre*-juridical values, stemming from specific histories, particular narratives, emblematic episodes, fundamental traditions of the European peoples, but in terms of the goodness of the goal that the theory or the design is aimed to achieve. To put it differently, the validation argument provided for the European Charter runs like this: since the European design is beautiful, then the ensuing Charter of Europe is good; since the former is appealing, then the latter is feasible; since the one is promising then the other is worth following; and so on. It is true that the reality of European history creates resistance and obstacles, but the ideal of European unification has such strength that it overcomes every objection. To support the validation argument and the whole design, a special optimistic European rhetoric was devised. Ironically enough,

in a world full of skeptics, only "Euro-skepticism" was condemned and criticized as impiety.

Habermas is the European intellectual and philosopher who more than
any other has defended this validation argument and the protective rhetoric
of the Charter. According to him, European constitutional patriotism stemming from a European constitution "can take the place originally occupied
by nationalism," and, as long as such patriotism grows, "it is to be expected
that the political institutions that would be created by a European constitution would have a catalytic effect."[7]

But this puts the cart before the horse (and the European Charter before
the European peoples), because the sense of belonging to a single political
body—which is necessary for a constitution to be recognized and lived and
not just written on paper—should come first, not last; before, not after. If
the Charter has to be the identity card of Europeans, their identity must *preexist* the issue of the document. Reversing the order is precisely a case of
constructivism, no matter how "enlightened": it is like hiding or wiping out
history, replacing it with a *tabula rasa*, and filling the gap with a tailor-made,
fully developed new course of action.

It is not difficult to understand what happened. Disgusted for many
good reasons by the European past, the intellectuals of constitutional patriotism, like their forerunners of the Enlightenment who were disgusted by
the old regimes, decided to ignore the real peoples and to look to ideal citizens. Devising a sort of new Declaration of the Rights of Man, two centuries after the first, was the only move they had once the specific histories,
peculiarities, and needs of the European peoples came to be considered
obstacles to knock out. It is precisely this constructivism that makes
the political unification of Europe a political cold fusion experiment. No
wonder the members of the Convention were not elected but nominated,
and that the European Charter failed as soon as it was put to the electoral
test. The fact is that the whole process of European unification lacks genuine democratic legitimization, and the resulting product—the Charter—
is weak. This is because neither of them has solid foundations. Both the
European design and the allegiance to the European Charter which constitutional patriotism is assumed to produce are too thin and too light to
give rise to a real European patriotism and an effective unification of the
European peoples. What is needed is not some other nice element to

introduce *into* the Charter, but a far thicker and heavier base to be found *outside* the Charter.[8]

A series of questions sheds light on where we have to look. Who are the bearers of those human rights the European Charter refers to? Individuals. Why do individuals have rights? Because they are citizens of a political and moral community. Why are some of these rights fundamental and inalienable? Because they are an integral part of human dignity. Where does this concept of human dignity come from? Our tradition. What tradition?

Surprisingly, when it comes to this question, which is the core of the whole enterprise, the Charter remains silent. Although the preamble states that "the Union is founded on the values of respect for human dignity," it refuses to take the next step and admit that the *Judeo-Christian tradition* is the main tradition in Europe, as elsewhere in the West, that supports the inalienable rights of the individual. It just says that Europe is "conscious of its spiritual and moral heritage" (Preamble to Part II), or that Europe has a "cultural, religious and humanist inheritance" (General Preamble). How did it come to happen that the drafters of the Charter made use of such trivial and misleading formulas? The answer is that their "enlightened" firm will to reject any external *pre*-political foundation induced them to disregard Christianity.

Habermas is again a case in point. In a debate with then-cardinal Joseph Ratzinger, he maintained that "systems of law can be legitimated only in a *self-referential* manner, that is, on the basis of legal procedures born of democratic procedures," and defended the view, inspired by Kant, that "the basic principles of the constitution have an *autonomous* justification and that all the citizens can *rationally* accept the claim this justification makes."[9] He then concluded that "the constitution of the liberal state can satisfy its own need for legitimacy in a *self-sufficient* manner, that is, on the basis of the cognitive elements of a stock of arguments that are *independent* of religious and metaphysical traditions."[10] But if the European Charter is to be self-sufficient and its validation independent of European traditions, then the European Charter disregards European history.[11] And this amounts to saying that Europe disregards itself. Why? Because—and here is my second thesis—European secularism has deprived Europe of its roots and has therefore rendered it just a vague, generic community of disembodied rights.

European Secularism

Secularism can be taken in two main senses: the separation of religion from politics and therefore the separation of church and state; or the implementation of public policies in terms of profane criteria alone. Although both senses draw a distinction between the public sphere and the private sphere, they do so in a different spirit and with different consequences. According to the first sense, the public sphere is an open space in which all religions are called on to play a role while the state remains neutral; according to the second, the public sphere is a closed space into which no religion is allowed entry because the state has its own view.[12]

Another distinction arises from the first. Secularism in the first sense makes it possible for religious beliefs to orient political decisions, and to give them fodder. Secularism in the second sense explicitly excludes the orientation of politics by religion. Needless to say, the first sense is American and typically liberal, because it derives from the English Enlightenment, while the second is French and typically Jacobin, because it derives from the French Revolution. The transformation of the first into the second marks the passage from secularism as an institutional regime to *secularism* as a political ideology. The differences between the two are enormous: the first allows a *social* dimension of religion, the second imposes the *privatization* of religion, or to put it in the terms used by then-cardinal Ratzinger, it imprisons religion in "the ghetto of subjectivity."[13]

In this respect two documents are worth mentioning and reflecting upon because they clearly reveal these differences.

The first is the report of the Stasi Commission in France on the principle of secularism and the public display of religious symbols. It states: "The spiritual and the religious cannot bear any influence on the State and must renounce the political dimension. Secularism is not compatible with any conception of religion that claims to regulate, in the name of the principles of the religion itself, the social system or political order." And it continues: "Secularism makes a distinction between free spiritual and religious expression in the public sphere, which is legitimate and essential for the democratic debate, and influence over it, which is illegitimate."[14]

The second document is the speech that Prime Minister Jean Pierre Raffarin made before the French National Assembly on February 3, 2004, in defense of the Stasi report. He said: "Today all the great religions in France's history have adapted to this principle. For the most recent arrivals, I mean Islam, secularism is an opportunity to be a French religion."[15]

It is clear that according to this view secularism is the fundamental, sacred, nonnegotiable creed regulating political institutions, the relationship of people with these institutions, and their behavior within society. Secularism is a sort of state religion with its own commandments and prohibitions. The obligation not to flaunt religious symbols in public is a typical case in point. But if secularism is a religion—indeed, the only religion that is admitted to play a role in the public sphere—then it places itself against every other religion, in particular Christianity, which is the religion of the European tradition. This antireligious secularism has devastating consequences for the unification of Europe and its place in the West. I will briefly mention three.

First, *secularism does not give Europe an identity*. This is the main source of the European paradox. Not only does secularism render Europeans cosmopolitan and nationless, it renders them stateless as well. Who are we? If we cannot define ourselves, I do not necessarily mean as members of the old "Christian continent," but even as the heirs to the Judeo-Christian tradition that more than any other has shaped our history, then the best we can offer to answer this question is the ostensive definition of pointing at the map. And even this is difficult, because where there is no clear connotation, there is also no definite denotation. The uncertainty regarding the borders of Europe, and especially the entrance of Turkey into the European Union, can be explained by the uncertainty over the definition of Europe. The fact is that concealing our history in the name of secularism means allowing secularism to obscure our identity.

Second, *European secularism is not inclusive*. By depriving Europeans of their own identity, secularism also keeps them from understanding and integrating those who have a strong one and intend to rely on it. As Benedict XVI has repeatedly recalled, it is the moral and spiritual crisis of Europe that gives rise to feelings of mistrust, dislike, and hostility in many Muslims. And it is this very same crisis that creates uneasiness in Europe. The European who meets a Muslim develops a sort of anxiety syndrome, surprised as he is by the strength of his faith. The Muslim who meets a European is afflicted by a sort of cultural shock, offended as he feels the lack of any sense of the holy or divine. The outcome is that the typically European fear of a clash between civilizations is itself at risk of becoming self-fulfilling.

Third, *European secularism divides Europe from America.* Europe is moving away from America not only because of conflicting economic interests (on world trade regulations, for example) and diverging political views (regarding the use of military force, for example), but especially because it does not understand or does not appreciate America. In particular, Europe does not understand or appreciate the profound and lasting sense of religious community and religious perception of a mission, both of which are widespread in American society.

Think of how American expressions are translated in Europe. What in America is called "civil religion" in Europe is called "bigotry." What in America is called "the spread of civilization" in Europe is called "the imposition of a lifestyle," the American way of life. What in America is called "the exportation or promotion of democracy" in Europe is called "colonialism" or "expansionism" or "imperialism." And so on for every relevant expression or term. It is no wonder if in the end what in America is called the "right to self defense" in Europe is called "appeal to the UN," and what on the American side is called "solution to a conflict" on the European side is taken as "appeal to the International Court of Justice."[16]

A European philosopher—John Gray—supplied an excellent example of these distorted translations. He wrote:

> According to the standard, social-scientific theory of advanced, knowledge-based societies, America should be following Europe in becoming steadily more secular; but there is not the slightest evidence for any such trend. Quite to the contrary, America's peculiar religiosity is becoming ever more strikingly pronounced. It has by far the most powerful fundamentalist movement in any advanced country. In no otherwise comparable land do politicians regularly invoke the name of Jesus.[17]

This misunderstanding is so deep that the difference between Europe and America on religiosity is blamed on the Bush administration and is usually considered to mark the moral and political primacy of the former over the latter. Habermas provides evidence also of this view: "In Europe," he has written, "a president who begins his official functions with a public prayer and connects his momentous political decisions to a divine mission is difficult to imagine."[18]

This is where secularism has led Europe: out of Christianity, out of the West, out of its own history. And this explains why the European paradox— the paradox of Europeans who are no longer Europeans—hinges on the secularization of Europe.

European Relativism

And now to face my third thesis, that European secularization is connected to the relativism dominant in Europe. "Connected" is a vague term, but I hope to clarify it and make it more precise.

Relativism in politics is a child of the crisis of liberalism. Two phenomena regarding this cultural event are relevant. On the one hand, the discovery of the pluralism and incommensurability of values—that is, the idea that there is no higher value that encompasses all the others, and there is no minimum value unit that measures all the others—has caused intellectual panic amongst liberals and has led them to conclude that liberalism, although it has been the philosophy of the Enlightenment and the fuel of modernity, is no longer suitable to our "postmodern" era. On the other hand, the secularist erosion of the Judeo-Christian tradition from which liberalism emerged—because, as a matter of historical fact, liberalism *is* Judeo-Christian doctrine—has pushed many liberals to take a further step and accept the theory that liberalism is merely one among many lifestyles. Which is to say, to embrace relativism.

John Gray's opinions are emblematic also in this respect. Regarding the four "key ideas" that according to him are typical of liberalism—individualism, universalism, meliorism, egalitarianism—he has concluded that "none of them can withstand the force of strong indeterminacy and radical incommensurability among values. Considered as a position in political philosophy, accordingly, liberalism is a failed project. . . . As a philosophical perspective, it is dead." The only thing that according to Gray can be said is that liberalism is "the only sort of regime in which *we*—in our historical circumstances as late moderns—can live well."[19] Or, as Gray also writes, what can be said is that "liberal regimes are only one type of legitimate polity and liberal practice has no special or universal authority."[20]

To defend this view, relativism had erected a protective belt around itself formulated in politically correct and ostensibly noble terminology, which includes terms like "tolerance," "openness," "respect," "state neutrality," "individual freedom," and so on. However, this terminology is insincere because it veils the very meanings of terms. These terms are so abused, so stretched, so consumed, that they no longer correspond to their original, proper referents. In reality, "tolerance" turns out to be equivalent to "compliance," "openness" to "indifference," "freedom" to "license," "neutrality" to "appeasement," "dialogue" to "surrender," and so on.

Relativism claims to have the best recipes for the inclusion of "others" and to be the best basis for the liberal state. But in reality the recipe is fairly poisonous, because by producing a crisis of identity, what relativism generates is precisely the exclusion of the "others." And, as regards the liberal state, relativism corrodes it by undermining those moral or religious values and principles that are its very base. If there are no basic values, if all values are negotiable, if primary intuitions about good and bad cannot be justified or argued for, if no way of life can be said to be better than another because all are incommensurable, then everything is permissible. Abortion as well as embryo experimentation, cloning as well as eugenics or euthanasia, gay marriage as well as polygamy. Not to mention appeasement of and surrender to fanaticism and fundamentalism.

This is where we see the worst consequences of what John Paul II called the "alliance between democracy and ethical relativism." As he stated in the *Centesimus Annus*: "A democracy without values easily turns into open or thinly disguised totalitarianism."[21] In fact, that alliance erodes the sense of limit, of the forbidden, of sin, of moral prohibition. The connection between European secularism and relativism is an ominous mutual reinforcement: secularism produces relativism and relativism nurtures secularism.

The European Crisis

I now come to the conclusion of my argument. How can we resolve the spiritual and moral crisis, more so than political, that is now spreading across Europe?

I do not have a special recipe. I hope that liberalism can be restored and brought back to those universalistic, Judeo-Christian-based tenets that gave birth to it and fostered it before it crossed the channel and then the ocean. But I am not sure that this is possible. What I can say is that if it were, then liberalism would find it difficult not to transform itself into a *conservatism* of some sort.[22]

Here too, another difference between Europe and America manifests itself. American conservatism above all aims to conserve the traditions of civil virtues and fundamental values that formed the bedrock of the religion of the Founding Fathers. But this is exactly what European liberals, as well as many conservatives and Christian Democrats, either are doubtful about or do not intend to conserve. The theory of constitutional patriotism was set out exactly for this reason: to replace, in a constructivist, "enlightened," Jacobin-like style, a still living tradition with a dead piece of paper.

I believe—I want to believe—that in America the situation is different. Old differences between Irving Kristol and Michael Oakeshott, as well as those between Kristol and Hayek, are emblematic examples. But it is not my intent to idealize America. I am convinced that it would be difficult for Tocqueville to write the same masterpiece about America today. And only with difficulty would an American Tocquetown (an equivalent of Tocqueville crossing the ocean in the reverse direction) perceive any great differences between Europe and his native country. It seems to me that the two shores of the Atlantic are, more or less, like the two sides of the same coin, because the moral and spiritual crisis is in large part similar in both. However, I think that the crisis in Europe makes the situation much more troublesome than it is in America. The fact is that while American history may still fuel American society, much of European history is a burden on the Europeans' shoulders.

Consider some historical epoch-making European events. In Europe there was a union between the throne and the altar. In Europe the French Enlightenment aimed to make a clean sweep not only of the Catholic Church (*écrasez l'infâme!*), but of the Christian religion itself. In Europe the critique of Christianity produced the Nietzschean idea that the Christian ethic is the morality of slaves. In Europe Marxism spread the view that mankind can live and be truly free only in the absence of God. In Europe Romanticism produced patriotisms that degenerated into totalitarianisms, and when these totalitarianisms provoked disasters and massacres, from a wizard like Heidegger arose the desperate and misleading cry that "only *a* God can save us." In Europe some of the foremost nation-states, such as France and Italy, constituted themselves against the church. And it is yet again in Europe that the Catholic Church invested a long time in coming to terms first with liberalism and then later with democracy. In light of this history, it is not surprising that someone happened to devise and work out a constitution in a closed room, believed that a new patriotism could be created in a philosophy seminar, and was convinced that European religious tradition is an obstacle to European unification.

I will conclude by repeating that I do not have a recipe for resolving Europe's crisis. But I would like to believe that, at a time when an increasing number of Europeans are disoriented, confused, and even frightened, there will be a sense of hope to pull us out of the crisis—one that will come from that new need for moral, spiritual, and religious guidance that seems today to be spreading across several parts of Europe. But this is just a feeling, not a prediction. The Enlightenment project to produce a godless society is ongoing.

Notes

1. Joseph Ratzinger and Marcello Pera, *Without Roots: The West, Relativism, Christianity, Islam* (New York: Basic Books, 2006), 109.

2. Irving Kristol, *Neoconservatism: The Autobiography of an Idea* (New York: The Free Press, 1995), 381.

3. Paul Feyerabend, *Conquest of Abundance: A Tale of Abstraction versus the Richness of Being* (Chicago: University of Chicago Press, 1999), 248.

4. On this crisis the analysis of George Weigel is illuminating. See George Weigel, *The Cube and the Cathedral: Europe, America, and Politics without God* (New York: Basic Books, 2005), and "Is Europe Dying? Notes on a Crisis of Civilizational Morale" (March 17, 2005), http://www.aei.org/publications/pubID.22139/pub_detail.asp.

5. *Treaty establishing a Constitution for Europe*, Article I-2.

6. See Jürgen Habermas, *Between Facts and Norms: Contributions to a Discourse Theory of Law and Democracy* (Cambridge, MA: MIT Press, 1996), Apendix I.; and Habermas, *The Inclusion of the Other* (Cambridge, UK: Polity Press, 1998).

7. Habermas, *The Inclusion of the Other*, 118, 161.

8. Habermas is clearly aware of this problem; he writes: "This notion of constitutional patriotism appears to many observers to represent too weak a bond to hold together complex societies. The question then becomes even more urgent: under what conditions can a liberal political culture provide a sufficient cushion to prevent a nation of citizens which can no longer rely on ethnic associations, from dissolving into fragments?" *The Inclusion of the Other*, 118. But if one adds to the thin constitutional patriotism such typical thick elements of European history and politics as the memory of the Holocaust, the critique of American unilateralism, the banning of the death penalty, the keeping of certain ways of life, etc., as Habermas does, then his view that the European Charter can be validated independently of *pre*-political presuppositions can no longer be maintained. For these "thick" elements, see Habermas, "Does Europe Need a Constitution?" in *Times of Transitions* (Cambridge, UK: Polity Press, 2006), chap. 7, and "Is the Development of a European Identity Necessary, and is it Possible?" in *The Divided West* (Cambridge, UK: Polity Press, 2006), chap. 6.

9. Habermas, "Pre-political Foundations of the Democratic Constitutional State?" in Jürgen Habermas and Joseph Ratzinger, *The Dialectics of Secularization: On Reason and Religion* (San Francisco: Ignatius Press, 2006), 28.

10. Ibid., 29.

11. In his endorsement of the European identity Habermas is clearly making use of his view about German identity, which, according to him, cannot depend on the "prepolitical crutches of nationality and community of fate. . . . A national identity which is not based predominantly on republican self-understanding and constitutional patriotism necessarily collides with the universalist rules of mutual coexistence for human beings." Habermas, "Yet Again: German Identity—A Unified Nation of

Angry DM-Burghers?" in *When the Wall Came Down: Reactions to German Unification*, ed. Harold James and Martha Stone (London: Routledge, 1992), 97. See also Jan-Werner Müller, *Another Country: German Intellectuals, Unification and National Identity* (New Haven and London: Yale University Press, 2000), Ch.3.

12. Applied to political parties, this distinction leads to Kristol's view: "A secular political party, in the traditional sense, has been neutral as between religions. . . . A secularist political party is neutral as between religion and irreligion." See Kristol, *Neoconservatism*, 372.

13. Cardinal Ratzinger, in an interview in *Le Figaro* magazine, August 13, 2004.

14. [Bernard] Stasi Commission, *La laïcité et la République* (Paris: La Documentation française, 2004), 31.

15. *New York Times*, February 4, 2004, http://query.nytimes.com/gst/fullpage. html?res=9D0CE2DB153BF937A35751C0A9629C8B63&n=Top/Reference/Times %20Topics/People/R/Raffarin,%20Jean-Pierre.

16. Quite rightly Roger Scruton has written: "The UN Charter of Human Rights and the European Convention of Human Rights belong to the species of utopian thinking that would prefer us to be born into a world without history, without prior attachments, without any of the flesh and blood passions which make government so necessary in the first place." *A Political Philosophy* (New York: Continuum, 2006), 23.

17. John Gray, *Al Qaeda and What it Means to be Modern* (London: Faber and Faber, 2003), 23.

18. Habermas, *The Divided West*, 46.

19. John Gray, *Post-Liberalism* (London: Routledge, 1993), 287, 288.

20. John Gray, *Liberalism*, 2nd ed. (Buckingham: Open University Press, 1995), x.

21. Pope John Paul II, *Centesimus Annus*, n.46.

22. To the best of my knowledge, Scruton in *A Political Philosophy* provides the best formulation of this conservatism in Europe. European intellectuals and politicians, especially those who are critical about the European Union but appreciate European tradition and its contribution to the civilization of the West, should pay more attention to his views and take them seriously.

16

A Response to Marcello Pera

Michael Novak

Senator Marcello Pera lays before us three powerful theses: (1) Paradoxically, Europe identifies itself today not by its deeply rooted history, but by a non-historical ideology constructed from philosophical abstractions. (2) These abstractions are necessary because Europe's political and cultural elites have deliberately chosen to maintain a stern secularist self-consciousness. (3) This stern secularist commitment feeds the insatiable appetite of relativism. Relativism, in turn, deprives Europe of its ability to make moral distinctions, and undermines its trust in its own ideals.

In briefer form: The paradox of an abstract and nonhistorical conception of European identity is required by deliberate ideological secularism, which issues in corrosive relativism.

In its large lines, Senator Pera's argument is quite brilliant, although there are individual judgments in it that might be disputed. Before raising one or two of those matters, it may help to explore the words "secular" and "secularist," which lie at the heart of the senator's argument. Wisely, Senator Pera sharply distinguishes the Continental meaning, based upon the ideology of the French Revolution, from the Anglo-American meaning, linked to the experiences embodied in the United States. But let us turn even farther back, if only for a moment.

The Enlightenment in which Europe now seeks almost the whole of its identity was a determined effort to reason as though God does not exist. This included confining religion, too, within the bounds of reason alone.

There were three myths embodied in the Enlightenment. The first held that prior to the Age of Enlightenment, virtually all people in Europe were simple believers, without skepticism, doubt, or questioning. The truth is, however, as even the Bible tells us, that at all times the circle of believers has actually been quite small, while the number of unbelievers has been vast. Both Jewish and Christian Bibles describe at length the large numbers of nominal believers, people who in practice do not believe. They are, Jesus said, like seed scattered upon the rock, or falling into thin soil, or languishing untended and unwatered. The faithful are frequently referred to as *pusillus grex*, a tiny flock. Contrary to the Enlightenment, there was never any simple, universal "Age of Belief." The widespread unbelief of the modern period may be distinctive, but it has many precedents in every earlier age.

Second, contrary to the rhetoric of the Enlightenment, many, perhaps most, of those who did undertake to practice as serious Jews or Christians had to make reasoned arguments, to themselves if to nobody else, as to why they became serious Jews or Christians while so many around them did not. One cannot read the confessions and *apologiae* of the many intellectuals who became Christians during the first four centuries (and every century since) without encountering numerous arguments addressed both to their earlier selves and to their friends, since they were making consequential choices that might lead to death or banishment.

A third myth of the Enlightenment may be more relevant to our immediate purposes. The great sociologist Robert Nisbet wryly pointed out the bigotry involved in the very name the Enlightened chose for themselves.[1] They called themselves the children of reason, the children of light, and they regarded all others, with some contempt, as the children of darkness and partisans of unreason and false consciousness. Implicit in this inherent bigotry was a Manichean metaphysics that divided the world into Light and Darkness.

Implicit also was a teaching of contempt, which would lead in time to history's cruelest and most extensive elimination of scores of millions of Christians, Jews, and other undesirables by self-proclaimed atheist regimes. That tradition of contempt lives on. In a recent book review in the *Washington Post*, for instance, the reviewer sounds the alarm that "the fundamentalists most dangerous to our future are not Islamic and foreign but Christian and homegrown."[2] He is describing the very same Bible-reading country people, outside the corrupt cities, whom Thomas Jefferson saw as the sturdy yeomen giving the moral life of democracy its ballast. From the War for Independence until today, these are also the young men who are most willing to fight and die for their country, and who supply disproportionate examples of valor under fire. It was their ancestors in southern Virginia who insisted, as the price for their crucial congressional votes, that James Madison work to amend the Constitution with a Bill of Rights to protect religious liberty. But the bigotry of the Enlightened goes on, undiminished.

Following in that line, I need to point out that "secular" is a concept invented by the Latin Christian West, as a way of working out the practical, political meaning of "Render unto Caesar the things that are Caesar's, and to God, the things that are God's."[3]

There are things that belong to the invisible kingdom of God, the eternal City of God rooted in God's own inner life; and there are things that belong to our lives in worldly cities such as Constantinople and Rome, Ravenna and Milan. The first carry with them a sense of the sacred, the eternal, the transcendent, the divine; while the second belong to the temporal order of space and time—to the brief time that each generation spends on earth, to the long sequence of generations down through history, and to the accompanying rhythms of earthly struggles for power and aspirations for justice.

In the Christian view, the secular and the transcendent are not a zero sum, such that if one loses, the other gains. On the contrary, it is the vocation of the transcendent to infuse the secular with a longing for liberty, justice, friendship, equality, and love, and to nudge the secular world—however slowly, generation by generation—toward a closer approximation of the "city on a hill," the shining City of God. But it is *wrong* for the sacred to try to intrude upon the legitimate autonomy of the secular, and wrong, too, for the secular to intrude upon the legitimate autonomy of the sacred. Secular power dare not be totalitarian, for it is limited by the power of the sacred. Sacred power dare not try to seize secular political power, for it must respect the duties that are Caesar's—or, in our time, democracy's. But neither can the sacred be confined solely within the privacy of the individual human heart, for it too lives in a City with its own public duties and responsibilities. The sacred realm is by its very nature both a communal and public realm and an interior, personal realm.

Thus, for Christians, "secular" is a good term, with positive connotations. The secular is not the whole of life, but it does have its own nobility and autonomy. Christians even have an obligation to work out their salvation by, in part, making contributions to the secular world. The term "secularist," by contrast, points to one who has made an ideology, a rival religion, out of secularism, and taken religion as his sworn foe. Since Voltaire, the number of secularists has grown, although in recent times at a far slower and more discouraged pace.

As secularists, Jürgen Habermas, John Rawls, and many others propose this bargain to their religious fellow citizens: "You may enjoy tolerance for your practice of religion, as long as that practice is private, and has no force in public life. The public square must be nothing but secular." This demand shows that secularist thinkers have made much less progress in adapting their zero-sum thinking to the persistence of religion in this world than the Catholic church has made during the past century in adapting its early resistance to secularist democracy, to the point that the church has now become one of the great forces for democracy in the world.

It is worth interrogating a little the implications of the rationalism so dear to the secularists. When rationalism acts alone, unaided by religion, where does it lead? With its allegiance to science, it leads us finally to what Albert Camus called the Absurd. Everything is chance. In the end, human life is meaningless. The narrative which scientific atheists such as Sam Harris tell themselves, loosely based upon the work of Darwin, is a sort of reductionism. It holds that, in the beginning, there were only the simplest of elements, and from their work upon each other through natural selection, and only after vast stretches of time, did more complex forms of life arise.

Yet in truth, it does appear from the work of scientists in physics that all the complexity that biologists claim has emerged only in recent times was there in the beginning. Lawlikeness, the impulse of inner motion toward the development of already existing inner potentialities, and a huge array of interconnections with other substances, are found in things both infinitesimal and vast.

For scientific inquiry, God may be insignificant and, in fact, *in principle* can never even be encountered. Insofar as science is based upon mathematics, the God of mathematics, so to speak, is a lawgiver, a luminous source of universally applicable signposts for scientific intelligence to identify and follow. To affirm the lawlikeness of mathematical accounts of the universe is, perhaps, as close as some persons come to affirming the existence of God. They cannot deny the power of intelligence that suffuses both distant galaxies and rocket travel in space, the satellites used for global positioning, and also the inner secrets of chemistry and sub-atomic energies.

Such persons may even want to take the next step, to affirm that this intel-ligence in the universe is the luminous Creator, praised by Abraham, Isaac, and Jacob.

But let us now take up Nietzsche's point: If God is dead, so is reason. "The question 'Why?' has no answer."[4] Taking Nietzsche's point, may we argue in the reverse direction? If you do accept reason and its mathematical models, its verified scientific predictions, and the vast array of reason's suc-cesses in penetrating the laws of the universe, are you not, in other terms, actually accepting the existence of God? So does the relation spelled out by Nietzsche work in reverse? From "If God is dead, so is reason," can one con-clude, "If nature is suffused with mathematical reason, then God—perhaps by some other name—exists"? Are scientific rationalists not declaring the glory of God in all they do, whether they wish to be aware of that or not?

This sort of reflection makes some wonder if there is a bad conscience among scientists and rationalists who affirm the validity of reason, only to deny the existence of God. They deny, that is, the Source of the intelligence whose most subtle and refined moves they devote their lives to tracing. In that case, it follows that the question "Why" has no answer.

Now that very phrase—"The question 'Why?' has no answer"—is Niet-zsche's most succinct definition of nihilism. In this way does secularism lead to nihilism.

⤚

There is a point implied by Senator Pera's argument which I would like to bring to the surface. In discussing some works by Habermas, Senator Pera suggests that even their very formulations rest upon hidden premises that Habermas does not, in his view, have the honesty to recognize. Whence comes the abstract model around which Habermas describes an authentic communicative discourse, in which each party respects the person and the argument of the other? There is no doubt that this model is attractive. There is also no doubt that Habermas is not describing a master-slave relationship, nor a lord-to-vassal relationship, nor the relationship of a powerful warrior to captives who are shivering in his presence until they learn their fate. Rather, the underlying concept that Habermas draws upon is the human person as described in Christian theology and philosophy: the incommensurable substance, unlike any other, yet made in the image of God, free, and worthy of being treated with respect and dignity. Whatever the rank or role of either partner in a conversation, in God's eyes (Judaism and Christianity insist) all are equal. There is no concept quite like this in Greek or Roman thought, and even when something like it appears in the Enlightenment its heritage is demonstrably traceable to premises that, officially, the Enlightenment does not accept.

If I understand Senator Pera correctly, he is writing that the paradox of Europe's new sense of identity, constructed around an abstraction in a non-historical world, is made necessary by its unquestioned and un-self-critical secularist commitments, and that from this same source issues forth in a self-condemning nihilism.

If all that is true, far from achieving its early promises, the secularist Enlightenment by this account is ending with a whimper. It seems unable to justify either its own distinctive identity or its own ideals, unable in this vastly religious age even to pretend to universal provenance, and unable to escape the tangles of its own self-proclaimed meaninglessness.

As a last point, I accept Senator Pera's fears that the United States may now also be sledding down the same decline as Europe. But the issue has not been settled yet. As I read the evidence, religious thinkers just now feel inspir- ited and optimistic, while secularist thinkers write as if they are spitting into the wind, without much hope of being widely heard, let alone prevailing.

Notes

1. Robert Nisbet, *History of the Idea of Progress* (New York: Basic Books, 1980).

2. Bryan Burrough, "Has the Right Gone Wrong?" Review of *The Conservative Soul: How We Lost It, How to Get It Back*, *Washington Post*, October 22, 2006, BW05.

3. Matthew 22:21.

4. Friedrich Nietzsche, *The Will to Power*, ed. Walter Kaufmann (New York: Vintage Books, 1968), 9.

17

Commentary

Robert Royal

One of the things I am constantly surprised at in the European discussion is that there is not more emphasis on the point Senator Pera made about secularism, which Michael Novak also touched on: secularism as a substantive position is not neutral. A neutral public space should be secular, i.e., open to both religious and non-religious arguments, not secularist. Secularism seeks to crowd out everything else, although we still have a slightly more robust notion of the secular, the properly secular, in the United States, which admits of some religious influence. I think we have to parse out that aggressive secularism and expose it, and say over and over again that it is a substantive position like Methodism, or Marxism, or Catholicism.

I also think we have to point to the roots of it and the rather violent expression of it in Voltaire. He could have said *Écartez l'infame*—we ought to discard religion. You do not have to crush it; you just get rid of it. But he chose a very different way to express his, as we would call it, "secularism"— he wanted to obliterate religion—*Écrasez l'infame*. There is at the very root of this secularism some kind of aggressive, militant attempt to exclude. And as is often said, if Voltaire were to come back today, he would be surprised that it is the popes who are defending reason, and not the secularists.

All that said by way of a preamble, I would make two comments about Europe, one optimistic and one rather pessimistic. The optimistic point, and it is worth having this on the table, is that rather large numbers of Europeans are still believers in spite of everything.

Russia, which for seventy years was under the oppression of the Soviets, is still (or is again) a place where 80 percent of the populace describes itself as religious. That is actually the case throughout most of the continent. The only two areas I know of in all of Europe where nonbelievers have been found to be a majority are the Czech Republic (for historic reasons) and the former East Germany. Even in France, which is always the test case, people report themselves as believer by large majorities—80 percent of the French describe themselves as religious believers. Now what exactly they believe in and what they believe this allows them to do, of course, is a different question. *Vive la différence*, we might say. But still the fact that there are 80 percent who describe themselves as believers is not an unimportant fact. It is actually roughly similar to the level of such self-description in the United States.

Now, that is the optimistic side of things. The pessimistic side relates to Senator Pera's comment about churches and state, and the very different American and European attitudes about the relationship between them. The British sociologist Grace Davie has said that the religious situation in Europe is "believing without belonging."[1] So you can have very high levels of religious belief among the people without their belonging or being attached to religious institutions.

Other things being equal, that might not be all that important. But without some kind of an institutional assertion of the Judeo-Christian worldview, I do not see how you have any effect on the surrounding society. Individuals are going to be isolated, and they are going to be pointing in different directions. In addition to the ideological drift in Europe, there has been this institutional drift; and the churches as institutions bear some blame for this, but they do not seem willing to fight the battles that absolutely need to be fought to regain their position.

This is a serious problem for the instruction of the next generation in particular. So there is much to be pessimistic about, but I think there is also the possibility that if attention is focused in the right way, there may be room for religious renewal in Europe.

Lee Harris

One of the essential points in Senator Pera's argument begins with the premise that in the West we have accepted the plurality of values. A second premise is that these values conflict and clash. And the basic thesis is that from these two principles you can derive the idea of ethical relativism.

But I think it's critical to understand that there is also another world-view you can derive from that combination of premises. It is possible to conclude that your own values are the values of the elite, of the chosen people, while the values that are incommensurable to yours are the values of the reprobate, the Gentiles. This is the way the Mormons felt; this is the way the Puritans felt; this is the way the Calvinists felt. It is the way many serious people have responded to the presence of a variety of strongly held values that seem to be incommensurable.

It may be true that no one becomes a believer because he thinks that this will be beneficial to the development of the Christian-European tradition—that is, the social utility of religion is not one of its selling points in practice. But it is nonetheless the case that very often in the history of Christianity, conversion came about because people felt they were offered the values of the chosen, of the elite; and this has been an enormous, motivating power in the development of Christianity, and, of course, in an even more explicit way, in the development of Judaism, too.

But nothing could be more at odds with liberalism. Liberalism argues that we must tolerate everyone, and that all are equal. Therefore, if I claim that I and my friends are the elect and the elite, I assault the fundamental liberal social compact. I would argue, therefore, that there is an antinomy between liberalism (which in key respects is a child of Christianity) and the historical mechanism that made the spread of Christianity possible.

Secondly, in response to a point made by Michael Novak, I am not so sure we can look at people like Sam Harris as being just a last gasp for secularism, or a new gasp for secularism. I think rather that what they demonstrate is something I would call "evangelical atheism."

Evangelicals in many religions tend not to be very conscious of the historical traditions of their faith; that is, they want to read the Bible and let the Holy Spirit illuminate them. Do not worry about St. Augustine or St. Thomas or any other theologian.

You will notice that people like Sam Harris or Dawkins are not conversant with church fathers and the like. They are armchair theologians who say things like, "The reason religion was invented is because people were afraid of death," overlooking the fact, for instance, that the Jews have an elaborate, wonderful religion in which there is no immortality of the soul at all.

I therefore think that what we are seeing today is a kind of trickle-down atheism, supported by a vague resort to science and the scientific; and it actually works the way conversion to Christianity once did. Once we hear the phrase "this is scientific" used to describe some argument or point, it means, "this is what smart people believe." This tendency is allowing the kind of evangelical atheism that is premised on very little theological knowledge of history or historical knowledge of any kind.

Note

1. Her book is *Religion in Britain Since 1945: Believing Without Belonging* (Oxford: Blackwell, 1994).

About the Authors

Stephen M. Barr is a theoretical particle physicist at the Bartol Research Institute of the University of Delaware. After post-doctoral work at the University of Pennsylvania, he became a research assistant professor at the University of Washington and associate physicist at Brookhaven National Laboratory before joining Bartol in 1987. Dr. Barr has also researched theology and philosophy extensively, and writes frequently about the intersection of science and religion. He is the author of *Modern Physics and Ancient Faith* (University of Notre Dame Press, 2003), and his work appears regularly in *First Things* and *National Review*.

Peter Berkowitz is the Tad and Dianne Taube Senior Fellow at the Hoover Institution at Stanford University. He is cofounder and director of the Israel Program on Constitutional Government and has served as a senior consultant to the President's Council on Bioethics. His scholarship focuses on the interplay of law, ethics, and politics in modern society. Dr. Berkowitz is the author of *Virtue and the Making of Modern Liberalism* (Princeton University Press, 1999) and *Nietzsche: The Ethics of an Immoralist* (1995), and has recently edited *The Future of American Intelligence* (Hoover Institution Press, 2005) and *Never a Matter of Indifference: Sustaining Virtue in a Free Republic* (Hoover Institution Press, 2003). His work has appeared in the *American Political Science Review*, *Atlantic Monthly*, *Chronicle of Higher Education*, *Commentary*, *Critical Review*, *First Things*, *London Review of Books*, *National Review*, the *New Republic*, *New York Post*, *Public Interest*, *Wall Street Journal*, *Washington Post*, *Weekly Standard*, and *Yale Law Journal*, among others.

Joseph Bottum is the editor of *First Things* and contributing editor to the *Weekly Standard*. His essays, poems, and reviews have appeared in the

259

Atlantic Monthly, the *Wall Street Journal*, *Nineteenth-Century Literature*, *Commentary*, the *Washington Post*, the *Wilson Quarterly*, and many other newspapers, magazines, and journals. His books include *The Fall & Other Poems* (St. Augustine's Press, 2001) and *The Pius War: Responses to the Critics of Pius XII* (Lexington Books, 2004).

Christopher DeMuth has been president of AEI since 1986. Previously, he was a practicing lawyer and consulting economist, taught at the Kennedy School of Government, and worked at the White House in the Reagan and Nixon administrations. His articles have appeared in the *American Enterprise*, *Harvard Law Review*, *Yale Journal of Regulation*, *Wall Street Journal*, *Commentary*, and other publications.

David Gelernter is a professor of computer science at Yale University, a national fellow at the American Enterprise Institute, and a contributing editor at the *Weekly Standard*. Previously, he was a member of the National Council of the Arts and a weekly culture-and-politics columnist at the *New York Post* and the *Los Angeles Times*. His essays have been anthologized in volumes including *The Best American Spiritual Writing* (Houghton Mifflin, 2004) and his articles have appeared in *Commentary*, the *Weekly Standard*, *Time*, the *Wall Street Journal*, *New York Times Sunday Magazine* and many others. Dr. Gelernter's books include *Mirror Worlds: Or the Day Software Puts the Universe in a Shoebox* (Oxford University Press, 1992), *The Muse in the Machine: Computerizing the Poetry of Human Thought* (Free Press, 1994) and *Americanism: The Fourth Great Western Religion* (Doubleday, 2007).

John C. Green is a senior fellow in religion and American politics at the Pew Forum on Religion & Public Life. He is a distinguished professor of political science at the University of Akron and serves as director of the Ray C. Bliss Institute of Applied Politics. Dr. Green's research centers on American religious communities and politics, and he is the author of widely cited surveys measuring the influence of faith on presidential elections. His recent books include *The Faith Factor: How Religion Influences American Elections* (Praeger Publishers, 2007), and the coauthored volumes *The Values Campaign: The Christian Right in American Politics* (Georgetown University Press, 2006), *The Bully Pulpit: The Politics of Protestant Clergy* (University

Press of Kansas, 1997), and *Religion and the Culture Wars* (Rowman & Littlefield, 1996).

Michael Greve is the John G. Searle Scholar and director of the Federalism Project at the American Enterprise Institute. He is also a member of the board of directors of the Competitive Enterprise Institute in Washington, D.C., and an adjunct professor at Boston College. Previously, Dr. Greve founded and directed the Center for Individual Rights, a public interest law firm. He is the author of AEI's *Constitutional Outlook* series; coeditor of *Environmental Politics: Public Costs, Private Rewards* (Praeger, 1992), *Competition Laws in Conflict: Antitrust Jurisdiction in the Global Economy* (AEI Press, 2004), and *Federal Preemption: States' Powers, National Interests* (AEI Press, 2007); and author of *Real Federalism: Why It Matters, How It Could Happen* (AEI Press, 1999), and *Harm-Less Lawsuits? What's Wrong with Consumer Class Actions* (AEI Press, 2005).

Lee Harris is an essayist for *Policy Review*, the bimonthly journal of the Hoover Institution at Stanford University, and a frequent contributor to the *Wall Street Journal's* "Opinion Journal." His scholarship focuses on multiculturalism and America's image in the Middle East. Mr. Harris's recent essays include "Marx Without Realism: The Intellectual Roots of America-Bashing" (*Wall Street Journal*) and "The Future of Tradition: Transmitting the Visceral Ethical Code of Civilization" (*Policy Review*). He is the author of *Civilization and Its Enemies: The Next Stage of History* (Free Press, 2004) and *The Suicide of Reason: Radical Islam's Threat to the West* (Basic Books, 2007).

Kevin J. "Seamus" Hasson is founder, chairman of the board, and president of the Becket Fund for Religious Liberty, a bipartisan, interfaith public-interest law firm that protects the free expression of all religious traditions. Mr. Hasson was previously an attorney at Williams & Connolly in Washington, D.C., where he focused on religious liberty litigation. From 1986 to 1987, he served in the Office of Legal Counsel at the Justice Department, where he advised the White House and cabinet departments on church-state relations. He has appeared as a commentator on religious freedom for programs including *The Today Show, Dateline NBC*, John McLaughlin's *One on One*, NPR's *Talk of the Nation*, CNN's *Talkback Live* and

Al-Jazeera. Mr. Hasson is the author of *The Right to Be Wrong: Ending the Culture War Over Religion in America* (Encounter Books, 2005).

Leon R. Kass, M.D. is the Hertog Fellow at the American Enterprise Institute and Addie Clark Harding Professor in the Committee on Social Thought and the College at the University of Chicago. Trained in both medicine and biochemistry, Dr. Kass served as chairman of the President's Council on Bioethics from 2002 to 2005 and executive secretary of the Committee on the Life Sciences and Social Policy at the National Research Council/National Academy of Sciences from 1970 to 1972. His widely read essays on biomedical ethics have dealt with issues raised by in vitro fertilization, cloning, genetic screening and genetic technology, organ transplantation, aging research, euthanasia and assisted suicide, and the moral nature of the medical profession. Dr. Kass's books include *Toward a More Natural Science: Biology and Human Affairs* (Free Press, 1985), *The Hungry Soul: Eating and the Perfecting of Our Nature* (Free Press, 1994), *The Ethics of Human Cloning* (AEI Press, 1998), *Life, Liberty, and the Defense of Dignity* (Encounter Books, 2002), and *The Beginning of Wisdom: Reading Genesis* (Free Press, 2003).

Roger Kimball is coeditor and copublisher of the *New Criterion* and publisher of Encounter Books. He lectures widely and is a frequent contributor of art and cultural criticism to publications including the *Times Literary Supplement, Modern Painters, Literary Review,* the *Wall Street Journal,* the *Public Interest, Commentary,* the *Spectator,* the *New York Times Book Review,* the *Sunday Telegraph,* the *American Spectator,* the *Weekly Standard, National Review,* and the *National Interest.* His latest books include *The Rape of the Masters: How Political Correctness Sabotages Art* (Encounter Books, 2004), *Lives of the Mind: The Use and Abuse of Intelligence from Hegel to Wodehouse* (Ivan R. Dee, 2002), and *Art's Prospect: The Challenge of Tradition in an Age of Celebrity* (Ivan R. Dee, 2003).

Douglas W. Kmiec holds the endowed chair in constitutional law at Pepperdine Law School. He was previously dean of the Catholic University of America School of Law, and, for nearly two decades, director of Notre Dame's Center on Law & Government, and the founder of the center's *Journal of Law,*

Ethics & Public Policy. Dean Kmiec also served as assistant attorney general, Office of Legal Counsel, at the U.S. Department of Justice under Presidents Ronald Reagan and George Bush. He is a columnist for the Catholic News Service, author of *The Attorney General's Lawyer: Inside the Meese Justice Department* (Praeger Publishers, 1992) and contributor to several volumes on the Constitution and individual rights. Mr. Kmiec is a frequent commentator on law for national news programs such as *Meet the Press*, the *Newshour*, and NPR's *Talk of the Nation*, analyzing constitutional questions.

Irving Kristol has been a senior fellow at the American Enterprise Institute since 1977. He is the founding editor of *The Public Interest*, a journal of politics and culture, and *The National Interest*, a journal of foreign affairs. Mr. Kristol has served on the President's Commission on White House Fellowships and the National Council on the Humanities, and is a fellow of the American Academy of Arts and Sciences. He is the author of several influential works of political thought, including *On the Democratic Idea in America* (Harper & Row, 1972), *Two Cheers for Capitalism* (Signet, 1979), and *Neoconservatism: The Autobiography of an Idea* (Free Press, 1995). In 2002, President George W. Bush awarded Mr. Kristol the Presidential Medal of Freedom.

Yuval Levin is a fellow at the Ethics and Public Policy Center in Washington, D.C., where he serves as director of the program on Bioethics and American Democracy. He is a cofounder and senior editor of *The New Atlantis: A Journal of Technology and Society*. Mr. Levin previously served as an associate director of the Domestic Policy Council at the White House and was chief of staff of the President's Council on Bioethics. He is the author of *Tyranny of Reason: The Origins and Consequences of the Social Scientific Outlook* (University Press of America, 2000). His scholarship focuses on federal domestic-policy programs, political philosophy, science and technology, and bioethics.

Charles Murray is the W. H. Brady Scholar at the American Enterprise Institute, where he researches human intelligence and social structure, marriage, family, and social mores, crime, and Libertarianism. Previously, Dr. Murray was a chief scientist at the American Institutes for Research in Washington, D.C., and a senior fellow at the Manhattan Institute for Policy Research. He is coauthor of *The Bell Curve: Intelligence and Class Structure in American Life* (Free Press, 1994) and author of *What It Means to be a Libertarian: A Personal Interpretation* (Broadway Books, 1997), *Human Accomplishment: The Pursuit of Excellence in the Arts and Sciences, 800 B.C. to 1950* (Harper Perennial, 2003), and *In Our Hands: A Plan to Replace the Welfare State* (AEI Press, 2006).

Michael Novak is the George Frederick Jewett Scholar in Religion, Philosophy, and Public Policy at the American Enterprise Institute. He has served as ambassador to the United Nations Human Rights Commission, head of the U.S. Delegation to the Conference on Security and Cooperation in Europe, a member of the Board of International Broadcasting, and a member of the Presidential Task Force on Project Economic Justice. In 1994, Mr. Novak was awarded the prestigious Templeton Prize for Progress in Religion. He has written and edited more than two dozen influential books on the philosophy and theology of culture, including *Belief and Unbelief* (Macmillan, 1965), *The Experience of Nothingness* (Harper & Row, 1970), *The Spirit of Democratic Capitalism* (Simon & Schuster, 1982), *To Empower People: From State to Civil Society* (AEI Press, 1996), and *The Universal Hunger for Liberty* (Basic Books, 2004). His essays and reviews have appeared in the *New Republic, Commentary, Harper's, First Things,* the *Atlantic Monthly, New York Times Magazine,* and *National Review.*

Marcello Pera was president of the Italian Senate from 2001 to 2006 and has been a sitting senator since 1994. Previously, he taught theoretical philosophy at the University of Catania, Italy, and became full professor of philosophy at the University of Pisa, Italy, in 1992. He is a vocal opponent of postmodernism and cultural relativism and has written for the Italian newspapers *Corriere della Sera, Il Messaggero,* and *La Stampa,* and the news magazines *L'Espresso* and *Panorama.* He is the coauthor of *Persuading Science: The Art of Scientific Rhetoric* (Science History Publications, 1991), *Scientific Controversies: Philosophical and Historical Perspectives* (Oxford University Press, 2000), and *Without Roots: The West, Relativism, Christianity, and Islam* (Basic Books, 2006).

Robert Royal is president of the Faith & Reason Institute in Washington, D.C. Previously, he has taught at Brown University, Rhode Island College, and the Catholic University of America, and served as editor-in-chief of *Prospect* magazine in Princeton, New Jersey. He writes and lectures frequently on questions of ethics, culture, religion, and politics. Dr. Royal's recent books include: *1492 And All That: Political Manipulations of History* (University Press of America, 1992), *Reinventing the American People: Unity and Diversity Today* (Eerdmans, 1995), *The Virgin and the Dynamo: The Use and Abuse of Religion in the Environment Debate* (Eerdmans, 1999), *The Catholic Martyrs of the Twentieth Century: A Comprehensive Global History* (Crossroad, 2000), and *The God That Did Not Fail: How Religion Built and Sustains the West* (Encounter 2006).

Roger Scruton teaches graduate-level philosophy at the Institute for the Psychological Sciences in Washington, D.C. and Oxford University. He has written widely on aesthetics, politics, and culture. His recent books include *The West and the Rest* (ISI Books, 2001), *Culture Counts: Faith and Healing in a World Besieged* (Encounter Books, 2007), and *The Dictionary of Political Thought*, 3rd edition (Palgrave Macmillan, 2007). Dr. Scruton is founding editor of the *Salisbury Review* and serves on the editorial board of the *British Journal of Aesthetics*. In March 2007, he took part in a public debate with Richard Dawkins, Christopher Hitchens, and A. C. Grayling on the topic "Are We Better Off Without Religion?" in which he argued that religion is both useful and necessary in society.

Index